Advance Praise

"Brutally honest, and brimming with rich metaphor and valuable take aways, it is instructive not only for family members (and other collaterals) of addicted persons, but also for the professionals who provide their treatment."

> — Robert B. Yankowitz, Ph.D., Assistant Clinical Professor of Psychiatry Ichan School of Medicine at Mount Sinai, and Chief Operating Officer (retired), The Bridge Inc.

"This is a heartfelt story, told in such a vivid, honest, and revealing fashion, that you cannot resist admiring the courage of the Hillman family in sharing it."

> — Marc A Whaley, MD, Distinguished Life Fellow of The American Psychiatric Association and President, South-Eastern Massachusetts Psychiatric Society

"If you have a loved one struggling with the disease of addiction, this is a must read for you and your family."

> — Shirley Knelly, Past President, Pathways Alcohol and Drug Treatment Center, Licensed Clinical Alcohol and Drug Counselor, Board Member, Maryland Addiction Directors Council

SECRET NO MORE

Lisa Hillman

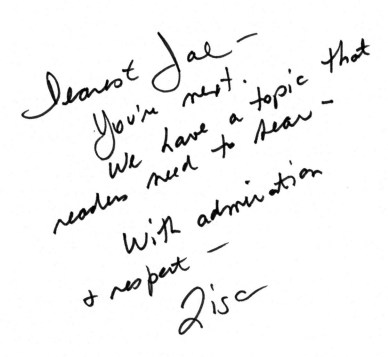

Dearest Jac —
You're next.
We have a topic that
readers need to hear —

With admiration
& respect —
Lisa

SECRET NO MORE

*A True Story of Hope for Parents
with an Addicted Child*

Lisa Hillman

Apprentice House
Loyola University Maryland
Baltimore, Maryland

First Edition

Printed in the United States of America

Hardcover ISBN: 978-1-62720-139-1
Paperback ISBN: 978-1-62720-140-7
Ebook ISBN: 978-1-62720-147-6

Editorial Development & Design: Mary Del Plato

Published by Apprentice House

Apprentice House
Loyola University Maryland
4501 N. Charles Street
Baltimore, MD 21210
410.617.5265 • 410.617.2198 (fax)
www.ApprenticeHouse.com
info@ApprenticeHouse.com

For Jacob
Vanish, o night!
Set, stars! Set, stars!
At dawn, I will win! I will win!

—Puccini, *"Nessun dorma,"* from Act III of *Turandot*

"When we bring things out into the light,
they lose their power over us."

—*Courage to Change: One Day at a Time in Al-Anon*

Contents

Acknowledgments

A memoir carries the risk of offending someone. In writing this book, I have tried to be faithful to the story as remembered through my journals and hours of reliving painful events and times. Seeking to recount these as truthfully as possible, I may unwittingly upset some people, even those closest to me.

The people and places are all real, though a few names have been changed. With references to Al-Anon I have sought to protect the anonymity of those involved. Therefore, some stories have been modified and some names changed. In some cases I received specific permission to use actual first names. I hope my revelations about Al-Anon will underscore my respect for this group and help to enlighten those who might benefit from it.

While this was a book I had to write, it never would have reached publication without the help of those whose encouragement and guidance were offered so generously: Libby Cataldi, for her inspiration and the long hours together sharing stories of addiction and love for our sons; Laura Oliver, for her professional guidance, instruction, patience and wisdom; Sheryl Sieracki, for her insightful editing; The Olives, my writing group, for cheerleading. I also am grateful for the students and faculty at Apprentice House for recognizing the importance of this story.

I thank my husband, Dick, for honoring the "don't talk to me before noon" rule, for being my first reader, and for believing in me. I thank my daughter, Heidi, for trusting the story. A special nod to Harry, our greyhound, who endured fierce hugs when memories were overwhelming.

Most of all, I am grateful to Jacob. Without his permission this story would remain forever locked inside my journals. He reminds me every day that only through openness and honesty can we hope to conquer addiction. I could not be prouder of the man he has become.

Prologue

Ten women and eight men sit in front of us on a Saturday afternoon. We are in the classroom of a treatment center, and they are the parents, grandparents, spouses, and friends of men and women upstairs, patients undergoing treatment for alcohol and substance abuse. Today is the biweekly Family Workshop session. My husband and I attend regularly to tell our story and to share our experience, strength, and hope. These families need to hear it as much as we need to tell it.

Sometimes when he is home for a visit, our son Jacob joins us. These become the best sessions, when the three of us give these families a glimpse of triumph over addiction, the salve their souls need to weather the next day, sometimes even the next hour.

Inevitably, while my husband or Jacob is speaking, my eyes fall on the reddening face of a mother. Her short, brown hair is a bit wild, untouched since she lifted her head from the pillow that morning. Nights give her some rest—when she shuts her mind against her child's absence—but soothing sleep never comes. She dabs at her eyes with a cream-colored tissue and streaks it with mascara. The day is warm, but her jacket is buttoned to her neck. On her lap her fingers twist and retwist the tissue. She never looks at us. Instead, her eyes close, then pop open again to stare at the small square of faded carpet at her feet.

I know this mother. I know how she suffers. My head and my heart hurt just to watch her.

She is the reason I share this story. Maybe—in the terrible, wrenching days that may lie ahead—it will give her hope, a talisman, a prayer, a candle by her bedside.

Chapter 1

The Phone Call

When the call came, we dropped everything and raced to the Outer Banks, where our son had just started the high school senior's rite of passage—beach week. The caller was a mother of one of the kids, breathless and direct. Jacob was in trouble. Big trouble.

As we barreled down Interstate 95, my husband driving, I watched the barren fields and billboards blur past my window. I pulled out my cellphone and made a quick call to my assistant.

"Mary, I won't be in today. A family issue has come up, and I need to go out of town. I'll be in touch."

That should quell the curious, at least for a few hours. I needed time to think. My orderly world had been overturned in an instant, like an eighteen-wheeler flipped by a storm. I stared absently at the dull landscape, my mind scanning the pages of the past weeks, months, seeking answers. When had this started?

There had been another phone call, many months earlier—ten to be exact. Jacob was just starting his senior year in high school. Dick and I were in the living room watching TV that night, which we seldom did. Normally, I'd spend evenings at events for the hospital where I worked, or curled up in our comfortable, small library at home, alongside Dick's childhood desk, which he'd repainted a high-gloss vanilla. Late in the day, sunlight would stream through the ceiling-high windows and set the copper-colored carpet aglow, beckoning like a hearth. Our library was where I often ended the day and prepared for the next. There was always preparation.

President of the hospital's foundation, I managed a staff of nine and a board of twenty-five. It was a big job—adrenalin-pumping, high-pressured—raising millions of dollars each year, and I couldn't get enough of it. Each time I experienced that thrill of getting a "yes" to a request for a six- or seven-figure gift, I wanted it again. That was real, a path I knew. No highway signs I couldn't read, no panic in my chest. No secrets.

I lived life out in the open. Dick did, too. Secrets just were not a part of our lives. Oh, sure, in the hospital with patients I always respected privacy, and with donors I was extremely careful to keep their confidence. But keeping secrets from each other and from the world was something that just wasn't in my family's DNA.

That started to change when the phone rang on a late August night. A secret began to worm its way into our home. I took the call in the library.

"Lisa? Hi, this is Phil Greenfield. How are you tonight?"

I recognized his name instantly. Greenfield was one of the most beloved teachers at our son's high school. It was the same school where our daughter had gone fifteen years before, and Greenfield had been one of her favorites, too. Why was he calling this late?

"Hey, Phil, how are you?" I responded, hoping the lilt in my voice masked the unease I began to feel. The setting sun seeped through the slatted blinds, striping the room gray.

"I'm sorry to bother you, but several of Jacob's classmates have come to me, and I thought I ought to share this with you." He paused. Silence on both ends of the line. Jacob's classmates had come to him? Why hadn't they come to me? Or Dick? We both knew Jacob's friends, and our home was always open to them. Nestled in the heart of the historic district of Annapolis, it was often the meet-up point for Jacob's friends coming from or going to almost anywhere in town. Phil Greenfield had gotten my full attention, but I was stunned by what came next.

"Lisa, they're worried about him. They say he's drinking. There also might be marijuana. They're seeing him hang around with a different set of kids, which is why they came to me."

Jacob was upstairs in his bedroom, most likely studying. He was just starting his senior year, preparing to apply to colleges like all his friends. Mr. Greenfield would be one of his advisors. Marijuana? Had he really said marijuana and my son's name in the same sentence? He must have gotten it wrong. He'd always liked Jacob. So why was he saying such bizarre things about him now?

"Are you sure? What do you mean different kids? Who told you?"

"Well, I don't know for sure which kids he's hanging with, but I can guess. I don't think the students who came to me would want me to reveal their names, but one was Ned."

Ned was one of Jacob's closest friends. Talented musically, he was big and friendly and very bright. He lived two blocks away and spent many evenings at our house. Jacob liked and trusted him. If Ned had gone to Greenfield, then there could be something to this.

"I can't tell you what to do," Greenfield went on, "but you might want to talk with Jacob."

The sunlight in the room faded. Charcoal shadows crept silently down the walls. At that moment, reality shifted. The copper-colored carpet turned black.

Chapter 2

Sharing a Birthday

As Jacob grew into his teens, he often quipped, "Oh come on, Mom, I know I was an accident." And why wouldn't he think that? I was forty-one when he was born, and in the late eighties that was unusual. Heidi, his sister, was already in her teens.

Although we'd never really discussed it, Dick and I always assumed we would have two children, but once Heidi entered grade school, the thought of having a second child just sort of faded. We both had gotten busy with our professional lives and were deeply engrossed in the town. Annapolis in the seventies and eighties was a growing community, firmly rooted in history and tradition. You were considered an Annapolitan only if you were born there. Dick, a true Annapolitan and natural-born leader, ended his practice as a lawyer to enter politics. With close friends urging him to run, in 1981 he was elected mayor. On election night we celebrated at the local deli with corned beef sandwiches served up with a dash of exhilaration and disbelief. His election meant a change for me, too. After several years as a newscaster for a Baltimore radio station, I now needed to work closer to home. When I learned that the local hospital was recruiting its first public relations director, I seized the opportunity, beginning a new career that lasted more than thirty years.

After his mayoral term ended in 1985, Dick took an administrative position in state government. Community service remained important to us both. We chaired several nonprofit boards, joined the running club, religiously purchased season tickets to the symphony and opera, spent summers hiking in the White Mountains, and built a wide and varied network of friends and colleagues. Heidi was an

A-student and on track for what most parents want for their kids: college, career, marriage, and family. Mornings, the three of us went in separate directions. Evenings, the road led us home, where dinner wrapped up our day like ribbon on a gift.

Then bad news hit. In July 1988 my mother was diagnosed with inoperable lung cancer. I had barely grasped the weight of her diagnosis when, two weeks later, I learned I was pregnant. Over tea at Mom's kitchen table, both of us giddy with my news, she promised to fight to see her new grandchild.

During the months that followed, I experienced both the wrenching sorrow of watching my mother slowly die and the singular joy of feeling the flutter and strong kick of new life inside me. My belly grew bigger; my mother grew thinner. When she asked for permission to learn the baby's gender—a fact Dick and I chose not to know—it was an ominous sign that she might not survive the nine months. In her hospital room we dreamed about the baby and tested various names: Jane for a girl, Jacob for a boy.

On a Monday in late March, my ninth month of pregnancy, my mother died. As I drove home from the hospital that day, a cruel rainstorm slashed at the windshield. Through my tears I screamed back: how could I live the rest of my life without her? In that prescient moment, I knew that the only way to face life without her was facing it one day at a time.

Funeral leave morphed into maternity leave. That's why I was home on Monday, April 10, the morning of Heidi's fifteenth birthday, to hear her pronouncement when she left for school: "Mom, you can have this baby any day you want, just not on my birthday." Six hours later, after an easy labor, she had a brother. In the delivery room, Dick and I marveled that our children—born fifteen years apart—would forever share the same birth date. Both the obstetrician and I were certain the baby would have arrived much earlier had shock and grief not shut down my body the day of my mother's death.

Hours later, neatly tucked under a white sheet and gauzy cotton blanket, I let my eyes wander around the semi-private room. The walls, like the curtain that cut the room in two, were cream-colored and bland. On the far wall a pale gray clock and a watercolor of boats broke the monotony. To my left, two windows reached for the ceiling, their milky blinds half hiding a small courtyard. Weeping cherry trees, just beginning to sprout tiny buds, tapped their branches against the panes. Weary from the last two weeks, I felt thick and billowy in a world gone beige.

The door opened. I heard something small but solid rolling along the linoleum floor. A clear, hard plastic bassinet grazed the curtain, and there he was—in full sight—my newborn son. The nurse rolled him straight up to the left side of my bed as I turned my gaze to find his.

"Here he is," she chirped. "He's all yours. I'll let you two get acquainted and be back in a bit."

The door closed. Finally, we were alone. She had died fourteen days before, almost to this hour, and now here was the grandson my mother would never see. I thought about the past nine months. It gave me such comfort to know she had known the baby was a boy, and that—like her—I would have both a daughter and a son. Most of all, I was grateful for the time we had spent musing over names. She knew him before I did: Jacob.

A tear pooled on my lower lashes, then another, as I took in this tiny new creature. Something red, outside the window just above the bassinet, caught my eye. Perched precisely at eye level was a robin, its head cocked, listening to my sobs. With a start, it swiveled its neck and stared straight at me, then at the baby. Through the mist I stared back at the bird's warm, ruby breast, its soft bob on the branch, and its uncanny interest in this mother and her newborn child. Then, swift and sure, it cocked its head once more and was gone.

Chapter 3

Meant To Be a Leader

Every mother says her baby is the most beautiful. By the time Jacob was three, his looks were stopping people in the street. A photographer-friend with whom I'd worked on marketing publications at the hospital asked if he could photograph him. He came to the house and had us pose on the stairs, positioning me close to Jacob to make him comfortable so the camera could zoom in on his beautiful face. He took a series of close-ups. Today, tucked safely away in the bottom drawer of an antique secretary desk, the striking black and white shots that capture my son's round hazel eyes, the pucker of his lips, the creamy white softness of his cheeks, are a memory I still treasure.

A glossy Baltimore magazine, which found me through professional colleagues, included me in a story on women over forty having babies. In the accompanying photos Jacob sits in the deep scoop of the bathroom sink, his chest naked, while I lean over him wearing a bright blue suit and pearls. I've always felt that the juxtaposition of bath time and me in my work clothes was a bit ludicrous. Still, the shot captures a laughing child with thick dark hair, blinking up at his mother while she laughs back. The magazine had a wide subscription. Some twenty-five thousand people witnessed the adoration I showered on this stunning baby boy.

When it came time for pre-school, I found one of the best. Hidden at the end of a leafy lane, planted on a small rise above one of Annapolis's many creeks, the school offered toddlers just the right balance of play and learning—everything they'd need to know to guarantee them a rich and happy life. On the first day in September, I walked Jacob into the tiny schoolhouse, hugged him, let go of his hand, and walked out, grateful that I was late for work. No time to think too hard about leaving my child in the hands of strangers for the first time, in a new place with other small beings he didn't know. I understood that this was how it was supposed to be, the next logical step in a child's life. He was only three, but already finding his independence from me.

It wasn't until Jacob's primary school years that I began to dream of what he might be like as an adult. In elementary school he developed an eye for anything that flew. Jets, cargo planes, helicopters, airbuses, he knew them all and could readily name them. His interest was fueled all the more when Heidi began dating Jon, a Naval Academy midshipman whose career goal was to pilot helicopters. Even Jon marveled at how Jacob could look up into the sky and easily identify a C-130 cargo plane. So it wasn't too far-fetched to envision Jacob as a twenty-year-old aerospace or engineering major, studiously poring over complex manuals deep in the bowels of an MIT library. MIT became a running gag for the family, but in my mind it was just shorthand for any Ivy League school or major university that would surely propel Jacob to make his mark on the world. Given a sister and parents who adored him, good genes, and obvious intelligence, there was every reason to expect Jacob would do just that.

An incident in elementary school revealed another side of Jacob that first suggested shyness, or a reticence to fit into the crowd. The school was known for putting on a first-rate musical each spring. All the top students, their parents, and many of the teachers got involved. For *The King and I* the music director wanted to cast Jacob on stage with other non-singers. But Jacob resisted, choosing instead to work backstage with a close friend. The two were very much alike. Quick to learn and even quicker to assess others, they preferred the shadows to the spotlight. I thought back to that photo shoot when Jacob was three—his large eyes and the shyness they held. There was a reserve, a holding back, a keen sensitivity to light and people and places. How would he handle that in other scenarios in his life? Would he always shun the spotlight? How could I help him, as he moved on to middle school and high school, to fulfill the vision his parents saw for him?

We imagined our son, born to us later in life, playing a starring role in whatever he decided to do, and earning great recognition for it. We saw ourselves attending ceremonies throughout his life—sitting in the very center of the auditorium, trying hard not to smile too widely, feeling our chests thump with pride, never taking our eyes off of him as he walked up to receive the certificate, the medal, the trophy or the handshake, saying a few words of gratitude, self-deprecation tingeing his speech, offering a high five to the principal or coach, bounding off the stage to the handshakes and man-hugs of teachers, fellow students, and teammates. It was a dream surely all parents dreamed. But we knew that for this boy, it would come true.

At the end of elementary school, Jacob escorted me down the aisle at his sister's wedding. Heidi's marriage to Jon, a Navy ensign, took her away from Annapolis. Like her, Jacob would grow up in a household as an only child. I worried about his feeling lonely and did everything possible to encourage his friendships with classmates.

In high school he continued to show that shyness and reserve, but it drew kids to him. Jacob was the quieter guy whom others turned to for insight or at least the punchline that could break up any tension. His class participated in the first International Baccalaureate program at the high school. That honor placed him with a core group of smart, well-rounded, witty, and interesting students. Dick and I knew them all, and their parents, too. It was the way high school was supposed to be. Our son would thrive in this cradle of camaraderie where the brilliance of colleagues would rub off, shaping and inspiring every one of them.

Despite his shyness and his teachers observing that this was a boy who held back rather than raise his hand, Jacob was recognized for his natural leadership abilities. The faculty chose him to represent the school in the Hugh O'Brien Youth Leadership program and sent him off to a week-long camp to learn what it takes to lead others. The little boy with the big round eyes who scoured the skies for planes might one day hold an important position, perhaps run for office as his father had.

He joined the cross-country team and the marching band, both mostly at his father's urging. Dick was a runner and a founder of the local running club. He also cherished memories of his school years as drum major with the marching band and wanted his son to enjoy a similar opportunity. Jacob's interest in music hadn't fully blossomed yet, and although he had taken piano lessons for a few years, that instrument wasn't suitable for a marching band. With the music director's approval, I trudged him off to a few fast lessons with the Naval Academy Band's top percussionist. It earned him a place with the school band, where he hammed it up a bit on the xylophone in "The Christmas Song." Meanwhile, being on the cross-country team forced him to eat better, get more rest, and bond with a motivated handful of girls and boys for meets at nearby schools.

Like most parents, Dick and I looked at our son through eyes filled with hope and love. We saw Jacob was soaring through high school, becoming the leader we knew he was meant to be.

Chapter 4

Just a Little Brandy
with Some Coke

Getting good grades was easy. In fact, most of life was easy for Jacob. He had friends, parents who worshipped him, and a future. Heidi was living in San Diego at the time, but the two talked frequently, and in some matters—especially with girls—she was his confidante.

To round out his life even more, when he was in his sophomore year Dick and I agreed to participate in a foreign exchange program. We welcomed into our household a sixteen-year-old student from Frankfurt, Germany. Martin was tall, blond, and brilliant. He oozed self-confidence, something Jacob still lacked. Instantly, he adopted Jacob as a brother, sharing his worldly ways, his ease with new people and places, and his knack for leading. Jacob warmed to him right away and was proud that Martin excelled at whatever he did, whether it was acting in the school play or playing tennis.

So it was natural that the two boys planned a reunion when Martin returned to Germany the summer before Jacob's junior year. Although Jacob never shared details, it was enough that they were together, and I trusted Martin to watch out for Jacob. Gertrude, Martin's mother, was a teacher, and I knew she'd keep an eye on them both. It was Gertrude who forced Jacob to send notes home. In one, Jacob wrote, "Well, about the beer and wine. I had some good beer in Berlin that was raspberry-flavored, so it wasn't as bitter. Had quite a few of those over the length of stay in Berlin."

A few days after his return, Jacob wandered out of the house one evening to greet me when I returned from work. In his hand was a glass half full of an amber-colored liquid. As he got closer, I smelled the alcohol. What astonished me most was how casual he was, the sublime ease with which he held the glass. I'd never seen Jacob holding a glass of beer or wine, let alone hard liquor, and the sight shocked me. I didn't hold back.

"Jacob, what are you doing?"

"It's just a little brandy with some Coke," he replied. His calm infuriated me all the more. Was he already tipsy?

"Jacob, are you crazy? You can't drink. What are you doing?" I couldn't understand why he couldn't understand how appalled I was.

"Okay, okay, Mom. Chill. The kids drink in Germany all the time. All Martin's friends drink," he grinned back at me. Was he drunk?

"Yes, but kids don't drink here. That's the law. Throw that stuff away. You're not supposed to be doing that, and you know it," I scolded.

He took another gulp and spilled the remaining contents onto the rose bed. We went into the house without further conversation. For weeks afterward, I tried to shrug off the incident. Jacob showed no other indication that he wasn't obeying the laws of Maryland or our household. Maybe this was just my seventeen-year-old son "post-Europe," still savoring the freedom of a different culture. But the picture of Jacob with that glass in his hand had unnerved me.

The following summer it was the adults' turn to visit Germany. Martin's parents invited Dick and me on a two-week trek to hike in the Alps and tour Bavaria with them. Getting that much time away from the hospital was difficult, but the Alps beckoned. The other concern was Jacob who was about to enter his senior year in high school. I'd heard and read so many stories about kids who get into trouble when parents are away. The parents' vacation was almost a cliché for wild parties and reckless behavior back home.

But this was my son. I trusted Jacob. He'd given me no reason not to. He had a summer job, and we lived in the heart of town with friends and neighbors nearby; surely we could leave him alone for two weeks. Heidi was still living and working in San Diego, but she would be accessible by phone if need be. I decided that Dick and I should go. As an added safeguard, more for my peace of mind than for Jacob, I paid a young woman to check on the house periodically.

The two weeks in Germany flew by. The Alps tested our stamina, and the high mountain huts rewarded us each evening with fireplaces, warming racks, and a soft bed at the end of a long day's climb. Martin's parents couldn't have been better hosts. The four of us became fast friends and reveled in one another's company.

Twice I phoned Jacob. Each time, the conversation felt one-sided. I recounted our visits to many of the places he had been to the previous summer. He shared little, but then, Jacob never talked much. He sounded—okay. I told myself there was no reason to worry.

As soon as we returned home, I sensed it. Something was wrong. Something heavy and sinister had tamped down the airiness of our home. The darkness emanated from Jacob. A different child greeted us. This boy gave off an unhappiness that shut down my expectations for a homecoming filled with chatty talk, unpacking, hugs, and look what we brought you, you love gummy bears, how did you do while we were away, we missed you and love you and are so glad to be home with you now.

Instead, just a few seconds after we entered the house, Jacob angrily accosted us.

"How could you leave me like that?"

"Jacob, what do you mean?" I was shocked at his outburst, confused by his rage.

"How could you just go away to Europe and not leave me any money or any food in the house? There was nothing here."

I looked at Dick, and he, too, seemed baffled. He responded right away. "What do you mean, leave you without any food? We told you that you could do your own shopping. That's why we left you the credit card. You could go the grocery store and get whatever you wanted. You could even go to a restaurant or do carry-out. We told you all that before we left."

"How was I to know I could do that?" said this sullen, dark boy. "There was nothing here," he repeated. "How could you leave me like that?"

The stunning revelation that Jacob had suffered while we were away hit us hard. What kind of parents were we? Off in Europe, laughing with German friends, while our son huddled alone and frightened at home. Still, we didn't get it. We had left Jacob everything he needed to care for himself for fourteen days—food, cash, a car, and a credit card. It was an odd, unsettling homecoming. We remained confused and a little shaken over Jacob's reaction.

Other clues that something was wrong sprouted over the next few weeks, like nasty little weeds poking sharp stalks up into the rose bed. There was a dark stain on the dining room floor. A chair in the living room seemed out of place. A few dishes were cracked or missing. Jacob finally confessed. Yes, he had had some friends over. No, it was never a big party, well, not *that* big. The police never came, or anything like that. It was no big deal.

Tired from our trip, disappointed at his greeting, we weren't pleased that our son had hosted a large party in our absence. Clearly, we hadn't been right to leave him alone. Trust or no trust, he was still seventeen, and things happen when parents are away, even to "trusted" kids. I hated the banality of it all. This wasn't supposed to be my life. My son wasn't born to make the same silly mistakes other kids made. A party in the dining room? Had he really allowed that? Didn't he know his script read a different way?

But once again, Dick and I shrugged it off. We tucked it away as just another adolescent rite of passage. Or so we hoped.

Chapter 5

No Drinking, No Drugs

When the phone rang a few weeks later—that late August evening just after Jacob had begun his senior year—Mr. Greenfield's warning upended all thoughts that anything in our lives would be scripted or planned. It was like a marathoner hitting the wall. Your breathing and pace suddenly falter, and your body fails. Drained and exhausted, you need to stop and suck in air.

I walked back into the living room where Dick still sat watching TV, mildly curious about who had called. The dimly lit room seemed even dimmer. My heart was racing, and my mouth felt dry. But my husband's impassive face steadied me as I recounted the phone conversation. In moments of crisis, I always was grateful that Dick had that ability to remain calm. Normally, I was a rock in crises, too, but this night's call was particularly unnerving. Dick didn't say anything at first, just stared at me, letting the news of his son's apparent marijuana use sink in, neither of us quite sure what to do next.

I called Jacob downstairs. He sounded irritated, a typical teenager annoyed that his parents were interrupting him. Flouncing into the room, he asked, "What's up?" Tall and thin, Jacob had the same pale complexion and dark, almost coal-black hair of his father. With thick expressive eyebrows against a pale face, he sometimes looked much older. My friends often told me, almost conspiratorially, "Jacob is so handsome!" I knew that. But I was never sure he did. He hunched his nearly six-foot frame on the sofa next to me, but a safe distance away.

"Jacob, Mr. Greenfield just called," I began. That got his attention. "He said several of your friends have come to him, and they're concerned you're smoking marijuana."

Then I committed the unpardonable sin, although I knew better. Never corner an angry foe. Always give him a way out. But without any forethought, I bluntly challenged him. "Are you?"

What could he say? To his credit, he didn't lie. Avoiding my eyes, he stared at the living room rug, shrugged his shoulders slightly, and replied, "Who told him? Who went to him?"

Clever tactic, I thought. Change the subject and focus on the whistleblowers.

"It doesn't matter. This is serious. Dad and I are concerned. If you're smoking marijuana, you need to stop. Just . . . stop." Even as I said it, I realized how moronic it sounded, but it wasn't until years later that I would understand how very naïve it was, too.

He shrugged his shoulders again, barely looking at me from beneath those thick eyebrows. "Okay? So can I go back upstairs now?" His face was impassive, difficult to read, like a shattered reflection in a splintered mirror.

When he left the room, Dick and I sat stunned. The phone call had triggered a tiny pinpoint of panic that settled deep inside me, like a mallet pinging against my heart, pumping adrenaline through my veins, pulsing chords of fear throughout my body and brain. I was a provoked animal, charged and ready for . . . I had no idea, but certainly something ominous and threatening had entered my household. I needed for this—whatever "this" was—*not* to happen. I needed to avoid looking at the dark shadow looming in the corner. But it was there, suddenly present, lurking in the hallway, following me everywhere in my house . . . like the warning signs on a pre-cancerous x-ray. This patient's going to need further testing. Schedule him for a biopsy so that we can be sure. It'll be hard on the family, but they'll just have to wait and see what happens next, because there's no overnight fix for this one.

I was definitely a fixer. Weren't all women? Didn't it come with being a mother? When Heidi was three, she tumbled down the brick front steps of the house and opened a gash just below her eye. All I had to do was scoop her up, race to the emergency room, hold her down on the exam table, and let out a sigh of relief when she got stitched up. That was easy. Accidents happen. Kids take tumbles all the time. But this sudden, frightening, amorphous blackness for which I had no name was altogether new, and if I thought about it at all, if I paused even long enough to give it a sideways glance, it was the most horrifying thing I'd ever faced. So I would just have to fix it.

The very next morning I used every resource at work to find someone to see Jacob. Pathways was the logical first stop. A freestanding substance use treatment center, Pathways was part of the local health system, and I knew everyone there. Without revealing any details, I phoned and asked the director for names of therapists in the area who might help young people. Helen Reines, the executive director, kindly responded without asking too many questions.

In addition to fear, the shame was overwhelming. I felt compelled to conceal that my son might have a drug problem. It seemed impossible, so incongruous, that this—"thing"—had crept into our family. Drug use lived in broken families, where fights erupted and husbands punched their wives in full sight of screaming children. No wonder those kids turned to drugs. But not in my clean household. My heart raced and face flushed when I considered the possibility that someone might find out. I needed to keep this secret from everyone, at least until I could get a handle on it myself.

The list of therapists was not a long one. Resources in general for troubled young people in our county were sparse. I picked one from the pile, a PhD psychologist whom I'd vaguely heard good things about, and swiftly decided that Jacob would see him.

At dinner that night, the conversation turned serious.

"Jacob, Dad and I love you very much, but right now we're worried about you. We don't know for sure what's going on, but you're showing all the signs of someone drinking or using drugs. You need to know that we'll do whatever it takes to protect you from hurting yourself or someone else. This is very serious, Jacob. We are very worried."

Jacob fought back, but not as vociferously as I had expected. At one point he said, "Well, we never had that talk when you're thirteen and your parents sit you down."

Really? Did he seriously believe that because we had never spelled it out we might condone his use of alcohol or drugs?

"Well, no," he said, "But maybe it got a little fuzzy." He again brought up his inability to take care of himself when we were in Europe that summer.

"Jacob," I said, "If it felt like we abandoned you, I am really sorry, and I apologize for that."

"Yeah, I know. I guess it showed me that I really can't do a very good job being on my own."

I studied his pale face, a child struggling to prove he was grown up, nowhere near the confident, open adult I hoped he would still become. In the end Dick stated firmly, "No drinking. No drugs."

Maybe he hadn't heard it at thirteen. But he did at seventeen.

Chapter 6

The Missing Bong

The next morning, after Jacob left for school, I went searching for the latest issue of *Time*. I'd subscribed since college, and now Jacob frequently read it. I loved that he had an interest in reading a weekly news magazine, and we often shared stories about whatever was covered. Did he have it? Was it near his bed? My search led to his room. Maybe in the drawer by his bed?

Then I saw it—a strange-looking, brightly colored, glass-like, twisted thing. All the educational sessions Pathways had presented at hospital-wide staff meetings came roaring into my brain. This was a bong. Hidden, hideous, and offensive, it was raw proof of Jacob's involvement with drugs. After scooping my heart from the floor, I called for Dick. Staring at the thing, we both jumped to the next fear: had Jacob depleted his bank account? Recently, he had asked our help in opening an account for him. We assumed he would deposit his paychecks from his part-time job as a barista at a local coffee shop. Much later, I marveled at how quickly we leaped from the sight of the bong to the thought of lost wages. Wasn't that what happened when there were drugs? Money suddenly disappeared? Already, I felt as though Dick and I were in a bad movie. Parents discover kid using drugs. Parents learn money is missing. How quickly we had gone from a beloved teacher's phone call to real anxiety about drug addiction in our household. This was tangible evidence. No longer could we deny Jacob's involvement, even though we tried.

A quick call to the bank confirmed that the account was fine. We agreed that Dick shouldn't cancel his annual volunteer stint for the Appalachian Mountain Club, and he left for New Hampshire that day, leaving me to face Jacob alone that evening.

Throughout my workday, I mulled over how to confront him. I hated confrontation. I just wasn't good at it. My boss had once counseled me that I'd never make a great executive unless I learned the subtle art of dealing with people who weren't measuring up. So I'd worked on it, and with my CEO as a great mentor, I'd gotten a bit tougher and more self-confident in tackling hard conversations.

When I got home, Jacob already was there. He hung around my room, chatting about school and a biology test, while I changed from business suit to jeans. I told him I'd made his first appointment with the therapist, and he seemed fine with that. We wandered back into his room. Eyeing him carefully, calculating his mood, I brought up my search for the magazine and why I'd opened the drawer by his bed. I watched for his reaction. For a fleeting moment, I thought there might be an explosion. But he recovered. He said it wasn't his, he hadn't smoked marijuana, he was just holding it for a friend. Most of all, he seemed stunned that I'd recognized what it was.

"So you have friends who are smoking marijuana?" I asked.

He didn't like the question. "No, it was a while ago. I was just holding that for someone."

"Okay, then," I responded, opening the drawer and reaching for the bong, "Let's get rid of it."

There was nearly a struggle, but with one swift move he grabbed the thing out of my hand, ran downstairs with me on his heels, opened the kitchen trash bin, and tossed it in.

Over dinner, the conversation again proved to be revealing. He was testing my knowledge. How did I know it was a bong, anyway? I reminded him of my affiliation with Pathways and that long before my current career I had worked at Crownsville State Mental Hospital, where I learned about mental illness and substance use. I was bluffing a little. I didn't want to admit that today's drugs went far beyond anything I could comprehend, from their make-up to their allure to the whole sordid drug "scene." It was all quite foreign and new to me, something I didn't want to face. Wasn't this handsome young man next to me at the dinner table headed for college and the happy, fulfilling life we'd set for him?

Jacob had other ideas. Lamenting the amount of homework he was getting, he said his interest in learning had been "beaten out of me." He vacillated between bemoaning his current school load and the college applications he faced, and expressing confidence that he would go to college, graduate, and one day have a good job. He talked and talked. One minute he wondered how he would ever be "ready" to be "on" his own if we were always on him, and the next minute he complained that we expected too much. I didn't get it. Shouldn't we allow him to apply for colleges on his own and not remind him of consequences if he missed deadlines? Well, no, he responded, not quite like that.

"Jacob, what I hear you saying is that you feel grown up, but you don't feel ready to do all of this by yourself."

"Yeah, I guess so."

"Well, I am "on" you now because of what we discussed last night. When I feel comfortable about your health and safety, then I'll back off a little."

Dick would be away for a week. Trying hard to maintain calm in the household, I felt isolated and alone. Over time, I would learn that's classic for addiction. Not only does it isolate the user, it can isolate the family as well. The worst part was the shame. I was embarrassed and terrified that someone would find out my son was using drugs. I wanted to trust Jacob. I wanted this new thing in our lives to go away, and until it did, I had to keep it secret.

The next morning brought a new horror. Taking out the trash, I had a bad feeling. Curious, I culled through the kitchen garbage can as its contents spilled into an outside bin. The bong was missing. Had Jacob really come back into the kitchen and retrieved it? Over the phone that afternoon, Dick asked me why I hadn't discarded it and gotten it away from the house. I'd simply have to confront Jacob again.

Leaving the office early, I beat Jacob home. More and more, I was finding reasons to be home. The prickly, uncomfortable mantle of watchdog was slowly forcing itself on me. Jacob came home with a friend, Chris, a tall, impressive young man, clean and focused, adept at foreign languages, a world traveler, someone I liked around my son. While Chris stayed downstairs, I called Jacob up to his room to question him about the missing bong. He appeared stunned that I'd actually searched for it in the garbage can. It was the first time the concept of "distrust" reared its head between us.

"Why were you even going through my drawers in the first place?" he countered. At one point, he almost said that he had returned the bong to the person who owned it, but when I zoned in on that, he squirmed. The conversation began to escalate.

"You know, Mom, I thought we were having a two-way street, but now I'm beginning to build a brick wall, and I'll just keep building it."

I backed off. The line between us was fragile enough. If I pushed too hard, Jacob would shut me out and then . . . what?

"I'm going to see the psychologist, right? If he tells you that I am okay, will you be okay with that?"

"Yes, all right," I relented. "That will go a long way towards helping me not to worry."

For the next several weeks, I tried to avoid Jacob's room. It was a typical teenage boy's room, the bed always a rumple of sheets and blankets, clothes in small clumps on the floor, notebook papers and folders littering the blue wall-to-wall carpet. Walking in the room was nearly impossible. I wasn't sure if the mess was a symptom of Jacob's internal chaos or just laziness. Regardless, the bedroom became a beacon, beckoning me like a siren to witness an emergency. For a while, I resisted. My son deserved privacy, and if he couldn't have it in the sanctity of his own room, then where could he? Besides, he was now seeing the therapist twice a month. I had promised Jacob that I would back off if his therapist told me he was "okay."

In a private session with Dick and me, the psychologist reassured us that Jacob was simply going through common anxieties that adolescents often face. Sure, he might be using a little marijuana, but that was not unusual at his age. His grades were otherwise fine, right? And no, he wouldn't tell us what he and Jacob discussed, but basically, we shouldn't be overly concerned.

Much as I wanted them to be, his words were not terribly reassuring. This experienced, highly degreed-professional seemed so sure that Jacob would be fine. He also knew a lot more about kids like Jacob than I did. So I should trust him and trust my son, right? The tiny pinging against my heart quieted, but it never stopped.

Chapter 7

Crossing Another Stage

Fall came, and Jacob was now a senior. Whether he was smoking marijuana or not, Dick and I couldn't tell, but he seemed to be obeying our rules. It was college-application time, and we were "on" him to secure his place in a school where he would be happy and challenged. While not stellar, his grades were still okay, and even Mr. Greenfield acknowledged that Jacob could get into some pretty good schools if he tried. With a lot of coercion and unabashed nagging from us, Jacob applied to several colleges, including Boston University, Emory, and the University of Maryland. I hoped for Boston University, imagining my son at least close to MIT—maybe for graduate school? I wasn't ready to give up my dream of seeing him on a university campus along the shoals of the Charles River, enraptured by college life and late-night coffee-fueled conversations with wickedly intellectual professors and witty, wide-eyed girls.

That autumn, a new friend of Jacob's appeared. George was everything Jacob was not: self-confident, sophisticated—even a bit worldly—and highly creative. He was headed for a career in drama and had even once used our kitchen to film a short movie. Along with George came other friends. Marty was a big, hulking kid. He seemed polite enough but rarely made eye contact and appeared awkward even in his own clothes. I knew little about his background other than that he lived with his mother. Jacob began spending more and more time with George and his friends.

The next warning came about a month later. Dick and I were called into school to meet with Jacob's counselor and his English teacher. The call surprised us considering by then Jacob had received acceptances from both Maryland and Boston. His college path was assured. Apparently, however, our son was in danger of failing for lack of handing in basic assignments. Just having this conversation with these professionals made me cringe. Something was wrong here. We didn't belong in this room, hearing someone critique our child. Maybe his grades had slipped these past few months, but at least two colleges wanted him. Lots of kids goof off their final semester in high school. Wasn't it permissible to allow him a little slack?

I felt that there was something else here that no one was saying and wondered if drugs were behind Jacob's change. And if I sensed it, didn't they? Why didn't they bring it up, much less help us do something about it? Why wasn't anyone talking about the real problem?

We listened politely to the teachers and expressed our concern. We promised to talk with Jacob. But I left both thankful that no one had brought up the issue of drugs and furious that they hadn't. It was my secret and my shame, and I might have raced from the room if they had mentioned it. But surely, as professionals in a big high school with more than 1,800 students, they faced this every day. How did they handle it? Why didn't they help me to help my son?

With no advice or offer of help from school officials, it was left to Dick and me. When we got home, we recounted the meeting to Jacob.

"Jacob, this sounds serious. Why aren't you turning in those assignments? You'd better get them done, or you'll flunk this class, and they can keep you from graduating."

Even as we said it, it sounded preposterous. Jacob Hillman? Held back from graduating? Even if there were drugs still lurking somewhere, certainly he would finish high school and move on. Other kids might not, those from broken homes or without parents. They were the kids who came from trash-littered neighborhoods where they didn't feel the arms of love around them every evening. Not like our house, where favorite foods filled the pantry and fridge, where fork, knife, spoon, and napkin neatly framed a porcelain plate on a pale yellow placemat that matched the walls. While I'm up, want me to get you more? Would you like more iced tea? How about more mashed potatoes? They're Cape Cod potatoes, the way we had them last summer. Dad made them especially for you, with chopped-up onions and garlic, just the way you like them. Another spoonful? At our table, there was no room for drugs.

Senior year slipped into spring. Jacob was invited to join a freshman honors program at the University of Maryland at College Park, and he accepted. In early April, a mother of one of the girls in Jacob's circle invited parents to get together to plan for senior beach week. By then, Jacob was turning in all his assignments on time, and the absurdity of his not passing had wafted away with the warm spring breeze.

At work, I faced the early stage of yet another major capital campaign. Now that the institution had moved to a new, sprawling one-hundred-acre campus just outside of Annapolis, people from surrounding counties had discovered it. The local hospital was fast becoming a regional medical center. We launched plans for a $450 million expansion to add an eight-story patient tower and a two-hundred-thousand-square-foot medical office pavilion. A study suggested we could raise at least $40 million within the next four years, and that became my new challenge.

In an infuriating, but ultimately fortunate, turn of events, Dick now was home most days. A new governor had cleaned house of political appointees; Dick was not one, but nevertheless he was asked to leave his post. The callous manner in which nearly 173 employees were fired in one day angered us. But eventually, always seeking to find the good in the bad, Dick and I realized it was fortuitous to have him home now.

They say kids need parents present even more in their teenage years than in earlier years, and that certainly seemed true with Jacob. He was active in after-school activities, like sports and the marching band, and spent time with friends at their homes, which made Dick want to be around to ensure his safety and well-being. With my hectic days, which often meant late-night meetings and events, I was glad to know that at least one parent was available. While we never voiced it, Dick and I assumed that just having an adult in the house every day meant Jacob would have the security he needed. We felt we were doing everything right, staying close to our son, to guarantee a smooth senior year. Certainly, no trouble could find him.

Even after the call from Mr. Greenfield and a few meetings with teachers near the end of the school year, Dick and I behaved as if all was well and didn't hesitate in allowing Jacob to enjoy beach week after graduation. As long as we were responsible enough to meet with other parents whose kids would hang out together in a rented, sprawling beach house on the Outer Banks of North Carolina, what could go wrong? Abby, the mom who called the meeting, would be in a condo nearby and would keep an eye on everyone. No drinking, and certainly no drugs, would be allowed. Twelve kids were going. Each was headed for college in the fall, got along with one another, and promised to watch out for each other. We parents were relieved that our children would not be doing beach week in Ocean City, Maryland, which was infamous for stories of binge drinking, kids falling out of second-story windows, and other youthful transgressions that headlined daily papers every June.

Graduation arrived. Held in a large arena near Washington, DC, that hosts horse shows and other large events, it was appropriately cavernous to accommodate several thousand parents, family members, and friends, each trying to get a glimpse of their graduate as she or he paraded into the giant hall. From seats seemingly miles away from the stage, the Hillman party of six—Dick and I, Heidi, Jacob's Aunt Helaine down from Philadelphia, plus two close friends—telescoped eyes to find Jacob among all the other blue-capped heads. Desperate to enjoy this milestone in my son's life, I tried hard to push away all worry about his possible drug use. For weeks, I'd avoided any conversation about it. Dick and I had settled into some sweet spring fog, wanting to believe it had been just a fleeting fancy in our son's life.

After he was graduated, he would kick up his heels this summer before buckling down to the serious, goal-oriented, mature student we knew he could be. When his name was called and the figurine dressed in blue gown and cap walked across the stage, we sighed with relief. High school was done.

After the ceremony, it was hard to find him, even at the appointed third-from-the-door white-post-facing the entranceway that was our designated rendezvous point. Once he finally appeared, he barely looked at any of us and announced that he was heading off with friends.

"But Jacob," I protested, "your aunt and sister are here and our friends. We thought we'd take you out for a bite to eat."

He acquiesced and came with us, but the rest of the evening was all too surreal. This wasn't how the post-graduation family festivities were supposed to go. When Heidi graduated from college, everyone came back to our house for crab cakes and beef tenderloin. With Jacob, all I wanted was an hour or so, uninterrupted by his friends, where he would be with his family, fully in the moment, sharing stories of what it was like to wait in line and to sit through all those boring speeches. Does anyone remember what their high school graduation speaker said?

Instead, once seated at a nearby restaurant, he pecked at his chicken wings, responded when asked a question, and perfunctorily apologized as he ran off to join waiting friends. My sister-in-law laughed it off. Typical of that age, she smiled. No big deal, everyone said, recalling their own high school graduations. Even Heidi couldn't begrudge her brother for wanting to dash off with friends on this night of nights.

I knew better. Something was wrong, very wrong, but I didn't want to face it.

Chapter 8

The Call from Carolina

When I reflect on Jacob's late-adolescent years, the horror is measured in phone calls. Each one brought another crisis. The call from Mr. Greenfield at the dawn of senior year had started it. Now, just days after graduation, came the call that changed everything.

Jacob had driven down to the Outer Banks the morning after graduation with Marty, the husky friend of George, who had his own truck. Instinctively, I worried about Marty and suspected he smoked cigarettes or drank at least, as most of the kids did. Dick and I knew little about him, other than that he hung out with the kids and George was one of his best friends.

It was a weekday evening, the sun setting on a typical, busy, June day. I picked up the phone in the kitchen. Abby's voice startled me. There was no introduction; she just charged right in.

"Lisa, Jacob's been arrested. He's in jail. The police picked him up with George, driving on the beach. He was headed to another house where some other students were staying. They found little bags of marijuana in his pocket and some other things. They took the truck. George went back to the house, and the police have Jacob."

Panic overwhelmed me, the same as when Greenfield called months ago. My brain couldn't process Abby's words as fast as she was slinging them. I didn't understand why Jacob had been arrested and George was free.

"So listen . . . I think I can get him out of jail. We got lucky because there's this cool attorney here, and he talked with the police, and they're letting Jacob go back to the house with me. But he has to be in court the day after tomorrow."

My mind raced. How could I "fix" this one? What happens next, and after that? After calling Dick into the kitchen and pulling him into the conversation, I thanked Abby and quickly formulated plans to drive to North Carolina the next morning. The rest we'd figure out as we went.

We were stunned—and yet, not really. We'd known all along that something was wrong with Jacob, but we hadn't wanted to acknowledge it was drugs or been willing to face that our son's sullenness was in any way connected with drugs. Nor could we, at that point, begin to understand how sick he was and was becoming.

The call itself hadn't shocked me. It only opened the door, giving me a peek into the painful understanding that our lives were becoming incredibly, horribly complicated. Shame overwhelmed me. Bad enough he was using drugs, but now arrested? Held, even for a few hours, in a jail? The ugliness of it made me sick. I tried hard not to think about him in that environment. Thank goodness Abby had gotten him out of there, because whatever "there" was, it had to be awful. And what if it made the papers? How would I ever face anyone in town again? Would my job be in jeopardy? I hated myself for thinking all these thoughts when Jacob was in such trouble, but they kept assailing me.

So if I couldn't instantly fix this one, at least I could get busy trying. Doing something was better than doing nothing. Jacob was in trouble, potentially serious trouble. I was his mother. I needed to act.

The next day before leaving for North Carolina, I phoned the attorney whom Abby had mentioned and lined him up to represent Jacob in court. His assistant sounded pleased that a family member was willing so quickly to shell out the five-thousand-dollar fee it would take to handle the case. And yet, I had the distinct sense that this woman knew this scenario quite well. It wasn't the first time an anxious parent had phoned Currituck County, North Carolina, willing to pay any amount to make things all right again for a son or daughter. I was grateful for her soft, kind voice on the phone, reassuring me that, yes, Robert Barnes was one of the best attorneys for this sort of thing and had a great way with young people. Just hearing this, and knowing we had a smart lawyer on our side, helped calm the panic I'd felt since Abby's call.

I'd spoken to Jacob only briefly the previous evening. He was barely audible over the cell phone, mumbling monosyllables to my questions. Are you okay? What happened? Why were you doing that? Crazy, dumb questions that blurted out from my despair and desperation. Questions that he couldn't answer then or even later and didn't even matter at the time. Just words—noise—to fill the black silence on the phone line between us.

When I spoke with him again, before leaving for North Carolina, he seemed glad to know that the cool attorney he'd met the night before would be his. In the background, I heard the easy, happy chatter of high school graduates on a sunny beach morning. I couldn't imagine what they were thinking about Jacob, or where George was, or who knew what, or if they even cared. I only knew I had to go to my son and help him through this terrible next day. Together, Dick and I would get Jacob back on track. There was still time to get this right. He had all summer, and the most important thing was to get him to college in the fall. He'd been accepted into the honors program; his dorm was all lined up. There were a scant two and a half months until a new life began for him. We just had to get this current ugliness behind us and keep him safe over the summer. We could do that. We could still fix this.

When we arrived in North Carolina, we gasped at our first sight of the house. It wasn't just a beach house. It was a mansion. Inside a gated community at the end of a cul-de-sac, it was a colossal, three-story, million-dollar modern home with a circular drive and elegant staircase. Who rents a house like this to teenagers, I wondered. Do these kids know how lucky they are to be in a place like this?

Entering the house, I took in the sweep of the large living area that stretched back onto an open deck. What struck me was the sight of teenagers—lots of them, ten or fifteen—clustered around a glass cocktail table, lounging on sofas, chairs, rugs, all in a bright, naturally lit, large room with a high ceiling, white walls, and back wall of all glass. My eyes squinted at the gorgeous expanse of brilliant blue Atlantic beyond. The kids were eating dinner, listening to music, engrossed in conversations. It was a scene from a movie. The air was bright, and they all seemed so happy, so comfortable with each other.

Expecting a far different scene, I found the setting calming. For an instant, I was glad that my son had enjoyed time here in this extravagant home with these happy friends. Taking it in, I had the acute sense that we'd walked in on a family.

My eye caught George seated on the far side of the room, talking with two other boys. He nodded to me but never got up. Jacob was nowhere in sight. In fact, none of the kids seemed disturbed or surprised to see us. Finally, one young man rose from the floor and came over to give me a big hug. It was Mac, another of Jacob's longtime friends from the track team, a boy with lots of family troubles but a sweetness that drew peers and adults alike to him. I would remember forever that Mac was the only one who greeted us, who hugged me, who seemed to understand the mess that was about to descend on our family. He knew mess, and he was sorry to see it visit us. Mac went to find Jacob.

A closed door off of the main room opened, and Jacob appeared. He was wearing a white tee shirt and jeans. With eyes cast down, he was trying hard to avoid looking at us. He smiled slightly but definitely was not happy to see us. Not now, not here, not this week. Then came the hard part.

"Jacob, let's go, "Dick said.

Jacob looked up. "Go? What do you mean, go?"

"We're leaving. Get your things. We need to go," Dick ordered.

"Well, I'm coming back, right? I'll be back later, right?"

The insanity struck me. Did Jacob actually think he was just leaving for a quick jaunt down to the courthouse? Yes, your honor, no, your honor . . . , then he would resume his happy-go-lucky beach vacation as though nothing had happened? Was my son really that far out of touch? Or really such a child?

With increasing force, Dick insisted he get his "stuff" and meet us at the car. There was nothing left but for us to turn our backs, say goodbye to Mac, and walk out of the house as quickly as possible, leaving Jacob to his farewells. We waited in the car for him. When he finally trudged down the long fancy staircase, one of the girls walked alongside him. Julia also was a good friend and from a good family. She loved Jacob as a brother, and the two would be lifelong friends, regardless of what life held for them.

"Jacob, what about your sweatshirt?" she called after him, holding a lump of gray cloth.

"No, you keep it," Jacob shouted back in his deep, husky voice. "I can get it when I come back."

And with that, he plopped into the back seat and slammed the door. Dick took off. Silence. Seconds later, he repeated, "I am coming back here, right?"

This time, I spoke up. "Jacob, do you really think that after what you've done you'll actually just go back to that house? Are you serious?" I felt the exasperation rising in my voice.

"What? I'm not going back? Really? Do you know what you've done? Taking me out of there? All my friends are back there. That's my family, and you're taking me away from them?"

Was the word "family" meant to jab at me, or was he just affirming what I, too, had felt back in that sunlit room? I made no reply. There was nothing to say. A few quiet seconds passed. Then, without any warning, within the dark silence of our speeding car, I heard a howl so loud and so strange that I turned to Dick and asked, "What was that? Was that a wolf on the side of the road?" It was unearthly, surreal. The sound wasn't outside the car. It was coming from inside, from the back seat. Jacob was sobbing, emitting a high-pitched wail so mournful it hurt to hear. He was screaming, howling. For a second

I actually wondered if a bullet had pierced the window and struck him. It was the painful cry of a wounded animal, but much worse. The sound was pure anguish, sheer despair, as though he were being slowly mutilated. It was horrible, and I shut my eyes against it as tears welled up.

"How could you do this? How could you take me out of there?" he sobbed. "I love those people. They're family. I'll never see them again, not all together like that. Never!"

What is pain? I wondered. Pain is something you point to. It's real. Show me where it hurts, the physician says, and you put a fingertip on your stomach or your shoulder or a wrist. But this? Where does *this* hurt come from?

Silence enveloped the car as the beautiful strands of North Carolina's Outer Banks streamed past the car windows. We rolled down the road, three prisoners in a cage, while outside, happy children and parents taunted us in front of gleaming vacation homes.

By the time we picked up dinner at a carryout and arrived at the motel—although how anyone would be able to eat I had no idea—Jacob had calmed down. The place was one of those nondescript roadside joints that people book in haste when someone is in trouble. I wondered what other miseries lay behind the closed doors, but I didn't care. We weren't going to be here long. Just overnight. Just long enough to get this all behind us.

Jacob followed us into the small room and dropped onto one of the two double beds, shoulders hunched, staring at the floor. No one said anything. After the violent eruption in the car, we craved the silence.

Silence was a thing that had become both a friend and a curse. So much not said. So many times I wondered, if only I had said something *then* . . . When he was disappearing at night, or hiding in his room, or going off to who knows where with George until 2, 3, or 4 a.m. When I couldn't sleep for listening for his footfall on the stairs to know he was home, safe, in his bed. When I was worried, too worried even to speak. So I let the silence take over because it was easier that way. To speak might conjure up terrible words and destroy whatever it was we had as a family. We loved each other. Of that, I was sure. But would facing it—this "it" that was shutting us down—destroy our love, too?

Tonight we had to talk. There was a court hearing in the morning, and we had to be ready. Jacob was facing two felony charges and two misdemeanors: not just possession of marijuana, but intent to sell it. The police had stopped him and George while they were driving Marty's truck across the beach, a violation in itself. They were heading for another house where kids from an Annapolis private school were having their beach week. Jacob was driving. According to him, George had let him carry "all the stuff" in his pockets, so when the police searched them, they only were interested in Jacob.

For the next three hours, Jacob opened up. Not only did he share the details of what led to his arrest, but he let loose a tirade of teenage fears and misery. Some of it made sense, but a lot of it didn't. I fought to stay quiet and let him talk, and he tried to stay calm. We all did. He told us he wasn't sure "how I can make it on my own . . . I don't know anything, Ma," he cried, "I don't even know how to write a check." He rambled on that he couldn't do anything. "I'm not sure I can make it in college. But I know I should go, because I have to. It's the only thing that's next." And then he said, "I don't know. Sometimes I think I'm becoming autistic." He said he hadn't written a thank-you note for a cousin's graduation gift. That worried him. Why hadn't he done that yet? He slid into anti-government comments and why do we have laws? Are we really free? When I tried the "Yes, Jacob, but with freedom comes responsibilities" response, he said, "Yeah, right, but I've been thinking about going to Spain."

As the conversation waxed from semi-reality to total senselessness, I wondered when he'd last smoked marijuana. He told me he hadn't smoked for more than twenty-four hours. Years later I would better understand the effect of drugs. That night Jacob was expressing deep anguish from a troubled soul, but he also was likely babbling under the effects of whatever was still in his bloodstream. That was the only explanation for a three-hour outpouring of genuine pain, intense anxieties over leaving high school and entering college, and outlandish thoughts of someone messed up with too many chemicals in his brain.

The next morning, I stole a few minutes to walk on the beach while Jacob and Dick slept. Sitting on a bench, I took in the pounding waves, the gray dawn, the scampering seabirds. I prayed for my son. For years, I'd kept a journal. Pouring my fears and worries onto clean, blank pages was a way to keep my sanity. On this strangest of mornings, when the three Hillmans were about to enter a courthouse where Jacob's future would be decided, the fear of the unknown was almost overwhelming. I wrote:

> *How can we help him? This is our job. I can*
> *line up the lawyer and the therapist. I can call in an*
> *army of professionals who are good at their trades.*
> *But this is my son and my flesh. I care more than*
> *anyone. How can I help him?*

I remembered what I'd told Jacob the previous night before we finally stopped talking and hoped for sleep: One day at a time. Let's focus on one day at a time. And I recalled what my father often had told me: Lis, if you take care of the little things, the big things will take care of themselves. I hoped we both were right.

Chapter 9

Our Day in Court

Dressed in suits, the three of us entered the Currituck County Courthouse. The cool, marble floors and whitewashed walls offered some relief from the hot, sultry day outside. A beefy-looking guard smiled us in through the security scanner, and we entered a wide, open hallway that held a row of oversized closed doors leading to the courtrooms.

Robert Barnes was easy to spot. He was standing at the far end of the hall, chatting it up with a guard who kept slamming his palm down on the desk and laughing heartily. Tall, lanky, clean-cut in a dark gray, striped suit, Barnes looked ever the local basketball star—Currituck County's favorite son, all grown up and serving his community. Everyone seemed to know him. His assistant had been right. The man had a command of the place. Eyeing us from across the broad hallway, he quickly finished his story with the guard, who let out a loud guffaw and slapped Barnes on the arm. Barnes strode toward us with the loopy grace of a man who knows the game and how to play it. Jacob was instantly taken with him. Like George, he exuded a confidence and ease that Jacob longed to have.

"Mr. and Mrs. Hillman and Jacob, I presume?" He extended his hand and tilted his head so we could make direct eye contact with his clear blue eyes. In seconds, he ushered us into a tiny side room and rapidly reviewed Jacob's case. Barnes reminded me of all the top-notch physicians I knew. They breezed into a patient's room, but once there, they gave that patient their full-faced attention. Even if it was only for a few seconds, it was focused, direct, eye-to-eye: You have my attention now, and I'm going to give you every bit of my years of training and experience to get you out of this mess and back to your normal and happy life. Trust me.

I did, and I liked Barnes immediately. We all did. Obviously, he'd been through this scenario many times. In minutes he laid out the plan. With one hand on Jacob's shoulder, in big-brotherly fashion he looked at my son and advised him, "Try to do the right thing. This was a one-time, spring break mistake. You're a college man. You're going to do all the right things it takes to be a productive citizen." Jacob nodded, mesmerized by this older guy's air of assurance, and we dutifully followed him into the courtroom.

I sat with Dick while Jacob joined a long parade of (mostly) young men, women, and adolescents who looked no older than he did, as they lined up along the far wall, awaiting their brief appearance before the judge. It was over in seconds. I wasn't sure what had happened until Barnes explained that his plan had worked, and here's what Jacob needed to do: Go home and be a good citizen. Stay clean this summer. Go to college in the fall. It wouldn't hurt to continue seeing a counselor; that would help later. Barnes would be in touch and—best case?—would work this out so that eventually Jacob's record might even be expunged.

In the end, Barnes secured for Jacob a clean future, at least legally. Jacob was given "PBJ"—the first time I'd ever heard that phrase applied to anything but what children ate for lunch. Barnes explained that at sentencing, later in the year, the judge might mandate community service and a letter of apology, but for now we were free to go. The entire experience had been unnerving and humiliating, at least for me. As an attorney, Dick was more familiar with courthouses, but certainly not with a member of his own family as a criminal defendant, let alone his only son. As for Jacob, did he realize how very lucky he was? He was arrested for possession of an illegal substance with intent to distribute, the three of us had endured shock and embarrassment at finding ourselves in a North Carolina courthouse on a summer's morning, the attorney would cost nearly $6,500—but Jacob would have a way out of the legal mess that could destroy his future. There would be another court experience in the months ahead, but for now he was given probation before judgment and sent home.

It would be an overstatement to say that we left the courthouse jubilant, but our relief was palpable. As we settled into the car for the ride home, the conversation quickly turned serious, just as it had the previous night in the dim motel room. From the back seat, Jacob commented on how smooth Barnes was.

"He's really a cool guy. Didn't you like the way everyone knew him? Maybe I'll do that, go to law school. Maybe I could be a lawyer."

"Jacob, you'd make an excellent lawyer. You like to analyze things, and you like to argue. You can do whatever you want to do. You know that."

"Yeah, but I really don't know what I want to do. I don't know. I'm not even sure it even matters."

The comment sounded so despondent, I lobbied back, "What do you mean, you're not sure it matters?"

"I mean, why even go to college if I'm not sure what I'm going to do? I don't know. I'm not sure what I'm saying."

"That's why you go. That's what college is for. So you can find out what you're good at and try different things that you'll enjoy."

"Yeah, but I'm not good at anything."

"Oh, c'mon, Jacob, you know that's not true. You're smart, you're good at math and computers, and you love music. There are all kinds of things you're good at."

"Yeah, but I'm not really that good. I mean, really, Mom, really? Why do you work? I know you work for the money and all, but why does it really matter?"

Staring straight ahead at the bland landscape, I reached hard to give this boy, who was sounding younger and more confused with each passing mile marker, something he could hold on to.

"Jacob, yes, I work to help support our family, but it's more than that. I like giving back. I believe we're here to make life better for others. If we're not, then you're right—what is it for? So it's important to me and to Dad that we give back to others, to help make their lives better. I don't know if you get all this, but I really believe that's why we're here."

The conversation was my first clue to how spiritually empty my son was. Like so much else in his behavior then, it caught me off guard. Despite years of attending synagogue, albeit not regularly, and his own religious training and bar mitzvah at age thirteen, Jacob was growing up malnourished. Not in his body—that I could feed—but in his soul, which I could not.

I was yet to learn that my son's addiction to drugs filled that emptiness for him and wouldn't let go until he found something to replace it. At first alcohol, and then hard drugs, helped him to fit in. He would later talk about how drugs helped him feel part of the crowd, washed away an insecurity that many adolescents likely experience, but for him seemed somehow more intense. He would talk about how drugs "filled a hole" inside him. And I would learn the irony that it's not enough for the addict just to back away from the drugs. There's still that hole. Something else has to fill it. That's where the spiritual part comes in. Not religion or even "God" necessarily, but something else greater than the addict is, and only he can find that for himself.

This was an incredibly hard and powerful lesson for me, and Dick, to accept—let alone for Jacob. The three of us, each in our own way, had to endure years of anguish to reach it.

Chapter 10

Summer as a Barista

Once home, Jacob faced a long summer, and I faced a huge worry. He was on probation. That meant staying clean and avoiding any tangles with the law. I feared the coming months more than he. I knew far better what another infraction might mean, and both Dick and I were focused on just getting him through this period in his life and into college at the end of August.

After all the kids returned from beach week, I arranged a meeting with George and his parents. Since the night of the arrest, I'd harbored intense anger at George, both for letting Jacob be the only one in that truck with "paraphernalia" on him and for deserting him once the police arrived. I had to be angry at someone, and there was a cavalier attitude about George that annoyed me immensely. I was pretty sure it was George who introduced Jacob to marijuana, thereby starting the chain of events that led to this tense meeting around our dining room table.

It was clear after the first few minutes that George's parents didn't quite share that view of their son. How could they? Didn't they love George as much as we loved Jacob? Besides, it *was* Jacob who had been arrested. George's parents felt bad about what had happened, and George said he did, too.

"George," I told him, "if you really are a friend of Jacob's, I need for you to help protect him this summer. He can't get into any more trouble. Understand? This is a pretty serious time for him. So if you really are his friend, you'll make sure he stays safe."

For their part, the two boys said little. They eyed each other across the table, smiled occasionally, but mostly tried not to look at one another. They were like two little kids caught pilfering candy from a grocery shelf. You knew damn well they wouldn't listen. The second they were out of earshot from their parents, they'd try some mischief again. The candy was just too available and too tempting.

As I'd promised Barnes, I contacted Jacob's therapist and signed him up for a few more months. When I recounted Jacob's experience at beach week and his probationary status, the therapist's reaction surprised me.

"Oh, really? He's been arrested? Well then, that makes this more interesting."

Interesting? Oh, good. Now maybe this PhD psychologist would pay attention to a young man who seemed to be getting worse, not better, and all presumably under his care. I felt angry and annoyed. This man was supposed to be one of the best adolescent therapists in the area and all he could offer was that now my son's case was more "interesting?"

Knowing it would help his court case, Jacob also agreed to a screening at the local substance use treatment center. Affiliated with the hospital, Pathways was a place I knew well. It was one of the few nonprofit substance use treatment centers in Maryland and, like the others, it struggled financially. Pathways counselors logged hours on the phones, arguing with insurance companies about getting the addict in for treatment. Often, the addict and his or her family would be sitting or pacing in the waiting room while a counselor begged and bargained with their insurer to gain them admission. The scene played out repeatedly day after day and still does.

Despite its failing bottom line, Pathways remained a top priority for the health system. Anne Arundel County was one of Maryland's worst in terms of drug use. Fortunately, the hospital's board was highly sensitive to the community's need. While these businessmen and women grew quiet whenever discussions focused on substance use, they never wavered in their determination to keep Pathways open.

As a member of the Pathways management board, I regularly

attended meetings there. But never in my years with the hospital did I suspect I'd be sitting in a bleak Pathways hallway on a hot June evening, waiting while my son was interviewed on the other side of a closed door by someone measuring him for the level of care he needed. When the door opened, the intake counselor, a large woman who looked mildly bored, simply pronounced, "Yes, he's a candidate for intensive outpatient treatment." Intensive? Was Jacob so far into drugs already that he required *intensive* treatment? It was one more cold slap, telling me that my son's problem was worse than I knew, and worse than I wanted to admit.

Intensive outpatient treatment meant that Jacob would attend Pathways three nights a week for six weeks. I was almost relieved. At least that would eat up some of the long summer nights. Plus, we would know where he was.

Meanwhile, Jacob had a solid summer job. He worked as a barista at a popular local coffee shop near Annapolis's busy City Dock area. It was a central gathering place for high school and college kids, as well as locals who liked the dark, smudgy feel of the place. Frequently, friends would mention to us, "I just saw your son at City Dock. He's so good-looking. What a great kid!"

Jacob practically lived at the City Dock Café all summer, often putting in extra hours because he liked the work and his co-workers liked him. There was something compelling, warm, and friendly about the dark, coffee-rich environment of the café, windowless except for the bowed glass panels fronting the building, facing the city Market House. Tables and booths stretched in the back, where Annapolitans and tourists lounged over steaming mugs of espresso and munched on simple breakfast sandwiches or homemade scones, talking local politics—always a favorite topic in any Annapolis café—or just catching up on each other's busy lives.

Often, I stopped in and ordered a coffee, dark roast please, just to make my visit legitimate enough to linger at one of the front tables so I could watch Jacob at work. Those were happy times. He seemed proud to have me watch him doing what he was good at doing. Customers seemed captivated by this tall, young barista with the shy grin who relished topping off their latte with an elegant figure-eight pattern of frothy foam. He moved quickly, kept the line of customers moving, remembered to smile as each one ordered. Here he was in control. He showed an air of confidence that I saw almost nowhere else. No wonder these were his best moments.

The hot, humid Annapolis summer days passed without incident, though not without worry. Since the arrest, worry was my constant companion. My anxieties rose and fell like a seesaw, teetering on Jacob's behavior. But he never missed work and seemed to enjoy his shifts behind the counter. These were my best moments, too. I stopped in to assuage my fears, to see him do something he loved, to know that he was safe, working, and happy. At these times, life felt normal, and I could almost relax.

But there were evenings I couldn't quash the fears. One night Jacob was in his room with a bunch of kids whom Dick and I knew and liked. As always, our home was a stopping-off point for friends heading downtown, and Jacob's room frequently filled with the sounds of high school graduates reveling in their last gasp of freedom before college. Around 11:30, a new group appeared at the back door. I was stunned to see George with a few friends I didn't know. The gang in Jacob's room seemed uneasy to see them, too, so I politely asked everyone to leave, explaining that it was a "school night" for me. Jacob left with them, saying they were going downtown and he would be back later.

Although it was unfair, for me George had become the symbol of everything that had taken Jacob off course this past year. My focus on him was irrational, but in my mounting worry I needed someone to blame. Jacob's problems had begun earlier than this year, before meeting George. Still, he was the one who kept Jacob out late, and he was standing next to Jacob on that North Carolina beach when the police arrested only my son.

Throughout the summer there were several late nights when I watched the bedside clock blink past one, and then two, wondering where Jacob was or when he would come home. Afraid to call him, afraid not to call him, I drifted off to sleep only after hearing the door close and his footfall on the stairs. The next morning, when I asked him where he'd been, I'd get only a monosyllable or the barest of explanations. But he never missed a day's work and kept his appointments with the psychologist.

I prayed that this summer of exhausting heat and worry soon would pass. The reward would be getting him to college. My job was to steer him towards that day when we'd pack up the car and head for College Park. Once there, the university would take over. He would love college life. The smart professors and dorm counselors there would know far better than I how to shepherd my son. He would get all the support and nurturing he would need to adjust and thrive in campus life.

We just had to get him there. All would be fine.

Chapter 11

Freshman Check-In

On the eve of Jacob's departure for the University of Maryland, I wrote in my journal:

> *For some parents, taking a child to college is an*
> *ending. Or a beginning. For us, it is more a continu-*
> *ation. Jacob has so much to learn about the basics.*

I had difficulty imagining Jacob taking care of himself, from handling laundry to writing a check, let alone finding his way across campus. Surely the university knew freshman like him; surely his seeming ineptness at even life's simplest challenges was common among kids his age. It was a little late to start blaming Dick and myself for sheltering him too much, making life too easy for him. Had we? Or was there something more serious in Jacob's offhand and oft-repeated comment, "I'm so not ready" for college?

Getting him to pack was excruciating. He had no idea what to take or leave. I imagined other households where mothers had gleefully gone shopping with their son or daughter, selected rugs or lamps, neatly folded tee shirts and jeans into clean canvas bags stacked smartly against the garage door for packing the car in the morning. Maybe it was different with boys? With Heidi, we had done all that and more. With Jacob, I could barely get him to stuff enough underwear into a backpack to last a week.

In typical fashion, the morning of check-in at Maryland I had to wake my son. He was never an early riser. At 6:30 a.m. I kissed the top of his head poking out from the sheets, and by 7 he was up. On the way out the door, he stopped in the library and knelt to kiss the dogs goodbye. At the time we had two greyhounds, Larry and Roman, and Jacob loved them both. He whispered a lingering farewell in Roman's soft, half-cocked ear. Goodbye to your home. Goodbye to your childhood. Time to grow up and take on a new world. Or so I thought, as he gave the dogs final hugs.

Once at the university, unpacking was easy because he'd taken so little. A clean garbage bag with sheets and towels, his backpack, one large suitcase, and his laptop. He'd already decided he could come home later for winter clothing. College Park was only a thirty-minute car ride from our house. The room wasn't air-conditioned, and it felt close to one hundred degrees. We headed across campus for the student union to pick up an Ethernet cable and fan. The place was buzzing with families just like ours—parents and kids scooping up last-minute items that they'd forgotten or couldn't fit into a packed car. The air was lively, light, and I breathed in the thrill of college life, happy that this is what my son was about to experience. As we left, I noted that I was carrying the fan and Dick the other items, to which my incoming freshman quipped, "Yeah, you're the woman. You shouldn't even be speaking!" I cuffed him on the head and held him close for a quick hug.

Back at his room, his roommate and parents were unpacking. After brief introductions, we learned that Caleb also was from a nearby town. His father was a physician and his mother a research nurse. It quickly became clear why he'd been paired with Jacob. Caleb was Jewish, and his birthday was April 10, the same as Jacob's.

The two had more than that in common. I learned from his parents that Caleb was disorganized, had blown off his last year of high school, and had no idea of his major. And there was something else. It was what his parents didn't say, and how they didn't stay long or linger to chat on what should be a happy day. It was enough to set off that pinging in my heart. The entire morning I had wavered between feeling light-hearted and happy for Jacob—breathing in the air of a vibrant college community, excited that he soon would savor all this—and acknowledging a deep-seated fear that he hadn't shed his dalliance with drugs. Or was it just a dalliance?

While Jacob struggled to get his computer set up, Dick gave me the sign: time to go. A quick hug and kiss, down the four flights of stairs, and out.

On the drive home, I felt a wave of both relief and sadness. He was gone. Out of the house. For most of the way I simply stared at the passing scenery and allowed myself to feel that same crushing heartache I'd felt leaving Heidi at college. The first day of nursery school revisited. Your little one is a grown-up now. Let him go. Let him grow. Time for others to tend to him, Mom. Your job is done.

That evening the phone rang. Dick picked it up and, hearing it was Jacob, I froze. But he only asked Dick to bring his skateboard next time because he needed a way to get across campus faster. It was so typical of him to forget it. My journal records:

> *Dick and I have started the room cleaning. Who*
> *knows what tomorrow or the days ahead will bring?*
> *Will he learn his way around campus? Buy books?*
> *Get to sleep at some point? Make new friends? Find*
> *the old ones? Allow himself the joy of everything*
> *Maryland has to offer? Grow up?*

The entry ended with what I later recognized as a prayer:

> *My son. My son. My son.*

Chapter 12

Freshman Failure

One of the nation's top public research institutions, the University of Maryland at College Park stretches across a sprawling 1,250-acre campus with thirty thousand students from nearly every foreign country. The place offered everything Jacob could ever want—friends, scholastic challenges, sports, girls—except the one thing he needed most: someone who could have foreseen the dark cloud of addiction descending.

Freshman year, Jacob got sicker, not better.

I don't blame Maryland for all that happened to Jacob. When someone has the disease of addiction, you can't really blame anyone for it. But I do begrudge the school for its seeming lack of trying. Drugs and alcohol were everywhere, and not just in fraternity houses. Yes, my son was eighteen, and the law entitled him to a great deal of privacy. College meant the era of parent-teacher conferences was over. That lifeline was cut, and it was now up to Jacob to seek help. It also was up to him to decide when and how much his parents should know about anything. Still, couldn't someone have called me? When we urged the dorm assistant or a professor we knew to "look in on him," there never was any feedback. As the year wore on, there was even less communication with anyone on campus.

During the first few weeks, phone calls became important. Tired of hearing how other kids were calling their parents, I phoned Jacob one evening. Big mistake. He sounded annoyed and shared little.

"Hi, Honey, how's it going?" I asked, trying to sound cheery.

"Okay."

"How's your roommate? You two getting along?"

"Yeah, he's okay."

"Have classes started yet?"

"Yeah. They're okay."

"Any plans for the weekend?" I prodded, hoping to hear about the football game, a lecture, a trip to Washington, DC, anything.

"Nah, not yet."

The call ended with an agreement to talk by phone every weekend.

The next weekend was the Labor Day holiday. Just as Dick and I were wondering when to phone Jacob, he showed up. It was Sunday evening. He'd hitched a ride home with a friend, supposedly to retrieve his shaver and to see a girl who worked in town and lived with her mom. The week between our phone conversation and his arrival gave us some perspective. Jacob looked and seemed great. Dick said to me, "He seems in control, not stressed. We need to leave him alone. He's figuring it all out—finding his classes, new friends, even where to eat. He seems fine."

I so wanted to believe that. My husband usually was right and normally astute at sizing up people and situations. After a chatty out-door supper at one of our favorite Main Street burger places, Jacob left us to catch up with Hank. While I didn't know Hank well, I knew that he was someone Jacob had met through George. That was enough to make me suspicious. I never knew where Jacob got drugs, and I never asked. To ask would admit that I knew he was using, or at least, that I suspected. Anyway, I couldn't imagine where that conversation would lead. It was ludicrous to think that Jacob would ever tell me where he purchased drugs. Worse, he'd likely deny that he did, and I feared the thought of cornering him into a lie. Until now, despite all the chaos of this past year, I still felt that Jacob was truthful with me. There was a strong bond between us, a taught line that tethered him to me, born out of the uncanny timing of his birth, this special boy whom I loved beyond breath, and who never would stray too far from the man he was destined to be. Just a week into college, and I still saw him thriving and achieving greatness some day.

Another surprise visit home happened two weeks later. Dick and I wondered what wasn't happening on campus to keep our son there. Where were the dorm leaders? Where was the professor or student advisor whose job was to engage these freshmen? Hadn't anyone noticed that this bright, promising Annapolis kid seemed totally disengaged from campus life so far? I was paying tuition and room and board, and had even given to the parents' fund. Why wasn't anyone paying attention to my son?

This time we had a longer conversation. Over a sandwich and fries from the Market House near City Dock, Jacob and I sat outside, watching boats troll up and down "Ego Alley," the narrow waterway where boaters parade their fancy yachts. Never much of a talker, Jacob chewed his food while I tiptoed among dozens of questions I was aching to ask. What I learned was disturbing.

"So, how about the food?" I began, picking a safe topic, "Are you eating in the cafeteria?"

"No, not much. I go there to get my food, though."

"So where do you eat?"

"Well, usually I just take it back to my room."

"Really?" Funny how responding with "really" was always a way to buy time. The image of Jacob eating alone in his room horrified me. What else did that signal about his life on campus? If he wasn't doing something as simple as eating in the cafeteria, then how would he meet anyone, make new friends, absorb what the college had to offer?

"What about your roommate? Does your roommate eat there, too?"

"No. He's not really around. He goes home on weekends a lot. I dunno. I guess we get along okay, but I don't see him much."

No cafeteria time. No connection with roommate. Silently, I checked off all the "normal" first-year college activities. What was holding Jacob back? He seemed more aloof and even more disinterested in academics than in his last year of high school.

There were more visits home, which should have been a warning.

So should the few times Dick and I visited him on campus. Usually, we met him outside his dorm and took him out for a meal—what every college kid loves the most. He never brought a friend, never asked if he could, although he knew we would welcome that. Lanky for years, he now looked skeletal, his skin all the whiter next to his black hair and downcast eyes. Sitting across the table from us, Jacob appeared gloomy and morose. It concerned me that he might be suffering some depression. Dick and I did our best to keep the conversation going. After dropping him off again at his dorm, I turned to Dick and said, "Well, that was fun." We both knew something was wrong, but not what, nor how to fix it.

Meanwhile, Jacob still had one more visit to the North Carolina courtroom. Postponed a few times, the date finally was set for late February. Once again we found ourselves in the Currituck County Courthouse with the impressive Robert Barnes as our guide. This time he wore a dark suit with a black sling over his left arm. Despite recent shoulder surgery, he was still a man on his game. After quick handshakes, he ushered us into a small side room and went through the drill. When it came time for Jacob and Barnes to stand before the judge, we stood behind them. On the judge's order, Jacob put his hand on the Bible and was sworn in. Later, when the judge asked his first question, Jacob reached again to put his hand on the Bible before responding. I caught the judge suppress a smile, then regain his rather bland facial expression as he said, "No, you don't have to put your hand on the Bible each time."

The judge began a slow litany, reading all the terms of Jacob's probation. Although it felt like hours, it was over in seconds. I felt myself relax for the first time since we'd left Annapolis the previous day. This must mean the judge was in agreement with Barnes: twelve months unsupervised probation, sixty hours of community service, and a letter to the arresting officer, apologizing for his behavior. At the end of the judge's recitation, Barnes flashed a thumbs-up behind his back for our benefit.

Before leaving the courthouse, Barnes stared Jacob straight in the eye, big brotherly style, and gave him a final pep talk. "You're a freshman in college now. You're in a great school. Life is good!"

For a second time in less than a year, we drove out of North Carolina, relieved to be heading home. In my journal that night I wrote:

> *What happens next is so up to him. He has to*
> *write that letter. He has to do the community service.*
> *He has to stay clean, not even a parking ticket, his*
> *lawyer said, and he has to pull the grades up this*
> *semester, too.*

And I closed with

> *The boy needs to become a man.*

By April, Jacob's pattern of coming home frequently from College Park was well established. Dick and I knew he was not happy there, but there didn't seem to be an alternative. This time he was home to celebrate his nineteenth birthday. Dick prepared a luscious dinner with all of Jacob's favorites: steak, Cape Cod mashed potatoes, and fresh broccoli. The thoughtful meal helped open conversation. Like everything about his life, Jacob's interest in class oscillated between marginal and none at all. He liked psychology a lot; he failed a math test. Linguistics was difficult; chem lab was fine. More often, conversations with him lapsed into psychobabble.

"Mom, why didn't you fix me when I was little?" he asked, picking up a piece of broccoli with his thumb and index finger.

"Fix you? What do you mean, fix you?" I tried to stay calm, ignoring his not using a fork. Conversations with Jacob often spiraled into inscrutable word games where I was on the losing end, groping for the right answer.

"You know, fix me!" Jacob rarely raised his voice but the words jumped at me. More calmly, he mumbled, "I don't know who I am anymore."

I recalled the night in North Carolina when I'd pulled him out of the beach house. Huddled in that motel room too tiny to contain all our misery, he had blurted out, "Maybe I'm becoming autistic." Something was grabbing hold of my son, something sinister, a demon I couldn't see or touch. When he'd fallen as a child and hurt his arm, that was easy. He complained very little, but after a few days I finally took him to see a favorite orthopedic surgeon at the hospital. One x-ray, and it was easy to diagnosis a tiny fracture. Jacob's pain was real. Rest the arm for a few weeks. The patient is young, the bone will heal. Don't worry, Mom. He will be fine.

There was no such absolution now. But it was clear that I had to try something.

"Jacob," I started slowly, holding my breath against his response, "why not consider therapy? Find someone you like at College Park? Someone you can trust?"

To my surprise, he didn't object. He even asked if he should see his old therapist again. I reassured him that we would pay for any help he sought. I suspected that drugs were still messing him up, but I couldn't understand why, nor did I have any idea of what he was using.

In fact, Jacob's disease escalated that year to such an extent that even he was surprised no one intervened. As he would subsequently tell me, "Sure, I smoked pot. Everybody did. I probably smoked every day." It was at Maryland that he used cocaine for the first time. He met a girl down the hall in his dorm and "did cocaine a few times with her in her room." She and her boyfriend, who lived off campus, used frequently. "One night I stayed up all night doing it. And then I went to a 9 a.m. class and couldn't handle it." Eventually, he was doing cocaine alone in his room. His roommate, too, was using, and was seldom around. "It was nuts," my son shared several years later. "I didn't know who I was. I was lost and confused, turned around. I'd never been on my own before. I just couldn't do even the little things."

But I didn't know any of this that night. "Jacob," I ventured tentatively, "I wonder how much getting high has messed you up?"

"Maybe," he said, "but that was in the past."

I was sorry I'd said that. Was he lying to me, or to himself? When Dick and I returned from the symphony later that evening, Jacob was still out. I felt the tug from the upstairs hallway. Torn between needing to know and violating my son's privacy, I often waded through Jacob's room to see if anything was there that shouldn't be. He knew the rule: No drugs in the house. I was like a bloodhound, hot on the scent of anything illegal under my roof. Sure enough, right inside of his open backpack were two tiny bags of dark green leafy flakes. I dug deeper and uncovered a box of baggies. My heart sank. Not only was he using, but—was it possible he was selling, too? Without thinking, I grabbed my phone and dialed his cell. He picked up after only a few rings. Feeling hot and panicky, and without so much as a hi, where are you? I fired at him.

"If there is anything illegal in my house, I want it out!"

Within thirty minutes he was home. His eyes were red, but he denied being high. He knows I have him, I thought. I started spewing the same speech that was sounding so old and tired, even to myself. I'd become some nagging fixture, this person who wouldn't let him get away with anything—except that he was.

It always began with, "You are nineteen. I know you don't have to listen to me. Marijuana can lead to other drugs." And because of his probation that year, it always ended with, "Jacob, it's worse for you. If you are caught using or selling, you're going to jail."

Saying such words terrified me, but the word "jail" cut through Jacob's fog.

"Okay, I'm going to leave the house," he said, "and when I come back it will be gone." Soon after he left, backpack in tow, he phoned to say he would spend the night at Hank's.

Doubts plagued me that whole year. I was sure Jacob was using, but I had no idea how to stop him. Since Greenfield's first phone call more than a year ago, there wasn't a website I hadn't read or a subhead I hadn't researched—"What Every Parent Needs To Know about

Drugs," "The Telltale Signs," "What To Do if You Suspect Your Child Is Using Drugs"—but these already seemed so sophomoric. What I wanted was someone to give me the words to say to my son, to hand me the script, just like I did for my CEO or board chair at the hospital. Give them the script, and if they follow it closely, then the event will flow perfectly, they'll end on time, and the audience will depart happy. I was so adept at directing others, but where was the script for my own life?

Work was my balm. The capital campaign was in its earliest phase, a sensitive time when I was needed most. This was the moment to meet with the largest contributors, mostly board members and former donors, to explain that the emergency department backed up every night and the hospital needed more beds. Their early support was critical to the campaign's success. My superiors wanted me there for the strategy sessions, prepping for those meetings. I had to coach my CEO and volunteers on what to say, when, and how. I pictured success, the donor's exquisite "yes," like a runner who envisions the quick snap of the thin blue ribbon at the finish line. The elation of securing a large gift for the hospital gave me the same high.

That "high"—was it anything like what an addict experiences, I wondered? And if it was, how could I help my son replace that addiction with something as positive as I had?

In reflective moments, I wondered if Jacob's addiction was genetic. As far as I knew, there was no alcohol or other substance use issues in my family. A son of a first cousin had gotten hooked on cocaine and other drugs in his early thirties. He'd lost a stunning wife, a career as a psychologist, his home, everything. Years later, he'd gotten clean, remarried, and started an entirely new life on a ranch in Georgia. That was as close as addiction came. Dick and I had never even tried marijuana. I almost had at college, but the idea of ingesting anything into my lungs scared me. And we barely drank. Maybe a glass of wine with dinner, but rarely at home. Sometimes I questioned if my penchant for work was an addiction. My father had been that way, laboring seven days a week in the grocery store he owned. I'd regarded that as his determination to give his children everything he didn't have—and he succeeded. His stamina and drive enabled my brother to attend college and medical school and me, college and graduate school.

Incredibly naïve, lacking so much understanding, during Jacob's freshman year at Maryland I made all the classic mistakes that parents with addicted sons and daughters make. I searched for the "cause" of the problem. Out of love and desperation, I kept trying to control a situation that was totally out of my control. I ached to find both a cause and a cure I was incapable of finding. I just didn't know it yet.

As uplifting as work was, it also posed a dilemma. It was ironic that I spent days and nights in a fast-paced, growing major medical center that treated people with all kinds of ailments, and yet discussion of substance use was still taboo. The hospital preached "patients and families come first." It was a deep, cultural value imprinted on doctors, nurses, techs, and housekeepers from their first day. And yet, when the health problem was drug abuse, there was a palpable difference. I lived in abject fear that someone would find out my son had a drug problem.

In my twenty-five-plus years at the hospital there had been occasional rumors of a physician or nurse who was being "counseled" or even "sent off" for rehab. Always whispered, these asides were kept quiet as much to respect patient confidentiality as to hide the notion that any caregiver might have a drug problem. On one occasion a well-liked internist made local headlines when his addiction to opiates finally disrupted his ability to care for patients, his wife, and himself. Even then, few in the executive suite talked about it. There was nothing they could do, except offer him a stint someplace in an out-of-state rehab center and hope he would get better.

During this time my heart felt broken most mornings, and my head throbbed from lack of sleep. Resigned to focus on the campaign, I simply dug in. Days passed in a calculated frenzy of meetings and donor visits. I loved my staff and the other executives. Life at the hospital gave me the reprieve I needed to feel normal, purposeful, and happy. At least there, I was somewhat in control.

Near the end of Jacob's spring semester, I picked him up at school on a holiday weekend. In the car he piped up, "I don't need to tell you this, but I have an appointment with a counselor Monday morning." I just listened, afraid to say the wrong thing, but I was pleased.

Later in the weekend, we argued.

"You know Mom," he began, "there's a personal side of me that you can't discuss."

Always afraid he would close the door, I said, "Jacob, I respect that you have a right to privacy. But you know we need to talk about the dope issue. There are just some people who can't smoke it. It messes them up, and until we address that, we aren't addressing what's really going on with you, right?"

He listened, shrugged his shoulders, his face bland, mouth turned down. We were in the car again, this time headed to Philadelphia to visit my brother and his family. That weekend, my sister-in-law Helaine and niece Jennifer, also a therapist, eyed Jacob carefully. They took me aside and expressed their worry. He seems depressed, they said. They urged therapy. Possibly medication. I didn't disagree, willing to take any suggestion. Their concern made me all the more panicky and even a little angry. Did they think I hadn't noticed this myself, that I couldn't see for myself every day how utterly miserable he was? Give me the solution, I cried inside. Tell me how to fix this. But no one answered.

Unable to recognize it at the time, I was suffering the same feelings of isolation, depression, and shame as my son. I couldn't bring myself to admit to anyone that Jacob had a drug problem, let alone a serious one, and I certainly couldn't admit how it was affecting me. At the time I knew little about how addiction can harm the entire family. Jacob was the one with a problem, not me. Unfortunately, it would get much worse before it got better—for both of us.

Chapter 13

Transferring Home

Despite Jacob's attempt to seek help from a counselor at Maryland, his grades ultimately decided the next move. It soon became clear that he would not be "invited" back for his sophomore year.

He was home, yet again, for a long weekend. It was early May, and the school year was ending. Dick and I were firm with Jacob that he needed a "plan." The conversations, like so many those days, vacillated between making sense and being total fantasy.

"I think my advisor likes me," he grinned. "She told me I'm actually doing okay. I saw my math professor, and instead of failing I'm actually doing okay there too. Same for linguistics and psych. I like psych, and maybe I'll major in it."

Aching to grasp something positive, I listened and hung onto every hopeful word.

"So if I take a class this summer, even though I could be academically dismissed, I can pull my grade point up," he went on. "You know, I can write a pretty good essay"—thinking he could write his way out of academic dismissal.

Then there was the issue of housing. Apparently that had been solved, too. A room had opened in a dorm he liked, a third-floor single. Naturally, that appealed to him, the supreme loner. He also admitted that he'd had three sessions with a psychologist in the counseling center, and that had helped him, too.

So, what's next? we prodded gently.

"Next, I'll look for a summer job."

Jacob also shared a tale that would petrify any parent. Likely, it's a common scene on college campuses and growing more common.

Just a few days before, early in the morning without warning to the students, Jacob told us, "someone from the government, the DEA or FBI," stormed into the dorm and "took away" one of two classmates in the room next door. It shook him up and "rocked the dorm." Apparently, the pair was running a successful business selling mushrooms and marijuana from their room. My, how ingenious of them, I thought sarcastically, profiting off a ready market for drugs. The only reason Dick and I knew about it was that Jacob told us. No word ever came from the university. In fact, communication with the university seemed limited only to paying bills. Like the health information privacy act in my world, the university had to abide by a law that protected students' privacy beginning at age eighteen. It galled me every time anything like this happened. Here was a patently illegal activity going on right under their noses, and the school had failed totally to nip it, until now. It was one more reason to turn against the university. It also filled my need to blame someone for Jacob's poor grades and flagging interest in academics.

Even more infuriating, Jacob admitted he liked the guys and had hung out with them, but the incident flat out scared him.

"I know what those guys are going to go through," he said.

"No, you don't," said his father, the lawyer. "For them, it will be much worse."

Of equal importance as the summer job—let alone a plan for the coming school year—was his need to complete the court-ordered community service.

Again, we stepped in. We suggested places to volunteer, people he might call, and handed him phone numbers on slips of paper. I even considered making the calls for him. It would be so easy. We knew everyone he might contact. But what would I say? "Hi, Claire? It's Lisa Hillman. Fine, how are you? Well, yes, you can help me. You see, my son was arrested last year for intent to distribute an illegal substance. So would you take him in so he can do his sixty hours of court-ordered community service?"

No. That I'd have to leave to Jacob.

Getting the community service stint turned out to be easy. Jacob narrowed his search to the SPCA and the Annapolis and Anne Arundel County Conference and Visitors Bureau, choosing finally the Visitors Bureau where he would greet tourists and share information about the town he knew so well. Friends of ours also worked or volunteered at the visitors' center. Occasionally, throughout Jacob's three weeks there, we would get reports on how polite he was, what a well-mannered young man. He's doing such a nice job, friends would say. You must be so proud of him.

If they only knew, I always thought. Yes, he is well-mannered and clever and engaging, but he's also so very troubled. Can't you see that? You really cannot tell what's going on behind that smile? I knew the drug use hadn't stopped, but I tried hard to believe it had. Jacob was working, and he was completing his community service. On the surface, nothing appeared unusual. Just another hot and humid summer in Annapolis. With each passing day I prayed that life would be normal again.

July brought a reprieve from the worry. Shortly after their marriage eight years ago, Heidi and Jon had moved to San Diego. Jon was stationed on Coronado, where the Navy has a large helicopter base. They were now expecting the birth of their first child, and Dick, Jacob, and I flew out there to attend a baby shower. The night before the party, after dinner at a nearby restaurant, Heidi tapped on our bedroom door. As calm as the night air, she whispered, "Shh . . . don't get up. I'm pretty sure I'm in labor. Jon and I are going to the hospital."

Yearning to follow, but respecting her wishes to make this a private moment, I counted the hours until dawn. Taking a long walk up the steep slope behind her house, I caught the panoramic vista overlooking the San Diego airport and the glistening Pacific, all blue and golden. My cell phone rang, and it was Heidi, my beautiful daughter, now a mother. This simple note in my journal takes an entire page:

July 26, Saturday, 8:26 a.m.

Born: Joshua Milton Anderson, 6 lb, 8 oz

Balboa Naval Hospital

Miracle.

His grandparents and uncle are in San Diego for

his birth, there for his parents' shower, but instead, he

arrives 3½ weeks early—and we are there!

Long before their marriage, Heidi and Jon, who is Catholic, had decided to raise their children Jewish. This meant that Josh's bris—the ritual circumcision ceremony—would be eight days later. We figured out the logistics, flew home to Maryland, wrapped up things at home and work, and flew back to San Diego the following weekend, this time with plans for me to stay longer to help Heidi. The bris was a small affair—several of Heidi and Jon's friends and my brother and his wife, Karl and Helaine, and their son, Bill, who lived in Los Angeles. During the ceremony I huddled with Heidi in another room, choosing to avoid that moment of brief pain for the infant, just as we had nineteen years before for her brother. The event boasted all the traditional Jewish fare with bagels, lox, whitefish salad, and the richest of éclairs. With such a small family, having Karl, Helaine, and Bill there increased my feelings of love and joy.

Given the day's purpose, it's not surprising that I remember so little about Jacob's being there. Photographs recorded his presence, but he easily could be overlooked. Like a shadow, he hovered, never really a part of the event, just a whisper beyond it. One picture shows the extended family gathered happily around Heidi holding Josh, all bundled tightly, the shot baby-centered. Jacob stands at the far end, looking at the camera with a tentative smile. He is rail thin. Pale, almost ghostly, his face shows the dark shadow of a beard, but the charcoal smudge looks sinister, a black smear threatening to wipe him out altogether.

After the bris, Dick and Jacob flew home; I stayed in San Diego for several more days. My mission was simple: take care of Heidi so she could take care of her son. There was grocery shopping, chopping vegetables for supper, fixing her a cup of tea. When Heidi and Jon went to the commissary to food shop, I had Josh all to myself. He slept the entire time, snuggled in his receiving blanket in his crib by his parents' bed. Later he snoozed soundlessly on my chest while his parents fixed dinner.

Despite the hospital's being an ever-demanding master, I determined never to let four months pass without seeing Josh. This baby would know his grandmother. I wanted to be the grandmother to Josh that my Bubbe had been to me, and that my mother had been to Heidi. My journal notes:

When you love your child, you watch them
become the adult you love. But it is a lifetime gift to
watch your child love her own child. It's a reflection
of your own love, and a gift from God.

The joy that Heidi, Jon, and Josh brought into our lives was in stark contrast to life with Jacob. Back home in Annapolis, our world continued to stagger between semi-normalcy and nightmare.

In August Jacob completed his community service. The formal note from the manager of the Visitors Bureau, dated August 27, 2008, affirms for the court that "Jacob has worked more than 60 hours at the visitors' center and has attended required training sessions. He has acquired additional training by visiting local historic sites and taking guided tours on his own time. Jacob will continue to volunteer here at the center through the fall, and has signed up for several shifts in September." I was relieved and proud to read the praise that followed: "I am pleased with the effort and attention that Jacob has put forth in his volunteering here at the visitors' center. I believe the other volunteers have appreciated having him around as well, as he has shared a different point of view with them, our typical volunteer being of retirement age."

That summer Jacob also found paid work. A good friend helped him secure a job at a new, trendy clothing store that had just opened in the Annapolis Mall. The mall was one of Maryland's most successful, a sprawling profusion of shops, eateries, kiosks, and name-brand department stores. If kids weren't hanging out downtown by City Dock, they were trolling the mall. For a brief time, Jacob also worked as a salesman and a model at a nearby men's store. It, and he, reeked of woodsy cologne, but I hoped that the job would boost his self-confidence.

Apparently it did. Jacob was soon dating a young woman he met at the clothing store. Chelsea Parks had just entered her senior year of high school. A wisp of a girl, she barely reached five foot two and weighed less than a hundred pounds. She radiated femininity—the kind that's fragile, a powder puff of time. With a sweep of shiny brown hair and creamy-white skin, she blinked brown eyes at Jacob, a damsel to save. In her, he found manhood and refuge.

Chelsea would be good for Jacob, I thought. Despite my concern that she was the spoiled younger daughter of affluent parents, she seemed fond of Jacob and happy to spend many afternoons and evenings allowing him to pamper her.

She was one of the reasons it didn't occur to me to question—until much, much later—where the money was going. When Jacob first got the sales job, he mentioned that his salary was a basic hourly rate plus counter tips his coworkers would divvy up at week's end. It wasn't much, but it was enough that he never asked his parents for money. I knew he was spending money on Chelsea, covering fast food, snacks, and movies without our help.

Assuming there would be money left over, we helped him open a bank account to start saving. Jacob had no major expenses. Unlike many kids his age, he didn't own a car. That had been a big issue in high school, but since we owned two cars and Dick was home most days, the SUV he normally used was available to Jacob. Once Jacob's drug problems surfaced, we certainly were not going to buy him a car. He knew that. After he started working, we promised to help him buy a car if he saved enough for the down payment. Thinking that would motivate him to save, we found it curious that he never seemed to have any money to deposit. We shrugged it off. If he had the use of Dick's car, maybe there really was no incentive to have his own.

Despite Jacob's bravado that he could pull up his grades, the University of Maryland—in an official-looking letter that arrived before fall—suggested he not return for a second year. Once more we made it clear that he couldn't live at home unless he had a plan. That included not only work, but school. So, without too much hassle, Jacob managed to go online and register for a couple of courses at the local community college. Known as one of the best such schools in the country, Anne Arundel Community College was a haven for kids like Jacob. It offered small class sizes, professors who lived locally and cared about their students, and a broad curriculum.

I yearned to feel hopeful again. Maybe if he liked his classes, he would get back into some positive groove. Maybe there would be a professor who would show some interest in him, and maybe if he continued to do well at his job . . . So many "maybes." I quickly went from hopeful to refraining from thinking too far ahead. The dreams I'd had of Jacob fulfilling an MIT career were rapidly disappearing. I kept those visions at bay, lest they fade forever. Instead, I tried to focus on today, not on what tomorrow might bring, taking my cues from Jacob. He rarely talked of his future. He seemed to drift day to day with little discussion on where it might lead. Except for his job, Jacob exhibited little initiative. That same lack of drive that plagued him the past two years continued.

Meanwhile, he resumed seeing the therapist he'd seen in high school and seemed comfortable going twice a month. But I had doubts about how much this was helping. I asked Jacob if I could talk to the therapist and got a typical response: shrugged shoulders, a nodding agreement. The therapist was guarded. With a little prodding during a one-on-one meeting, he opened up and shared his observations of Jacob. Jacob was a great kid. The therapist really liked him, and they had a good relationship. He was suffering from fairly typical anxieties that most kids his age have about growing up, leaving home, being independent. He had lots of fears that many kids have. Was he still using drugs? Yes, he was smoking some dope, but the therapist didn't really see that as a big problem. He was advising Jacob just to try to modify his use, tone it back a bit, and he should be fine.

I left his office bewildered. I'd never heard that "toning it back a bit" was a therapeutic recommendation for someone showing signs of substance abuse. But I had no evidence that Jacob was using anything but marijuana, and I yearned to believe this psychologist. He was on our medical staff at the hospital. He was recommended by people I trusted. There were always people in his waiting room, and his appointment secretary made a fuss when you wanted to change an appointment. If such a man said Jacob would be fine, shouldn't I believe him? I wanted to. I wanted to let go of all the mounting fears and worries. I wanted to know the ending to this story, that Jacob would find his way, that he would be happy and find joy.

Later, I would learn not to trust professionals in the mental health field, especially those in substance use disorders. I would learn to adopt a healthy skepticism when it came to anyone who treated my son and to trust my own intellect and curiosity about what might be best for him. But that summer, with no one to rely on and few to confide in, I turned to what mothers always turn to: maternal instinct. I would rally and argue and fight for what was best for my child, like the snarling lioness protecting her only cub. But unlike the lioness, I had no idea of who the real predator was.

Chapter 14

It Took Away the Pain

Early in 2009, two events at work distracted me from worries about Jacob. Anne Arundel Medical Center boasted a stellar reputation in the region. The CEO, Martin "Chip" Doordan, was rounding out a forty-year career there, during which his strong, steady leadership had allowed the institution to become one of Maryland's fastest growing health systems. The hospital was now planning its second major expansion in less than a decade—an eight-story patient tower and a seven-story office pavilion—which would catapult it to the third busiest hospital in Maryland in just a few years.

Over the course of nearly thirty years at AAMC, I'd risen to the ranks of the executive suite and now held two titles: president of the hospital foundation and senior vice president for the health system covering legislative and public affairs. My professional life gave me busy, rewarding days and asylum from the chaos at home. I also enjoyed a relationship that few there held: I was very close to Chip. As we worked together through the minor and major crises that affect all large healthcare institutions, Chip learned to trust my ability to guide him through the public maze of reporters and politicians. The respect was mutual. Something of an icon for his wisdom, humility, and kindness, he was one of the reasons I stayed at AAMC, despite offers to work for larger organizations.

About this same time, a new hire—an exceedingly bright young woman, Victoria Bayless—was a fast-rising star in the hospital hierarchy. Tori had joined us from a multi-hospital healthcare system and had the experience that AAMC needed. Easy to like, clever, and intuitive, Tori soon became someone to consult on major decisions affecting the hospital's future.

So it didn't surprise me when Chip confided one morning that he was eyeing Tori as his successor. What did surprise me was that he was planning to retire. Until then, I hadn't considered an end to my career at AAMC. My days were full and fulfilling, building the foundation into a high-functioning and respected organization. But if Chip was considering his departure, even though I had a solid relationship with Tori, then maybe I should be planning my retirement as well.

Adding to my duties, Chip asked me to help with the transition, which would take two years. My role would be to handle all communications, gauge reaction both internally and externally, keep the board members and hospital leadership informed, and stay close to Chip and Tori. Despite the additional workload, it was a privilege to become a confidante to both leaders.

With all the changes occurring at the hospital, I rarely got home before 7. Weekends were filled with community functions, catching up on professional journals and writing, or just trying to supplement lost hours of sleep.

Meanwhile, at least on the surface, Jacob was doing well. He finished his first semester at the community college with all A's and B's and made the dean's list. He also changed jobs. Preferring coffee to retail, he found another barista position, this time in a shop behind the mall on a busy boulevard with easy parking. The place featured both coffee and tea and soon became a destination for residents, commuters, and lots of people Dick and I both knew. Again, we began hearing, "I saw your son today. Boy, what a great kid."

By this time, I accepted that Jacob wasn't taking the traditional path to college and career. It was reassuring to hear praise from others, even more so given my constant anxiety about him. Kind words about him not only filled me with pride, but also assuaged the deep pain inside that this was a young man who held secrets, whose life was not what it could or should be. I wondered how others couldn't sense the graying shadow that followed him, sometimes settling in just below his eyes, where dark circles revealed a torment that maybe only I could see.

Now that he was living at home, Jacob resumed his old friendships with local kids. That proved to be another worry. The very fact that they were still in Annapolis made me question if these kids were just like Jacob—lost, directionless, searching. I also feared they might be using drugs.

Despite my constant worry, this was a relatively calm period in Jacob's life. He liked his job and was doing well at the community college. Although Chelsea had started college in New England, she still was a presence in his life. And Jacob had met another young person who would be important to him—Scotty, who rented an apartment nearby and worked at several jobs in town. Somewhat of an enigma, Scotty was five years older than Jacob but oozed adolescence with a sandy-haired look and an aesthete's thin body. He was the modern-day hippie, savoring every moment, with or without joy, not asking for much, just taking whatever the day offered. With a poet's soul, Scotty was drawn to Jacob's darkness and became his friend.

I later learned Scotty was never a drug user. He had a calming influence on Jacob and even got him a part-time job during the holidays at an eyeglass shop on Main Street. Jacob enjoyed hanging out with Scotty at the store and quickly learned all the brand-name frames. It was Scotty who got Jacob to go on a weeklong, all-expenses-paid trip to the Dominican Republic just after New Year's, a perk for good employees. Naturally, I worried about Jacob's going on a trip like that—with anything he wanted available and paid for—but Jacob returned jubilant and refreshed. It wasn't all sleeping till noon and umbrella drinks by the pool. Even amid the self-indulgence, Jacob took in the poverty of the local people, a new experience in his sheltered life.

Years later, Jacob would tell me that this was a good time for him. "I was using less" and "it seemed less cool or popular."

Meanwhile, despite pressures at work, time to visit my grandson in

California was still sacred. So were big family occasions. In February, the whole family gathered in Atlanta for a young cousin's bat mitzvah. Looking forward to a family reunion weekend, I booked adjoining rooms in the hotel.

The weekend began happily enough. Heidi and Jacob spent some quiet time together, time they rarely shared since they lived on separate coasts. For many years Jacob regarded Heidi as a confidante. Despite the fifteen-year difference in their ages, he would talk with her about anything, especially girls. The two had spent hardly any time together growing up. He was three when she left for college and eleven when he escorted me down the aisle at her wedding. They were almost a generation apart, but still there was closeness. He respected her instincts. She had been through college and working years and had emerged on the other side with a husband and son. For Jacob, that was proof enough that she could be trusted to know a thing or two.

But since his senior year in high school, Jacob's drug use had been seeping into their relationship like a slow, poisonous drip. I always suspected that Heidi knew more than she revealed. Closer to Jacob's generation, she could see it, smell it. In the soft, quieter moments where a brother and sister sometimes meet, perhaps he had talked with her about his using, his anxieties about life, and just about everything. I imagined that in the shelter of their bedroom, Heidi and her husband whispered a blend of concern and disgust for her brother. Jon, a naval officer given to toughness and rigid self-discipline, was well aware of how alcoholism and drugs could wreak havoc. He had counseled young men and women and eyed them sadly as they stuffed duffel bags and slammed lockers shut under strict orders to vacate the base. Inappropriate use of alcohol and certainly of drugs meant dishonorable discharge, swift and sure.

With the military as her moral guidepost, it was no wonder that Heidi distanced herself more and more from Jacob. She knew, intellectually, that addiction was a disease, and that morality had nothing to do with it. Still, that couldn't stop her from feeling deep-seated anger at her brother for slowly destroying his life and for causing such pain in the family. At a time when her own life was soaring with a newborn son and sunny days in San Diego, it was no wonder her anger at Jacob grew into resentment and frustration and fostered growing isolation from him.

While I sensed all this, I was helpless to prevent it, just as I was helpless to prevent Jacob's growing drug use. I'd read enough to know that addiction affects the entire family. Feelings of anger and resentment are common. What I didn't know then was what wiser people would teach me much later: "You didn't cause it, you can't control it, and you can't cure it." Another thing I didn't know then was that our family was heading into the worst throes of the disease. Like Jacob, Dick, Heidi, and I each were suffering from frustration, anger, hurt, and hopelessness. It's ironic, I would later reflect: the family feels the same wrenching emotions as does the abuser.

In Atlanta, an incident occurred that further fueled Heidi's anger.

The bat mitzvah ceremony went smoothly. Grateful for the hours to sit quietly with my family in the glow of the synagogue, witnessing this ancient ritual and beautiful, thirteen-year-old cousin recite Hebrew prayers perfectly, I savored the morning. Afterwards, family and guests enjoyed the traditional oneg shabbat—the meal after the service—stuffing themselves with bagels and lox, egg salad, brownies, fudge-topped cookies, and ribbon cake. In the afternoon, we retreated to the hotel to change clothes and took a long walk through the posh, suburban neighborhood. After stopping at a coffee shop, we headed back to our rooms to rest before the evening party.

The nighttime affair was in an older Atlanta suburb, in a graystone building that had been converted from a private home into a popular restaurant and reception hall that catered to large parties. Guests entered through a long hallway that opened into a dark, wooden bar. Beyond the bar, a wide ballroom was set with tables that surrounded a large dance floor. Dim lights, loud laughter, and the peals of schoolgirls just turning into teenagers filled the night.

For most of the evening, Dick and I sat at our table or wandered through the bar, catching up with cousins, enjoying a slow dance, and trying to endure polite chatter with people we'd likely never see again. Frequently, I retreated to the far end of the bar where Heidi had found a quiet corner to nurse Josh. After the bat mitzvah girl, Josh attracted the most attention. Family and strangers alike couldn't resist cooing over the sweet sleeping baby cuddled in his carrier or blinking blue eyes up at their silly grins.

Maybe that's why we all lost track of Jacob. When it came time to leave, amid the hugs and happy wishes and farewells, he suddenly appeared outside and sidled up to me as we headed for the car.

"Did you have a good time?" I asked.

He mumbled something. His slow, slurred speech shot through me like a thunderbolt. In the car, everyone chattered about the evening. Jacob sat silent and withdrawn in the backseat while I tried to subdue a mixture of fury and fear, wondering if anyone else was noticing what I was.

Heidi, Jon, and the baby—and Jacob—all went up to the room. Dick and I took the car to get gas since we were leaving early the next morning for the eleven-hour drive home. When we got back to the suite, Heidi opened the door.

"Jacob threw up."

"What? Where?"

"In the living room. Over there. Jon cleaned it up."

"Oh, my gosh. Really? Is he okay?"

"I dunno. Talk to him. He's your son."

And with that, she turned her back, retreated into her room, and closed the door. The dismissal stung, but I couldn't blame her. I found Jacob slung across his bed, still dressed, half asleep. The smell of alcohol was strong. Pressing my lips together lest I let loose words he wouldn't hear, I pulled a blanket over him and turned off the light.

In the darkness, conflicting thoughts assailed me. Sure, my mind said, plenty of guys Jacob's age drink and get drunk. They throw up, too. How would a "normal" twenty-year-old have handled that evening? Too old to dance with thirteen-year-old girls, and with no one his age there, what should he have done? It was an awkward evening at best. But how "normal" is it for someone with an arrest record for carrying illegal drugs and a trail of years using other drugs to get so inebriated that he disappears from a family reunion? I knew that his behavior was one more signal of where Jacob was in his life. Lost, and suffering from that shyness he'd had since childhood, he swallowed alcohol to fill the hole. Much later, Jacob revealed that he'd taken Valium before the alcohol, compounding his delirium. Just as he had at Josh's bris, he'd found a way to blot out the entire evening. A giant eraser wiped away his visage completely from the family photo, leaving only the empty space where the cousin known as Jacob should have been.

My son had a problem. It was a big one that was growing worse. And I was helpless to help him.

Once home, our lives returned to the business of jobs and school and a professional trip. That year I was chair of the Association for Healthcare Philanthropy, an international membership organization of some five thousand fundraisers in the United States, Canada, and Australia. The association's top executive invited me to accompany him to the annual meeting of fundraisers from all over the world in Sydney, Australia, and Dick would be my guest.

With friends promising to look in on Jacob and close neighbors watching too, I felt as comfortable as possible leaving him. He was, after all, almost twenty-one, in school and working, and certainly capable of caring for the dogs and bringing in the mail. Hiring someone to stay with him would seem demeaning, and we had no relatives close by. I was left to trust him for the nine days we'd be away.

Unlike our trip to Europe when Jacob was seventeen, this time he seemed to manage fairly well. When we returned, he greeted us happily, the house was in order, and even the two greyhounds looked healthy and well fed. What I couldn't see was that his abuse had escalated. Our absence had given him unquestioned use of two cars and the freedom to drive to Towson, just outside Baltimore. There, Jacob found easy access to a drug that would be his ultimate seducer—OxyContin.

Later, he would tell me "a friend from Towson texted me about prices of Oxy. I went to Towson to get it, and it took away the pain." The phrase baffled Dick and me. What pain? As non-addicts, could we ever understand what that meant, especially in a family where a child was given everything he wanted or needed? Jacob had parents who adored him, a sister who cared deeply for him, and sufficient means to meet nearly all of his desires. So why this? Why drugs? It wasn't supposed to be like this. Not in my family. Not my son.

OxyContin would dominate Jacob's life for the next two years. At the time, I'd never even heard the name. Like many unfamiliar with substance use and the world of drug users, I assumed he was only smoking marijuana. He was still attending community college, finishing his first full year there and doing well. He continued to work at the coffee shop and readily accepted the extra shifts they offered. I rarely questioned what he did with his money. We assumed he was depositing some into his savings account. The promise of a car was still there, if he saved enough for the down payment.

The insidiousness of addiction caught us unaware. Like a serpent, it slithered slowly into our lives. Just as sinister, its sister demon, delusion, masked how I faced each day—showering and suiting up, meeting with colleagues, asking people for money, smiling and radiating genuine gratitude, sharing with Dick in the evening, and starting it again the next morning. Despite my anxiety, I couldn't face the reality of what was happening. If I pretended that Jacob wasn't really a drug user—he only smoked weed, like a lot of kids did, practically everyone I knew had at least tried it, even lots of adults—then I could still apply lipstick in the mirror each morning and smile in the hospital halls throughout the day. What was far more horrifying to consider was that he might be using something worse than marijuana, drugs whose names I didn't know and couldn't imagine how he used them. And if that was true, then what could I possibly do about it? How could I stop him? The questions welled up from a black, open hole—was that where the serpent lived?—a chasm so deep and dark that if I dared peek inside, it would suck me in and pull me down into its bottomless cavern. Better not to look at all.

But the signs kept popping up. Since he was living at home, Jacob asked if he could change his room. I thought he meant to paint it, straighten it up, or organize his desk so he could study there. Not quite. He had something very different in mind. On craigslist he'd found a huge, overstuffed sofa. It would become the centerpiece of his room, his life. At night he would retreat to the tufted, cheap, faded beige cushions, his command center for opiates, where he'd misguide his ship and sail off into clouds that took him farther and farther away from us and from himself.

With the help of Scotty and some other friends, he lugged the thing into his bedroom during a weekend we were away. Now Jacob's queen-sized bed was against the left wall, his desk faced the door, and behind the desk this ungainly, fading, plush couch rested against the windows. When Jacob sat on the couch, his back was to the windows, and he faced the door. His computer was positioned in the center of the desk so that its bulk blocked his face. Anyone entering the room wouldn't see him.

Some might have quipped that Jacob was building his "man cave." To me, the sight was frightening. My son had cleverly created a place to hide. Tucked away upstairs in his room wasn't shelter enough. He had to build a fortress inside the room for added protection. Facing the computer, his back to the windows, he could withdraw completely. It was even more frightening because Jacob never used the desktop computer; he used his laptop exclusively. The big, hulky desktop had been sitting on the floor, awaiting its disposition. Now Jacob had found a use for it.

With the redesign of the room, other strange things happened. Jacob had never told me, like some kids do, not to go into his room.

But there was an unspoken agreement that we respected each other's space. He almost never entered our room. In fact, the only other room in the house he ever occupied was the kitchen. Otherwise, it was a straight shot from the kitchen door—the door to the street that we all used—to his bedroom. He wasn't a TV watcher. For anything he wanted to watch, he'd use his laptop. Given his permission, it wasn't unusual for me to enter his room, drawn by a perverse need to check on his life. Whenever I did, I had to pick my way carefully. The dark blue wall-to-wall carpet was a sea of debris: piles of faded jeans and basketball shorts, scattered pages from notebooks, printed homework assignments, worn textbooks left open, gum wrappers, thin packages of mints, pencils, bits and pieces of torn-up envelopes, letters, cellophane, and scrawled notes from Jacob to himself.

One morning, against this blue ocean of chaos, an odd color glinted. I couldn't help but see it, shiny and small beneath Jacob's desk. If he were seated on the sofa, where he now spent most evenings, it would be at his feet. Silver. Thin sheets of aluminum foil. I eyed them curiously, afraid to see them there, wishing them away. At first, I had no idea what they were. But when my brain finally calculated what they meant, the sight alarmed me. Like a detective uncovering new evidence, I was curious to know what it was, yet terrified where it might lead.

An odd dance began. I tried to avoid Jacob's room, but it was still my job to keep my house clean, and this was a room in my house. At the very least, I had to tidy it up. When I did go into the room, I'd scoop up obvious litter and discard it, the foil included. Some blind force compelled me each time I entered his room to scan for the foil and get rid of it. Those thin, shiny pieces of paper had black smudges down the center, as though someone had burned something on them. I'd never smelled anything burning in his room. Jacob knew that smoking of any kind was forbidden in the house. Since my mother had died of lung cancer, I abhorred cigarettes, and my children knew it.

But the fear and images those pieces of foil fired in my brain forced me more and more to avoid entering his room altogether. I was like the little kid watching a horror movie who covers his face when the monster appears, yet stares through spread fingers to watch it eat all the people.

Jacob never questioned why snippets of trash went missing from his room. Likely he didn't notice. He didn't notice Dick or me much at all. We were far more focused on him. At least, I was. Often, I stopped into the coffee shop when he was working. Just as when he worked downtown, it comforted me to see him behind the counter, smiling at customers, filling their coffee cups, making sandwiches, joking with co-workers. He seemed so healthy, just a college kid working a part-time job, growing up. Maybe he had some problems, but all kids did.

When summer came, Jacob settled into a full-time schedule at work. Much to our delight, he ended his first year at the community college with A's and B's and promptly signed up for courses the coming fall. His grades and steadiness on the job reaffirmed that he was right in wanting to come home from College Park. Things were going according to plan.

Or so we wished.

Chapter 15

Love Lost and Turning Twenty-One

The alarm went off at 5:20 every weekday morning. I was in the gym by 6, working through a drill that included machines and treadmill. I had my routine. Thirty minutes on the machines, thirty doing cardio. Against pale heather walls and a polished oak floor, men and women lifted weights and stretched, emerging from locker rooms freshly showered, sporting suits and smart shoes, toting gym bags and briefcases, off to the office.

Everyone was happy at the gym. You couldn't be unhappy when you had to focus on breathing or feel that delicious stretch with your arms reaching for the ceiling and your legs set wide apart. If you kept moving, misery couldn't find you.

Like the gym, the hospital was also my refuge. If I just kept moving, I could get through it. The capital campaign was nearing yet another critical phase. We were four million dollars shy of our goal with just eighteen months remaining until the ribbon-cutting ceremony and the campaign's end. In the office I was the calm one, the person everyone looked to for guidance, the cheerleader who turned any setback into opportunity. If staff members returned from a meeting with a potential donor empty-handed, I would review each step. What went wrong? What else could you have said? Stay close, I would gently coach them; just keep doing the right thing for the donor, and one day the gift will emerge.

I lived a schizophrenic existence. Patient, positive, and in control at work. Lost and frantic at home. If my staff only knew, I thought. If they only knew the tragedy that's playing out right now in my house, upstairs in that darkened bedroom-cave, if they saw what I see, how could they ever trust anything I tell them? A mother who can't even fix her own child. How could I fix anything else?

Shame and fear of exposure settled in like a heavy shroud. There were times I actually was terrified that someone would find out my son was using drugs. How would that affect my job? Would people refuse to give me their money if they knew I was the mother of an addict?

I dressed elegantly, but the weight of shame hung on my shoulders every day. My appearance had to stand up to multi-millionaires. I had to represent the hospital with dignity and maturity and with the polish to ask others for seven-figure gifts. Mornings, when I buttoned the silk blouse and latched the thick strand of pearls around my neck, I glanced at the face in the mirror and tried not to stare. Who was this woman? Hair carefully blown dry, makeup artfully applied, the face in the mirror looked back with haunting eyes, gray shadows pooling beneath the mascara, red lipstick pressing the mouth into a thin, taut line. Smile, I would tell myself. You look so much prettier when you smile.

A family ritual that helped sustain me was the shared dinnertime. Many evenings I stayed late at the hospital for meetings or attended functions in town. But as often as possible, Dick and I preserved the dinner hour for Jacob. Jacob knew that, too. If he wasn't at work, he would join us and take his seat on the banquette behind our square oak table. The banquette framed two sides of the table beneath windows that looked out on the busy historic district street. Conversation was easy. So was keen observation of how everyone was doing.

Since Dick was home during the day, he became chief cook, and he was wonderful at it. His love for his family simmered in the home-made, rich spaghetti sauce, sizzling garlic-laced steaks, and buttery mashed potatoes, all among Jacob's favorites. He tried to make meals that were well-balanced and nourishing and served them with flair on a finely set table. Gratitude oozing from me, I'd arrive home after an eleven-hour day to find bowls of steamed broccoli or cauliflower, fragrant baked chicken, or a boiling kettle of linguine ready to soothe a starving stomach.

Food was plentiful and delicious, and Jacob should have eaten well, but often he barely finished half of what was on his plate. Tall and thin, he took his looks more from my side of the family. Dick was lean, too. Our family was physically active. Weight control had never been a problem, but Jacob now led the pack for fewest pounds per inch.

Dinner on the table, we called Jacob downstairs from his cave. The twenty minutes or so it took to consume the meal were check-up time. This was when I could most closely observe my son, take a mother's medical scan on the general condition of this boy I loved so much: the slump of his shoulders, the gray cast of his forehead and cheeks, wrists like wishbones, eyes half-open with lids that fluttered like window shades battered by a storm.

Jacob appeared exhausted. It was a look he wore frequently now and often at dinnertime.

"So, Jacob, how was your day?" I tried for airy conversation.

"I dunno." He eyed the steak and fluffy mound of potatoes, arms loose at his side. Silverware sat still as sentries, bordering his plate. "Okay, I guess."

"School? Anything happen today?"

"Nah, not really. I did get a call from work. I'm getting extra shifts this weekend, so that's good, I guess." He speared a piece of steak. "How about you guys? How was your day?"

By the time the conversation switched to us, Jacob took a few bites of meat and seemed to lose interest. He slouched back against the padded back of the banquette, his eyelids closing.

"Jacob, you look tired. Are you all right?"

"Yeah, Ma." He pushed back, voice rising just slightly. "You know I get up early for school, and I'm working. Yeah, I'm tired. That's all."

Dick sat quietly, eating his meal and looking at his plate, but following the banter between mother and son. When he'd heard enough, he calmly spoke up with just the smallest edge to his voice, "Well, if you're that tired, you should go upstairs and go to bed."

And with that, Jacob hauled his body out of the seat, set his still-full plate on the kitchen counter, and silently passed from the room.

Silence had become the sound that our home made these days. Ours had never been a noisy household. Neither Dick nor I were shouters. Whenever we'd gotten angry at Heidi or Jacob as children, we'd adopted a calm approach. Lowering our voices soothed the crisis better than yelling. But lately, the volume in the household had turned down so low there was no sound at all.

One night Jacob surprised us. He seemed more animated than usual and opened up the conversation on his own.

"Hey, can we talk about something?" Knives and forks stopped mid-air. "Would it be okay if . . . I've been thinking . . . Chelsea and I have been talking, and . . . would it be okay if I visited her Valentine Day's weekend?"

Chelsea was at school in Connecticut. In her freshman year, she still dominated Jacob's social life. The two spent hours Skyping late into the night. Even though Chelsea reminded me of a pampered, high-strung puppy, I was grateful for the relationship, since it was one of few Jacob had that seemed healthy and normal. She made Jacob happy, and so little did.

We discussed details of the trip. Dick agreed to give Jacob the airline tickets; the rest of the weekend would be on his own dime. Jacob beamed. College kids visited each other on far-flung campuses all the time. But for Jacob, this was a very big deal. A young man who showed no initiative in other areas of his life, he'd planned this visit on his own. I was thrilled for him and silently applauded his stab at independence, his reaching out for adventure, however small.

But the trip was a disaster. What was meant to be a romantic weekend with a girlfriend, complete with an expensive plush teddy bear and a bracelet from Tiffany's, instead marked the beginning of the end of their courtship. When Jacob got home, he said he'd gotten ill—some flu, or maybe something he ate. So he and Chelsea hadn't been able to do much, and they really hadn't had a very good time. He felt bad about getting sick, and it had ruined everything. It was all his fault, and that made him feel even worse. He knew he'd disappointed Chelsea, and the whole weekend "really just wasn't good."

Years later, Jacob explained what really transpired. He'd gone off to Connecticut with no thought of what might happen without opiates in his system. With his drug habit escalating, his body needed a certain level of opiates just to function. Missing the drugs, his body simply revolted. He started cramping, suffering severe stomach pains, chills, even the shakes. To his alarm, he recognized he was going through withdrawal.

Jacob's relationship with Chelsea and her family soured after that weekend. When Chelsea first went away to school, Jacob developed an affinity for slipping out evenings to visit her mom at her house. The Parks lived on the Chesapeake Bay about twenty minutes outside of Annapolis. It was natural for Jacob to be there when Chelsea was home, but I didn't understand what drew him there when she was away.

"I like Mrs. Parks, and she likes me," he'd say when I questioned him. "She's lonely. Mr. Parks travels. He's away a lot. I'm company for her."

I supposed that made sense. Mr. Parks was a high-level executive in an international land development company, who travelled several times a month. So Jacob was right. His wife frequently was alone in their large, empty house. And it wouldn't be unusual for Jacob to have friends who were adults. He was close with my friends and was having difficulty finding friends at home, since most of the kids he knew were away at school. I had met Mrs. Parks, and she seemed like a decent woman. A doting mother, she liked Jacob and enjoyed joking with him. Besides, he missed Chelsea, and being in her home made him feel closer to her.

What I didn't know was that Chelsea's mom suffered from several health problems. Chronic back pain topped the list. She often took pain medication, and prescription drugs filled her medicine cabinet. It was easy for Jacob to slip into the bathroom, shut the door, and scan the inventory. Surely a few pills would never be missed, especially given the ample supply of his favorite, OxyContin.

Though she never discussed it with me, Mrs. Parks apparently had confronted Jacob early in his relationship with Chelsea. The previous year, she suspected Jacob was not only using, but possibly selling drugs, and she told him flatly, "You need to stop this, or you can't continue to see my daughter."

The door closing on the Parks family was one more loss in Jacob's life, and it was a big one. He admired Mr. Parks for his success as a businessman and the material things it brought his family. He genuinely liked Mrs. Parks and felt sorry for her pain. Chelsea had filled him with a joy that nothing else did.

After the Valentine's Day visit, Jacob narrowed his activities. He continued to go to work and class, but he was falling rapidly into serious addiction. As he told me much later, "There was a day that year when I knew I was an addict. I just remember feeling it. It was just me and Oxy. That's all I wanted."

Because of Jacob, Dick and I began narrowing our activities, too. Addiction was slowly worming its way through our household, eating away at the strands of normalcy and routine that thread lives together. We had to limit Jacob's use of the car, and that meant one of us had to drive him to work. Jacob had sideswiped enough lampposts in town to wreck the passenger side mirror more than once. Late one night, he misjudged the garage and crunched the front fender. Getting the car fixed cost time and money. It was more of an irritant than anything else, but it reflected Jacob's steady and increasing drug use.

Dick and I took to adjusting our calendars, trying to ensure that one of us was home evenings, weekends, whenever Jacob was. We never actually discussed this. It happened as naturally as robins in our backyard swapped places to protect their nests.

That spring my staff and I prepped for the hospital's sole fund-raising event: the annual gala. Unlike many fancy balls hosted by non-profits to make money, this one actually did. It also gave the hospital staff a chance to show off an institution that was worth showing off, to mingle with people of wealth, and to foster relationships that would blossom into much larger gains. The gala always was a very big deal.

Dick hated the galas and would use any excuse to avoid attending. Since I worked through the event, it mattered little if I went solo. But this year the gala was April 10—Jacob's twenty-first birthday. Dick and I thought it might be memorable for Jacob to attend as my guest and to volunteer his help, especially since he had no other plans. Even though we never voiced it, it also was a way to protect him on this important day.

True to their kindness, my staff made a genuine fuss over Jacob. As soon as we arrived in the glittery hotel atrium, Mary, my assistant, wrapped an arm around his thin frame—decked out in black tux and tie—and ushered him to the registration table. There he sat, one of the youngest among the nine hundred guests he helped to check in, bright lights glinting off his smooth, white forehead, black hair as slick and shiny as a shoeshine, his smile—when he gave it—as warm and sweet as springtime itself. I took one long, loving look at him before drifting off to welcome the gala sponsors. I wanted to remember this good-looking young man on his special birthday just this way, grinning back at me with the barest whiff of self-confidence as if to say, Hey, Mom, look at me. How cool is this? I'm in the big leagues now. At this fancy ball. Checking in all these rich people. Pretty cool.

The glow didn't last long. By the time we reached the seated dinner portion of the evening, I wondered if Jacob was tipsy. He was quiet at the table, and I knew the situation had to be awkward for him. What would a twenty-one-year-old part-time community college student have to say to a sixty-seven-year-old hotel developer or a retired physics professor who managed his family's foundation? Particularly a kid who was shy and unsophisticated in the role he had to play that evening. Still, Jacob seemed even quieter than usual.

As typically happened at this event, staff members wafted over to the table and whispered updates in my ear. Mary appeared with the latest scheduling notes, laid her hand on Jacob's shoulder and smiled at him, and let me know gaily that she and the registration table volunteers had been plying him with champagne cocktails to celebrate his big day.

Great, I thought. How's he going to handle this? It was the first time I was forced to face the question: what was worse for Jacob—alcohol or drugs? Could he drink alcohol and be fine? What started all this was marijuana, and the only other drug I knew he had used was OxyContin. At the time, I understood little about how addictive Oxy is, and I hadn't yet learned enough to know if there was any difference between alcohol and other drugs. All this rapidly churned over in my mind while I kept up a warm smile and watched the auctioneer hawk a week's stay in the Azores, a three-carat diamond bracelet, a river cruise on the Danube for six.

The gala encouraged guests to stay overnight and enjoy a brunch the next morning. Among other reasons, it was the hospital's nod to protecting those who drank too much and had no business driving home. During gala planning, it hadn't occurred to me that the group might include my son. By the time the band played the last dance and the few dozen guests lingered over coffee and trays of Krispy Kremes, Jacob had long disappeared.

I found him upstairs in my hotel room, slung across the adjacent bed, sleeping soundlessly. Gently, I slid off the slick, patent leather dress shoes and considered what to do about the rest of the rented outfit, destined to be a rumpled mess by morning. Who cares, I sighed, exhausted from the strain of smiling and standing in heels for nearly seven hours, let alone trying to keep track of Jacob.

Staring at the length of my son in his tuxedo, stretched across the freshly turned down queen-sized bed, I thought: this is his twenty-first birthday. Let him end it in style.

Chapter 16

Revelation

Work continued to be my refuge. Less than a year remained on the campaign, with some three million yet to raise. People were counting on me to make it happen. Long-term donors were mulling over pledge requests; a generous few had promised to give more when the time was right, and now it was. I coached staff and board members to stay focused and secure the remaining gifts.

While managing the campaign, I also handled communications during my CEO's final year and the transition to his successor. As the incoming CEO, Tori was forming her own team, and I worked hard to ensure my place on it. It meant many late nights, often catching up on sleep on weekends. My social calendar was booked with hospital functions, sparing time only for a long weekend trip to San Diego to see my grandson, now two. Friends missed me. But it was all I could do to manage work and get through worry-filled evenings at home.

Nights were the worst. Once in bed, Dick and I typically read. We were each in book clubs, so there always were stacks of books on our side tables. I tried to keep up with my club's monthly choices, but mostly I read just for distraction and to bring on sleep. Long after Dick was snoring softly, I'd turn the pages, steal a glance at the clock, turn the next page. Jacob wasn't home. The downstairs hall light was still on. It was a household rule that the last one upstairs turned off the light. No matter how exhausted or hung over he was, Jacob somehow always managed to turn off the light when he hit the upstairs landing.

So it became easy to know when Jacob was home—or not. Waiting for that light to go off, I glanced repeatedly at the bedside clock. The tiny, battery-powered box became both friend and demon.

Its black face blinked minutes in a fierce neon-orange, flashing images of horror. Where was Jacob? I tried to picture him from the snippets he shared: maybe awash at one of the county's street-end beaches? Or hidden away deep inside the bedroom of any of the odd characters he'd met in the last few years? These were kids who still lived at home, kids whose parents looked the other way while they stashed themselves in a basement bedroom where no mom ever ventured. While I didn't recognize it at the time, these were kids just like Jacob.

It wasn't every night. Some evenings Jacob would mutter "G'night" and disappear into the cave of his room. Door closed, it was eerily quiet. I ached to tap on his door before I turned off my light. I yearned for reassurance that he was all right. If I could just say "Good night" in person, I might reach some part of him that was still normal, healthy, or sane. Instead, I'd creep into my room and lie awake under the covers, afraid to disturb him and the shaky stability and silence of our lives.

The nights he was out were terrifying. The bedside demon blinked 1 a.m., 2 a.m. I strained for the sound of his footfall entering the house or the street door closing. My head throbbed with lack of sleep, but my body pulsed awake and alive. Sometimes my heart raced so hard the bed couldn't contain me, and I paced the upstairs hallway. Dick, meanwhile, somehow found the strength to sleep. I marveled at how he could sleep when our son was who knew where, doing who knew what.

While my relationship with Jacob was becoming increasingly fragile, I was certain of one other: my love and respect and need for Dick. I needed him to be exactly as he was: calm, strong, willing to listen to my anxieties and just sit beside me when I cried. Just as in so many other areas of our lives, there were times I questioned him for answers he couldn't possibly know. But at least he listened to me ramble. He let me do the hard work of trying to help Jacob because I was the one with the healthcare connection. But he was no better at this addiction thing than I was. Though we were lost when it came to helping our son, I was determined that Jacob wouldn't harm our marriage. There were too many stories of bad things happening to kids—drug abuse, car accidents, even deaths—that destroyed couples. The wise words of an older woman I knew kept ringing in my ears: "You gotta go home from the dance with the one that brung ya."

Despite Dick's strength and support, nights became a surreal suspension of all I knew and understood. They were endless panicky voids. Worry engulfed me like a great prehistoric bird, flapping its black wings at my heart, wrapping me in its sickly grip, beating at my heart and face until tears trickled down my cheeks. And it would return the next night, and the next . . .

Occasionally, when it got so bad I just needed to hear Jacob's voice, I'd reach for my cell phone and call him. He rarely answered, and if he did, it was only a monosyllabic answer. Yeah, I'm fine. Sometimes I would try texting. Even that took enormous thought and energy. What could I text to ensure he would respond? Something light, not too worrisome, or he'd ignore me. Find the right words, I would challenge myself in the pre-dawn hours. I'd opt for, Hey, getting late. You okay? I would barely breathe until he responded: Yeah. Home soon.

Only his footfall on the stairs could beat the thing out of the shadows. I would hear him switch off the light and softly enter his room. He would close the door. He was safe. The clock would fire an orange 3 a.m. I'd close my eyes, relieved that he was home.

The thought that Jacob could overdose or die barely whispered at the edges of my nightmares. I didn't know at that point how bad his habit was, or even what he was using. A close associate in city government had lost his nineteen-year-old son to a drug overdose. The incident was hushed up. The paper reported only that the teenager had died, not from what. It was typical of most drug overdoses you'd read about, young people ages nineteen, twenty-two, twenty-three, who just died. They'd leave a loving father and mother, a sister or brother. The obits usually were short, just a paragraph or two. *He loved animals and biking and his golden lab, Bo. He leaves a loving grandmother, two brothers, and his friend, Jill, who always will remember how his smile would light up a room.*

And then, like dandelions gone to seed in spring, these children were gone.

In May, my professional association invited me to a national meeting in Cleveland. Jacob's classes at the community college were over for the semester, and Dick and I thought a trip to the Rock and Roll Hall of Fame and a few days away would be a nice family treat.

And it was. While I attended meetings, father and son enjoyed touring Cleveland, went to an Indians game, and met me for evening events. With my professional colleagues, Jacob was quiet but charming, as always. They complimented me on how mature he was, what a smart young man, so cute. I loved having him there, catching that shy smile from across a room, or the glint of his amber eyes after a joke. The trip was a happy, brief respite from all the worrying at home.

Like the storybook Dutch boy who presses his finger against a hole in the dyke, the Cleveland trip was just a stopper on mounting pressure. This time, the swelling wall of water wouldn't hold. In the airport, waiting for the flight back to Maryland, the flood poured out.

Jacob admitted he was in trouble. Real trouble. Seated next to me, head down, he told me he'd been using OxyContin for some time. He'd racked up nearly nine thousand dollars on four credit cards and had no idea how to pay it off. His grades were in from the community college, and he wouldn't be graduating. Despite a B in human sexuality and an A in health, he'd flunked accounting.

"I need help, Ma," he cried, head down. "I really need help."

The two of us sat together in the small waiting area. Dick had gone off to buy food for the plane. Passengers paid no attention to the tragedy unfolding next to me. Businessmen in dark pinstripe suits heaved luggage straps over their shoulders, girls chattered in cutoffs and flip flops, a woman chased a runaway toddler, a skycap pushed a wheelchair conveying an old man with a tiny, yapping dog in his lap . . . they all swirled past while I tried not to breathe. Any inhale or exhale, and I might miss an anguished word of my son's torment that was now gushing out as we sat motionless on thin, hard plastic seats in Southwest's waiting area.

It was far worse than I'd imagined. Jacob was using heavily, and now real money was involved. The vague dream of seeing him in cap and gown evaporated. So much evaporated. My pulse started racing. Despite the relative safety of the airport, I closed my eyes and saw, in fast, blinding seconds, the black horror that came only at night when I struggled to sleep, felt just the faintest flutter of its wide, wicked wings against my face and chest. My boy. My beautiful son. Caught in such ugliness. This wasn't supposed to be. This wasn't how I would raise this child of mine, born in a time of unfathomable sorrow, meant to give joy, never destined to bring such shame to me or to our family, and certainly not in this silly little airport in Cleveland, Ohio.

When Dick returned and we lined up for the plane, there wasn't time to talk. He had no idea that everything in our lives had suddenly changed—or perhaps been made clear. No more delusions about Jacob's drug problem. It now even had a price tag.

Once home, the three of us talked. Jacob's confession wasn't something we could ignore. There had to be a plan. In the first of what would be many plans that summer and fall, Jacob promised he would dig out of this mess. First, he handed over the four credit cards. Next, he agreed to focus on his health. He even agreed to go back to Pathways into the outpatient program, or to see a counselor. Whatever we wanted, he said.

His ready compliance should have signaled another warning, but it didn't. Loving parents, wanting to help our son out of this mess, Dick and I calmly and methodically ticked off the steps needed to fix the problem and get our son well again. On the plane ride home, I'd gone straight for his health.

"Jacob, how about if you just take the summer off? No classes. Just focus on your health. Rest. Eat better." The mother in me kept at him, oblivious to how absurd these words were, talking as though my son had a bad case of mono or flu and not a life-threatening addiction. But I kept on, craving calm because it was the only way I could get us home. "Really try to get yourself well and healthy, and you can resume classes in the fall?"

What most worried Jacob was the money. Dick said we would cover it, for now, and Jacob would begin to pay us back from his work. He agreed to everything we suggested. He was clearly panicked. For the moment, he was willing to say or do anything that might clear the way.

In my journal after the Cleveland trip, I wrote:

> He's hitting bottom, or at least a bottom. And
> through it all he is sweet and helpful and good. What
> a dichotomy. Doing bad, secret things, but so pleas-
> ant . . . O my sweet boy, I pray you find your way.
> Yours is to be a greater life than slave to a habit.
> As your mother, I pray that I find the wisdom and
> strength to be and give you what you need now.

Chapter 17

Vacation Breakdown

The tension at home had grown worse. Jacob was working and dutifully attending outpatient sessions three nights a week. But I knew things were not right. He still disappeared and often came in after midnight. The pattern was exhausting not just him, but Dick and me as well, and one day I'd had enough.

"Jacob, I need to get up early for work. You know I'm a light sleeper, and you know I listen for you to come home. I'm sorry, it's just the way I am. So when you get home at one or two in the morning, I can't sleep."

He listened, avoiding my eyes.

"So can we at least agree that on weeknights you'll get home by midnight? So I can sleep?"

He nodded, "Sure, Ma."

"And that means Sunday nights, too, since that's a weeknight for me."

"Okay, Ma. Whatever you say."

The spare words allowed the delusion to live. I still believed I actually could bargain with him, that I was talking to a rational adult who could reason and think through his actions. Even then, I had no idea how strong a hold drugs had on my son.

That summer, desperate for something positive to look forward to and the chance to bring some normalcy into our lives, I rented a house at the beach. I wanted to give the family a carefree week together. Summers in Rehoboth Beach, Delaware, had been part of my growing up, and I wanted the same for my family. An online search turned up a comfortable, five-bedroom cottage three blocks from the waterfront.

It seemed a perfect one-week rental for our immediate family, including the Andersons—Heidi, Jon, and Josh, now two, and Heidi's in-laws from New Jersey, who would drive down for a few days.

Heidi's father-in-law, Joe, and mother in-law, Peg, both in their eighties, were retired educators. Peg had been a teacher, Joe a former administrator from a large New Jersey school district. They'd raised five children; Jon was their "baby." Since the Andersons still lived on the West Coast, Peg and Joe didn't see their youngest often, so this would be a welcome visit and a chance to visit with their newest grandson. Including them in our beach time would enrich the week for everyone—especially, I hoped, for Jacob. Jacob was rarely around older people. It was a constant sadness for me that he never knew his grandparents. My father died the same year Jacob was born, just six months after my mother. Dick's parents died when Heidi was little. Perhaps our two houseguests might offer our son, and me, some comfort and wisdom.

By now, Jacob was in outpatient treatment at Pathways, but he was depressed and miserable. If the week at the beach didn't become the postcard-perfect family vacation, it did reveal more about Jacob's disease. Despite a houseful of people, he slept late every morning. Some days he didn't appear until well after noon, and then only to trudge to the bathroom and fall back in bed. Even the infectious giggle of a scampering two-year-old didn't draw him out. He spent almost no time with anyone. Later, I learned that he wasn't using that week, and withdrawal was adding to his misery.

One evening early in our stay, I took a long walk on the boardwalk with Jacob. He came alive at night, and we enjoyed time alone together, even during his worst days. It wasn't unusual for us to stroll around downtown Annapolis on a weekend and sit at the City Dock or near the Market House and watch cars and people pass by. One of his favorite pastimes was to imagine the stories behind the people we saw. He loved naming the cars, especially the Rolls Royces, Lamborghinis, and Ferraris.

In Rehoboth, we drifted together down the boardwalk, doing much the same—eyeing the people, making up stories about their lives. Then the conversation turned serious. Jacob confided that he hadn't been clean. Despite going to Pathways obediently three times a week, he was still using. He said he was trying, but everything was so hard. Leveling my eyes on the boardwalk, I took in every word, listening for what he didn't say, afraid to speak, grateful for his honesty, grateful that he was honest with himself, and that he was still talking to me. Perhaps because of Joe and Peg's presence that week, he surprised me with an unexpected comment: "I don't even know my grandparents. I know nothing about them!"

The next evening at dinner, Dick recounted for Jacob the lives of his paternal grandparents. He told the stories as only he could—both seriously and laced with hilarious humor. Everyone laughed. Jacob listened intently.

After the dishes were cleared, Jacob remained at the table. Everyone else had scattered to their activities—novels in the living room or light sweaters on the screened porch to watch other vacationers head for the boardwalk. Many evenings, I watched families trundle past, toddlers aloft broad shoulders, moms pushing carriages with tiny arms and legs reaching out, light chatter breezing by in the cool night air, heading for a cone of cotton candy, mint chocolate chip ice cream, caramel corn, the excited sweet voices of pure summer innocence, and *after we get ice cream can we take off our shoes and play in the sand? Aw, Mom, please? Dad, can we?*

Inside the house, Jacob sat at the dining room table. Afraid to leave him alone, I sat there, too. Except for the one conversation on the boardwalk, I'd tried several times to get him to open up.

"Jacob, is there anything I can do for you?"

"No, Ma," he'd say, eyes down, never meeting mine.

"Would you like to do miniature golf one evening?" That was one of his favorites.

"Yeah, maybe."

"Anything special we can get to eat? Or get from the market to fix for dinner one night?"

"I dunno. Steak maybe. It doesn't matter. Whatever everyone else wants."

"How about coming down to the beach with us tomorrow? I bet Josh would love for you to help build a sand castle."

"Yeah. All right. If you wake me. I dunno."

So this time I didn't even try to open conversation. Jacob sat absolutely motionless, staring at the table. It felt like hours, but only a minute or so ticked by. He was almost catatonic. Nothing in the room moved.

Slowly, with no sound, he crossed his arms and placed them on the table. In excruciatingly slow motion, he lowered his head until his forehead rested on his arms. I stared, baffled, not knowing what to do or what might happen next. A few more seconds ticked by. From somewhere in the scrunched-up huddle of his frail body, I heard low, soft sobbing.

Rarely were there tears in our household. All their lives, both Heidi and Jacob had been happy and healthy children. Tears were relegated to the rare cut lip from falling on the brick sidewalk or, thanks to growing up in a Navy town, the sudden announcement that a cherished classmate was moving far away.

The only memory I had of Jacob crying was when he broke his arm during kickball at school at age seven. He complained for days before I took him seriously enough to get him x-rayed. When the orthopedic surgeon showed me the films confirming the fine, broken bone in his radius, Jacob grinned at me from the examining table, "See, Mom, I told you!" And of course, there was that horrible day in North Carolina, when I pulled him out of the beach week mansion after he'd been arrested. His unearthly cries from the back seat of the car as we drove away could hardly be dubbed tears—but I would never forget that sound of anguish and pain.

Jacob was the product of a long line of men who never cried, let alone show their feelings. It was characteristic of his father and grand-fathers to shield their emotions. When a tragedy happened, an illness or death, their way was to grow stolid, to be strong for the rest of the family. Jacob had certainly watched his father act that way as he grew up. I couldn't think of a time when my husband had cried, and never in front of the children. So it wasn't surprising that Jacob would grow into adolescence without learning how to reveal his feelings, especially if they were dark or painful.

Tonight, inside this happy beach house, Jacob sat lifeless, forehead resting on folded arms on the table, tears dropping onto his knees and the stubby weave of the carpet. Gently, ever so softly, I touched my hand to his shoulder and slid it slowly down his back. I sat there, stroking and caressing his back, as I did with our greyhounds when they suffered bad dreams. But unlike with our hounds, this unnerved me. The silence was frightening. Jacob said nothing, and the tears kept falling. He was lost, incapable of finding his way, incapable even of asking for help. So we sat, a mother who ached to do anything she could to help her son, crying inside herself, and a young man in such pain the words wouldn't come.

Then, they did. Slowly, he lifted his head and said, "I know they're looking down on me now. And wherever they are, they understand the terrible pain that I am in, even more than you do."

"You mean your grandparents? Well, yes, I hope they do. They would have loved you very much, just as Dad and I do."

My comeback was lame, and I knew it. I just couldn't penetrate the world where Jacob wallowed now. Depressed, isolated, he was pushing me and everyone else away. He sat at the table only a few minutes more, and abruptly went back to his room.

Soon afterwards, Joe joined me at the table. I wasn't sure how much of Jacob's meltdown Joe had seen, but he opened up with a tell-ing conversation. Did I know there was a time in his career with the New Jersey school system when he worked with a colleague trying to help kids with addiction? He had my attention. It was such a big and growing problem in his school district, he said, and still was.

Here was this eighty-two-year-old man, still so vibrant and filled with years of experience as a teacher and administrator, sharing a story about his attempts to help young people with addiction. I had never discussed Jacob with Joe. Maybe Heidi had. But he knew for sure, and here he was, engaging Jacob's mother in a sane, rational discussion on substance use in the young.

The two of us sat at the table long after Jacob had left, Joe talking about the difficulties in getting his school system to open programs for kids with substance use problems. We were two adults having a quiet and deep conversation about addiction. What Joe also was doing, although I never knew if he was aware, was offering me a life-line in a sea of misery, a few quiet moments to regain some sense of normalcy, and I was forever thankful for his kindness that evening.

The week wore on, a seesaw of emotions for Jacob and for me. He managed to make it to the beach a few late afternoons, enough to impress upon Josh a future memory of a tall, gangly, pale man with thick black hair who filled buckets of seawater for the moat around his nephew's castle.

The final evening of our stay, Jacob seemed ill. Joe and Peg had left. It was just the immediate family, having a farewell supper on the porch. Jacob pushed back from the table, hand on his stomach, eyes half closed.

"Jacob, what's wrong?" I asked, out of earshot of others.

"Ma, I think I'm going through withdrawal."

He admitted he had not taken Suboxone for "more than a day." In his own way, he was trying to get clean, and to him that meant no drugs at all. He never liked taking Suboxone, a relatively new drug, but a psychiatrist in Annapolis had prescribed it. Although not quite the panacea that the medical world hoped for, if taken as prescribed it supposedly reduced the urge to use. Still hoping that doctors knew more than I did, I urged him to take a pill. He left the porch and returned a few minutes later, saying he felt better, "if only mentally."

By then, we were alone on the porch. The rest of the family had gone inside to pack, clean up the house, put Josh to bed. The night was still, humid, thick with memories of the week. Suddenly, Jacob teared up. I felt his sob more than heard it. He laid his head on the table, his arms a pillow, like he had a few nights before. The air was soundless except for the soft crying of my beautiful boy.

"Jacob, Honey, what is it?" I touched my hand to his back. "Sweetie, please tell me. What can I do to help you? What is it? Jacob, please, I can't help you if I don't know what it is."

Without lifting his head, he snuffled, "Mom, I hate this!"

"Hate? You hate what?"

"That it's over. It's all over. The week is over!"

I almost let out a huge sigh of relief. Although somewhat extreme, at least this was a reaction I could understand.

"You mean you're upset because we're all going home tomorrow?"

He shot up his head. "Yeah, of course, aren't you? I mean, this has been so great. Hasn't it? To be with all of us together and have Heidi and Jon and Josh here. It's just so nice. And now it's over. It's just over!"

It wasn't what I had expected to hear. I was almost delighted that the time together had meant that much to him, but how to comfort him now? And what about his over-reaction? A twenty-one-year-old crying because a week at the beach was over was far from normal. What to do about that?

There were so many times when I felt as lost as Jacob. Wasn't there anyone I could call, right then, to ask, please tell me what to do—now. In a world of instant communication, wasn't there a red button I could press to ring up help for my son? I only wanted someone smarter and more educated in the world of drugs, addiction, depression, and adolescent anxiety to tell me what to say and do. Please, just feed me the words to help my son right now. Damn it, where's that red button, and why isn't anyone answering?

His plight, his disease, made me feel totally inadequate most of the time. There was no script for this new life I'd entered. The drama unfolded without rehearsal. I couldn't read ahead. I simply had to respond when Jacob tossed me the lines.

That night, I sat with my hand stroking his back, praying that my love for him and fierce desire to help might soothe him. Yes, I reassured him, I was sad, too. Leaving the beach with my family always had been tough for me as a kid. Posters in the five-and-dime advertising back-to-school supplies made me shudder. That meant Labor Day was coming soon. And that triggered a whole routine of to-do's: pack up shorts and tee shirts and sandals and all our beach stuff—towels thick with the smell of suntan lotion, rubbery water wings that the mothers made us wear—stuff Monopoly and Candy Land and all our other games and toys and coloring books and crayons into big brown paper bags, and shove them into the trunk of our car for the long, hot drive, with the windows all the way down, back to the city.

As a kid, I'd had the whole summer. Jacob had only one week.

The trick, I knew, was to carry the joy and power of the week into life at home. Vacations with people you love restore and energize you. You take them with you into the office Monday morning, when colleagues say, "How was your vacation?" and you respond, "Really nice," but what you really want to share is your daughter's smile made brighter by the new color on her face, and the giggle of your grandson when the waves tickle his toes, and the warm clasp of your husband's hand as he takes yours while the two of you stroll along the boardwalk, your children walking just ahead, where you can see them, and you know for those precious moments, soon to be sandy memories, that they are healthy and safe.

Could I ever impart this to my son? Not then, and not for a long time. I didn't know that the transition to work and home would be harder than we could imagine.

Chapter 18

Where There's Life, There's Hope

When we returned to Annapolis, Jacob seemed to bounce back. In the evenings he borrowed the car to attend regular outpatient meetings at Pathways and resumed work at the coffee shop. At home he was helpful and even considerate. He registered at the community college to begin classes in the fall with the goal of graduating in December. When he talked, he made sense. Overall, he looked and sounded better, brighter, stronger.

But that wouldn't last.

One evening, just three weeks after the beach, I tossed Jacob a casual question, fully expecting him to say yes. We were in the kitchen. I was cleaning up after dinner, and he was helping me before heading back upstairs.

"Hey, Jacob, did you pass your 'pee' screen the other day?"

At Pathways he was subjected to both routine and unannounced drug screenings. He hated them. It meant peeing in a cup, sometimes under the eye of an attendant. I'd remembered that he was due for a test shortly after Rehoboth. His counselor, Derrick, cautioned him that going away for a week and missing outpatient meetings would mean an automatic urine test when he got back.

To my total shock, Jacob responded, "No."

I stopped drying the plate. My eyes locked on his.

"No?" was all I could respond. "No? What does *that* mean?"

"They found Valium, Ma," he began, eyes down, "and I'm outta Pathways, I guess."

"You guess? What do you mean, you're out of Pathways? Jacob, what are you telling me?"

"I dunno, Ma. You can talk to my counselor if you want. The Valium was just from this guy who owed me money, and that's how he was paying me off. It's really no big deal. Call Derrick if you want."

"Do you want me to call Derrick to see if you can continue at Pathways?"

"Ma, I don't know. It doesn't really matter. Whatever you want. Do what you want. I'm feeling stronger now. I want to attend meetings and keep things going, but I don't know. What do you think? Maybe I should see a psychologist."

Before I had a chance to process this new turn and the jumbled confusion of his words, one of Jacob's former high school classmates tapped on our kitchen door. Mary was beautiful, talented, serious, the kind of young woman Jacob should be seeing. She sensed she was interrupting a tense conversation. Jacob looked at me, eyes pleading to let him go. I greeted Mary warmly, genuinely liking this girl. The two disappeared upstairs and later went downtown to meet other old high school friends. I knew that with Mary Jacob would be safe, or so I hoped. It always cheered me to see him with her and other friends from high school, now home for the summer.

A pattern was emerging. Jacob would drop a bomb: he's still using. Then he would disappear into the relative normalcy and safety of high school chums.

The roller coaster of addiction wreaked havoc with my emotions, one minute chugging up the hill, the next sliding down. It paralleled Jacob's universe. I panicked to discover and rediscover that he was still using, swallowing pills, hiding truths. Just as abruptly, my pulse slowed to see him with Mary, the good guy high schooler grinning alongside the prettiest girl of his dreams.

He'd been kicked out of Pathways. I had no idea what that really meant. Could a healthcare institution deny treatment? How could they turn a kid away without some other referral? Jacob plainly wasn't telling me everything, and I resolved to learn more.

The next day I could barely wait to get into my office, shut the door, and phone Pathways to reach Jacob's counselor. Derrick agreed it would be a good idea for Jacob, Dick, and me to meet with him. In all my dealings with Pathways, I tried hard to play it straight, to be just the mother of a patient. Although a senior vice president in the health system, I wanted to be treated like any other family member. My natural sense of fairness—not to mention the deepening sense of shame over my son's condition—urged me to fight for anonymity. Even walking into Pathways to meet with Derrick caused me angst. It helped that it was an evening appointment, so the people I knew weren't on duty.

The meeting was eye-opening. Once more, I learned that addiction masks a surprise around every corner. Discovering how serious your son's drug addiction is, is like a long, slow walk through an abandoned building, dark and dank and boarded up for years. Behind every door is a horror story. And just when you think you've opened the last door and heard all the terrors, you discover there is still another door, and another...

You aren't prepared for what you hear, either. Just like the meetings with Jacob's counselors in high school, when they tried to tell me my son wasn't doing well, I found it hard to comprehend whom they were talking about. Jacob Hillman? *My* son? Are you sure you haven't mixed up your records? It happens, you know. Mistakes like that happen all the time with the thousands of medical records you must have, and I'm not angry that you've confused my son with someone else. You don't even need to apologize. Let's just end this meeting so we can all get back to our normal lives.

Derrick's opening was a killer.

"Your son has been taking some very dangerous drugs. What's best for him now is to go 'inside' for a twenty-eight-day stay, at least."

Derrick explained that Jacob had been dismissed from the outpatient program because he'd reneged on his agreement. When he entered the program, he signed a pledge for a "higher level of care" if he failed the drug screen three times, and he had. Jacob denied using

OxyContin. We didn't ask, nor were we told, what the "dangerous" drugs were. It was just as well. That small, closed-in room couldn't have contained my terror if I'd heard the names of the drugs my son was using. If I didn't know what they were, I could still delude myself that maybe his addiction wasn't that bad. Not *that* bad.

But here was an addiction counselor, supposedly someone who knew far more than Dick and I did, strongly recommending that our son enter an inpatient rehab program. Okay, my mind quickly reasoned, we can do this. Now what?

Jacob calmly stated he did not want to go.

"No, I really don't want to do that," he began. "I feel better. I feel like I'm on the right road now. I've learned a few things here. Last night I went to an NA meeting, and I've been going to other meetings. I want to keep trying."

When pressed why he didn't want to enter inpatient treatment, he repeated his refusal.

"No. I really don't think I need inpatient. I'm going to meetings and I'm doing okay. And I don't want to mess up my job, 'cause working is important, right? School starts soon, and I gotta do that, too, right? So, no, inpatient would just mess all that up for me right now."

Neither Dick nor I knew how to respond. We agreed that his job and school were both important. And he did seem, at least on the surface, a little better. He never missed work, and his manager seemed happy with him. So how bad could it be?

What we didn't understand was how sick Jacob really was. Derrick knew. His practiced eye could see farther down the road. He knew Jacob was headed for disaster unless he got treatment. And the only way he could get it was to accept it. Which, at least this day, he did not.

Trying to help us, Derrick suggested alternatives. He told Jacob to "find yourself a sponsor. Get a 'temporary' sponsor if you need to, for now." He also advised a contract with us. "You agree to stay clean and sober. You will go to meetings, attend school, work at your job.

That's the contract. And if there is any break in this, then you'll do the twenty-eight-day program."

Three pairs of eyes were on Jacob. He stared at the floor.

"Yeah, okay. I guess that's fine. But is that it?"

Derrick: "What do you mean, is that it? Jacob, that's a lot."

Jacob: "Yeah, I know, but what about the other things?"

"What other things?"

"Well, that I sometimes feel, I dunno. Like I don't fit in. I don't belong. It's just sometimes I feel like I'm not really there."

I remembered that Jacob had once told me he felt like he was disappearing. Another time, he'd said he thought he was becoming autistic. Maybe Derrick needed help understanding Jacob.

"Jacob, do you mean you feel awkward in some situations?" I offered.

"Yeah, I guess that's it. There's just times I don't know what to say and I don't feel right, like I don't belong there, I guess."

Derrick nodded, but I wondered if these thoughts from a troubled young man might have challenged his credentials. As the session wound up, he asked Jacob if he would consider talking with a counselor, someone outside of Pathways, and Jacob said yes right away. We left the meeting with Derrick promising to recommend a counselor. In the car heading home, we said little. So many words, both said and unsaid, had passed in that little room.

What I felt most on the ride home was hope. The revelation that "your son is using some very dangerous drugs" shocked and scared me, all the more so because it conjured up an image of Jacob I didn't want or wasn't willing to accept. To me, he was still the promising, funny, straight-A student whose mere presence could light up my life. I refused to let in any other image. It was too frightening. "Dangerous drugs" spelled an ugliness I'd never known or could possibly imagine.

Throughout Jacob's illness, hope was something that never left me. Even amid constant worry and fear, I clung to hope. Maybe it was irrational, given the bad news we kept getting. Or maybe it was that I'd always been inherently positive. It certainly buoyed me professionally. How else can you weather the hard work of asking people for money and accepting the possibility that they might say no? Being positive is one of the many traits I inherited from my mother. She refused to wallow in misery. "Don't morbid," she'd often quip, knowingly turning the adjective into a verb. Others admired that about her. "Your mom is such a positive person," they told me, even during her illness. "She's always smiling. So gracious and lovely."

In my worst days of fear and anxiety over Jacob, I drew strength from her. If my mother could face cancer for so many years and stay positive throughout her illness, then I could do that for my own child as he lived through his.

Despite my will, despair popped up when I least expected it. It often happened—of all places—at the gym. Weekday mornings I'd be at the machines, pumping the shoulder press in my normal 6:30 a.m. routine, when a clear understanding of how bad things really were would hit me. The raw hurt of living with Jacob's disease would sear into me. Hidden inside a body that I somehow kept moving, shielded by sweat and grimace, I felt terrified, sad, lost. The music didn't help. The drumming thrump of popular songs, the same we listened to in the car, made me think of him. We'd be driving somewhere and he would hook up his iPhone, blasting the music through the car speakers. "Did you like that one?" he'd ask, choosing songs to please me. We both liked mournful tunes in minor keys that told stories. Occasionally, he'd listen to rap, but mostly he went for lyrics that dug into your heart. He liked classical music, too, a byproduct of the years he accompanied us to Annapolis Symphony Orchestra concerts.

Listening to his music at the gym, I could shut my eyes and let the tears hide behind closed lids. Inevitably, some mother I knew from Jacob's high school days would come into range and ask, "So how's Jacob?" I'd smile, choke my thoughts, politely answer, "Oh, he's fine . . . ," and quickly turn the question around to her son. As she rattled on about how her kid was doing in his second year at Stanford, majoring in physics, planning graduate school at Caltech, and interning for some famous West Coast company, I'd listen politely and hurt all the more. Hearing stories from other mothers of how Jacob's high school friends were thriving only deepened my sadness. Why their sons and not mine?

There were moments in that gym when I despaired so deeply that I wondered not about Jacob's life, but about my own. I knew that what I was feeling was depression. I just didn't recognize to what depths Jacob's addiction was hurting me. All the classic signs were there—intense feelings of sadness, fatigue, isolation, a lack of interest in everyday joys—and at times they overwhelmed me. At home, and especially at work, I tried hard to suppress them. After all, I was the positive one in the office. It was up to me to lead the team to victory in the campaign. No time for wallowing in disappointment or sadness. No time to "morbid." We had money to raise and a ribbon cutting to plan, so let's get on with it.

But weekday mornings at the gym, sadder, scarier thoughts filled my head. Eyes closed, a pulley with weights forcing my arms up over my head, stretching my core, I sought release from the unbearable sorrow crashing down on me. There were moments when my mind flirted with this thought: it doesn't matter if something happens to me. If I get sick now, or there's an accident that takes my life, it's okay. I've had a good life. I've been very blessed. And finally, in my blackest moments, there in that brightly-lit gym, with blood-pulsing energy pumping all around me, this darkest of thoughts was the only one that gave me relief: if living gets too hard, I can always end it. The word "suicide" never actually entered my mind. Instead, it was just a comfort to know, like a good fallback plan, that if living became too sad or too hard, if my son continued to use and slowly killed himself, then I could die, too.

One morning, as I practiced leg lifts, a woman appeared in front of me. It had been years since I'd seen Ronda. Dick and I knew her from the first synagogue we'd joined in Annapolis. She and her husband had two children, one a boy, but that was all I could quickly recall. We'd never been close, and I'd lost touch with what she was doing now. She told me that she was now a real estate agent, struggling with the economy, but aren't we all?

"I don't know how you can do what you do, raising money at a time like this," she went on. But she was confident the market would pick up. She asked about my family. I recounted how Dick was doing, and Heidi. Then she asked about Jacob.

"Jacob is, well, he's just okay," I answered. For some reason, Ronda standing in front of me had gotten my full attention. I let the leg extension bars go slack as I tried to focus on her. "I'm a little worried about him right now, but I think he'll be okay."

Then I remembered.

Thirteen years earlier, her eleven-year-old son was killed in a freak swimming accident at summer camp. At the time, the tragedy rocked our tight community. Parents didn't lose eleven-year-old sons, and certainly not like that. And months ago, Ronda had lost her husband to cancer. She was alone now, building a real estate career, attending the gym most mornings, measuring her life one contract or calorie at a time.

Now standing squarely in front of me, her eyes penetrating mine, this woman whom I'd not seen in at least ten years softly said, "Well, where there is life, there is hope."

Chapter 19

Hope Tested

In early August, Dick and I flew to Cape Cod to spend a long weekend with one of our oldest friends. A psychiatrist, Marc was one of Dick's fraternity brothers at Hopkins. Happily married to his second wife, Marc's first wife was an alcoholic, a fact he hid from us for decades.

That weekend we relaxed into the easy, summertime lifestyle of the Cape. Marc took us out on his boat in search of lobster, and the four of us, with total abandon, belted out the theme song from the movie *Indiana Jones*, a Cape Cod family tradition. Reaching the lobster pots in the remote, quiet cove, we turned our voices to "Hello Lobby" in sync with "Hello Dolly." We wrapped our fingers around the heavy chains and hauled them, slippery with seaweed, from the seabed, excited to see our catch.

It didn't matter that the cages came up empty. The sun glinted off Pleasant Bay, there was the whole night and another day in front of us, and we laughed just to be together.

Marc knew about Jacob. I wanted to corner him and let him play psychiatrist to our dilemma, but I didn't want to abuse our friendship. He gave me an opening when he asked how Jacob was doing, and I told him the story. He listened patiently, as psychiatrists do. I studied his face to see how much he was really getting. We were taking one of our early morning walks, walking through the woods behind his house. About every third sentence he nodded, encouraging me to keep talking, which I gladly did. It was a relief just to talk so freely with someone who understood. He didn't offer any new advice or suggest anything I wasn't already doing. He knew we were about to try a new counselor for Jacob, that we were staying close to our son, and that I loved him so much I cried to talk about him. He offered to send me a few names of addiction specialists in DC, but otherwise, he just listened. That alone helped.

Once home, I eyed Jacob carefully. That was typical after a few days away. Part of me was still pure mother, checking my child's vital signs after a brief separation. The other part was detective. I hated to leave him now for fear of what he might do to himself if I weren't there. He was too old for me to hire a babysitter, but I worried whenever we left him. So we didn't leave often. Dick and I had slipped into an unspoken routine of checking each other's schedules to be sure one of us would be home when Jacob was. Except for the trip to Cape Cod, we were careful not to be away. I actually thought that our very presence might keep him safe, that just being there would protect him or block the drugs. If Dick and I were around, Jacob might not use drugs, or he'd use them less, or at least he'd avoid more serious trouble. Such is the insidiousness of addiction. I still thought that my actions could save my son, change his behavior, turn things around.

Jacob said he'd been fine while we were gone. He'd had an odd bout of nausea, some vomiting, likely something he'd eaten. He told us he'd been clean, and we believed him. Or chose to.

About three weeks later, just days before the start of Jacob's fall classes, Dick sent me an email at the office: "After work, go to the coffee shop. Jacob is not having a good day."

The email alarmed me. I closed my office door and phoned my husband.

"What does your email mean?"

"You were right. He didn't go to meet Chris. I was just out walking the dog and happened to run into Chris. He said he hadn't seen Jacob this morning."

Oh God, I thought. I didn't want to be right. Earlier that morning Jacob asked if he could borrow the car to visit with Chris at a nearby bagel shop. Chris was leaving for college that day, and this would be

Jacob's last chance to see him. We loved Chris. He was one of Jacob's closest friends. Tall and confident, Chris was brilliant, on a PhD path, and destined to make his mark. He also was always kind to Jacob and to us.

So when Jacob asked if he could see Chris, I said "yes." It made me happy whenever Jacob spent time with his "normal" friends. I shrugged aside the passing thought that he might be lying to me—just another fleeting moment of denial, among so many.

"So I don't know where he was," Dick went on, "but he didn't come back for about two or three hours."

Jacob's shift ended at 7:00 that evening. Somehow I pushed through my day, fighting hard to tamp down rising panic. At 6:45 I pulled into the parking lot facing the shop. From my car I watched the workers doing their end-of-the day chores, stacking outdoor chairs and tables, sweeping the sidewalk, locking the doors. I didn't see Jacob until he walked out. It was immediately clear that he was under the influence of something. His gait was off, more like a shuffle than a walk. He tried to wave goodnight to a fellow worker, but his hand never made it into the air. He slid into my car, stared briefly at the glove compartment, tilted his head back against the seat, and let his eyes slowly close.

It was pointless to try to have a conversation, but I tried anyway.

"So how was work today?" My forced jauntiness made even me ill.

"It was okay," he slurred back. "I'm really tired."

"Jacob, we need to talk about this morning. Remember when you said you were going to go visit Chris?"

I realized trying to talk to him now was ridiculous. Jacob was nodding-off in the car, his head alternately leaning back against the headrest and dropping nearly to his knees. If it hadn't been so serious, it would almost be amusing. He looked like one of those men you see across the aisle on an airplane, who falls asleep the minute the plane takes off, head bobbing back and forth from the headrest to the air in front, startling himself awake, only to fall back again in deep slumber.

When we got home, I met Dick's gaze as Jacob moved past us and went straight to his room. We knew Jacob was using, but we had no idea what to say or do.

It was shocking to me that he could work in that condition. Hadn't his co-workers seen how compromised he was? Didn't they say anything to him? I wondered about his boss. Surely she knew Jacob was using. How much longer would she put up with that?

Dick and I knew Jacob's boss. She lived near us downtown and was an older, mature woman who cared about the shop and her staff. I knew from Jacob that she had taken a personal interest in him. Jacob was easy to like, so that didn't surprise me. What did was how long she let Jacob work there.

One Saturday morning I was walking along a popular shop-lined street in the neighborhood when she happened to come up behind me. As she drifted past, she said, quietly, so only I could hear, "You know, Mrs. Hillman, Jacob is a fine boy. You have every reason to be very proud of him. If he can just get his problem under control . . ." Years later I would learn that she, too, once fought addiction and has remained clean and sober for more than twenty years.

One of the reasons Jacob held on to his job so fiercely was money. When he first began working in high school, Dick and I hadn't paid much attention to what he made. That was his business and we assumed he was depositing his paychecks into his savings account. The promise we'd made in high school when he first asked for a car still held: save enough money to match a down payment and we'd help him buy it.

Jacob rarely asked us for money. We knew he used whatever he made at work to pay for fast food, an occasional movie, polo shirts on eBay, or treat a girlfriend, as he had with Chelsea. It never occurred to us to ask him to cover anything else, like food or gas or certainly not rent.

Shortly after the day he'd taken the car, ostensibly to visit Chris, Jacob asked me to help him with his bank account. Something didn't look right to him, and he had questions. Why he showed his online statement to me, however, was either out of pure ignorance or a subconscious way of crying for help for something far more serious than an accounting error.

The evidence was right in front of me. The day before he had asked to visit Chris was a payday, and Jacob's account showed a direct deposit of $198. The next day, when he would have met Chris, the account showed a withdrawal of $180 from a bank in Edgewater, a community about five miles south of Annapolis. Why had Jacob driven to Edgewater and withdrawn that much money, I wondered.

Many of the pieces were missing, and I wasn't smart enough then to sort them out, but it was clear that Jacob's addiction was moving into new territory. If he lied about why he wanted the car and covered up his trip to the bank in Edgewater with the ruse about seeing Chris, what other lies or cover-ups had there been? Or were ahead?

Jacob's lying was new, or at least had taken this new turn. He'd surely been hiding so much from us for months, years, but now, here was a brazen story poorly told. He'd asked us for the car to see a friend whom he hadn't gone to see. It was the first time we could corroborate the lie. As we stared at the computer screen's unblinking truth, it also was the first time we couldn't deny what was happening. In my head, it escalated his addiction to a far more frightening level. My kids always were truthful with me, and certainly about anything important, like using the family car. Trust was a basic tenet of our family. We didn't lie to each other. There never was a reason Dick, Heidi, Jacob, or I had to cover up anything from one another—until now.

As this new reality emerged, another fact was clear: Jacob had broken the contract made in Derrick's office. The verbal agreement to remain "clean and sober" hadn't lasted a week.

It was time to take action.

Chapter 20

Searching for Help

Whenever a problem confronts me, my response is to dive in. At work, if something went wrong, it was easy to gather staff, dissect the problem, assign who would do what, and fix it. A frequent issue was maintaining accurate donor records. Given that we were in a multimillion-dollar campaign, our record keeping had to work flawlessly. With ease I'd pull together a small team and agree on a solution. Everything we did well was a team effort, a mantra that hospital leadership espoused every day.

It was the same on those rare occasions when something more serious went wrong. The chief nursing and chief medical officers would pull together whole teams of staff, covering every facet of the patient's care—nursing, pharmacy, lab, sterile processing, dietary, housekeeping, and security——and analyze, step-by-painful step, what had occurred. The goal was not to affix blame, but to prevent its ever happening again. I sat in awe of my fellow professionals who shared their intelligence in a methodical, thoughtful process to ensure that whatever happened would never happen again. Despite their professional demeanors, their hearts were breaking for any pain they may have caused. It wasn't unusual for a nurse or tech to lower her head and let the tears fall. Inevitably, a colleague would place an arm around the suffering nurse's shoulders, murmur encouraging words, and coax her to return the next day.

Spending days and nights swathed in a healing, therapeutic environment that cared so deeply for others, I was stung all the more by the absence of it in my life outside of work. The teamwork with others, the camaraderie and consoling hug, another's understanding heart, were all lacking. I was alone facing Jacob's addiction. Except for Dick, I had no one.

The shame of my son's actions kept me isolated. But that's how I wanted it. At the time, I was terrified that anyone, even my closest friends, would find out Jacob was using. What would that say about me? What kind of mother was I if my son was a drug addict? Clearly, I'd failed the most basic purpose of my earthly life. It was impossible for me to face the fact that this child who'd come from my womb was now ingesting unknown and dangerous poisons into his body, that same precious miracle of cells and blood and veins that my own body had helped to form years ago. I had to fix this, or hadn't I failed as a mother? No, this was a problem Dick and I would deal with privately, just as we were, by ourselves. It wasn't a topic I would even consider bringing up with close friends or family. When others asked about Jacob, I'd wave them off with, "Oh, he's okay. You know how boys are these days," and deftly turn the conversation to their own children. People always were more ready to talk about themselves than listen anyway. So it was easy to deflect attention away from Jacob and away from me.

I'd cultivated that talent of turning the tables almost to an art. It was a skill I'd honed over years in development and from days as a reporter. Development professionals—and journalists—speak little about themselves. The aim is to engage others about their families, their interests, their hopes and dreams—not yours.

When Dick and I went to parties or anywhere there was a large gathering of people we both knew, I'd do a quick scan of the room and check for those who might ask about Jacob. Steeling myself for their questions, I quickly consulted my mental file on their families: which one had a daughter at Williams, who had the son at Stanford, and what was their youngest's name? I'd load the arrows in my quiver, ready for a pre-emptive strike.

Steeped in silence and secrecy, Dick and I faced the challenge of seeking help for our son while shielding our privacy. Shame hid my soul from others. But I was Jacob's mother, caregiver of the family. It was up to me to find him help.

My only outlet was Pathways. At least the staff there knew about Jacob, and I trusted them with confidentiality. Telling his counselor that Jacob had broken the pledge made sense and was within the safety of what I could do.

Helen, the director of Pathways, who is as kind as she is patient, also knew. I'd confided in Helen when Jacob first came home from beach week and needed that round of outpatient counseling. Like me, Helen had hoped that Jacob's "problem" was simply a typical adolescent experiment with marijuana. Surveys of county high school twelfth-graders showed more than half had smoked marijuana before they graduated. But Helen knew better. At one point, she even looked at me with her big, understanding eyes and said, "Lisa, I am so sorry."

So it was Helen I called to inquire about inpatient treatment centers. She responded right away that, of course, there was Pathways. I'd already ruled that out. It was too close. I couldn't imagine having my son under treatment for drugs in a place where I was on the board, let alone under the roof of my health system. Nor did I think Jacob would go for that either.

She understood immediately and recommended two or three other places. One was in a neighboring county, run by a woman named Peggy, who took in young people like Jacob and allowed them to continue their jobs or college. Helen thought the place had a good reputation. Pathways staff knew Peggy, a practiced and caring woman, and admired her for converting a six-bedroom home into a halfway house for young men.

I seized upon Peggy's name and phone number. In the purely irrational way that addiction takes hold, Peggy became the person who would save Jacob. It was now mid-August. Jacob was set to resume community college in two weeks. Just three courses shy of earning his associate's degree, he was determined to finish this semester. There were occasional references to continuing college after that, and although it was vague, he seemed to have a plan. I had to help him fulfill that plan and not allow drugs to become a distraction. Maybe Peggy could fix all that.

Making a connection with Peggy became my newest obsession. She wasn't easy to reach. Between her schedule and mine, we finally connected by phone one harried weekday morning.

Yes, she thought she would have a room available, and, yes, she had clients who left the house each morning. Two had jobs. Another young man drove to the community college each day and returned in the evening. Jacob would have to be drug-free and agree to all the house rules.

"That sounds perfect for him," I responded, growing hopeful that maybe I actually *had* found a solution to present to Jacob. "Pathways doesn't think he should be living here, and if he comes to your place, then he can still start school and finish it this semester as he wants to do."

I'll never forget what she said next.

"Lisa, if he is still using drugs, school won't matter. Nothing will matter. I know you want him to go back to school, but it doesn't matter when he's supposed to start. There are so many losses with this disease. School's just one of them. He'll never finish there, anyway. Until he gets his drug problem under control, nothing else will matter."

Stunned by the harshness of her response, I thanked her and said I would talk with Jacob and let her know. Her words horrified me. They forecast a reality I wasn't willing to accept.

That weekend Dick and I found a quiet time to talk with Jacob. It was Saturday night, and he'd just gotten home from work. He seemed tired but clear. Dick opened the conversation by telling him, calmly, that he'd broken the contract with us. This meant the next step was inpatient treatment.

"So, Jacob," I jumped in before he could respond, "Helen at Pathways recommended this really nice halfway house in Calvert County. It's near here, and the woman who runs it sounds like she knows what she's doing. She has six other guys who live there and work or go to school. You could live there and go to school from there. We'd work out the car thing. It sounded like a pretty good place. Should we go see it?"

Jacob listened, his eyes blank, lips closed tightly. When I stopped my exhortation, aware even as I told him about Peggy's place that my imagining him there was a fantasy, he erupted.

"No, I will not go there. I won't go inside. It will ruin my life."

Dick and I exchanged looks. I responded first, totally misunderstanding his reaction.

"Ruin your life how?"

"I'll be too far behind in school. Look how far behind I am now!" He nearly spit the words at me, Mom, the idiot. "My friends are all in their junior year already. No, absolutely not. I want to go to school, and I'm applying to UMBC, and that's it. That's what I want to do. I'm not going inside."

So despite the contract and the counseling, we'd come to this impasse. The German cuckoo clock in the front hallway ticked, and the little mechanical bird chirped nine times. I looked at Dick, who was staring at the rug. Jacob didn't move. After the interminable silence, I suggested we talk to Derrick, his counselor at Pathways. The three of us agreed to meet with Derrick as soon as we could.

That happened the following Monday night. I was quickly learning that addiction counselors are pretty busy, and unless it's a life-threatening crisis—an ambulance or police at your door—you wait until they can get back to you. To Derrick's credit, he arranged a late-night conference call for us after his normal day ended. At 9:30 p.m. we huddled in our downstairs library and put Derrick on speakerphone.

"Hi guys." Derrick's attempt to sound cheery fueled my impatience. "Tell me what's going on."

The three of us sat mute, each waiting for the other to begin. I hoped Jacob would start. The silence rankled me.

"Derrick, Jacob has broken the contract. We're not sure what to do next," I finally said.

Derrick came back right away, aiming for Jacob. "If that's true, Jacob, then you need to go inpatient."

Jacob sat next to me on the sofa. He kept his eyes down, only looking at the phone when he spoke.

"No, Derrick, I can't do that. I'm not going inside."

"Listen, man, you're either in or you're out. This time it sounds like you're in."

Jacob shook his head. "Nope, I'm not." And he left the room.

I clicked Derrick off speaker, picked up the receiver, and asked him what to do next. As calm as the night air, he said, "Well, if he uses again, and it sounds like he's going to, you could ask him to leave."

The idea was preposterous. A stupid, silly joke. If the topic had not been so deadly serious, I could have laughed. Ask my son to leave? Where would he go? It wasn't anything I was willing to consider, and I told Derrick so.

"Derrick, it's hard to kick out your own son."

"Yes, I know. But what choices do you have?"

A ridiculous image of Jacob walking out of the house with a stick over his shoulder and a cloth bag tied up with tattered tees and jeans, headed God knows where, darted across my vision. Jacob had never tried to run away from home, had never even wanted to be away from home very long. Our longest separation was his two weeks in Germany with Martin, our exchange student, a time that I felt started him on the path to today. I knew Jacob would be frightened if he were forced out of his home, and the thought frightened me just as much, maybe more.

Realizing he must have been too forceful in suggesting a step I was nowhere near ready to consider, Derrick asked if seeing a family therapist outside of Pathways might be the next move. I latched on to the idea—anything to keep Jacob close, to forestall that inevitable moment when I'd have to tell my son, you can't live here and use.

That time was approaching.

Chapter 21

May God Bless and Protect You

Stink bugs. Richard's office had become a haven for them. In the fall of 2010 Anne Arundel County was suffering its worst stink bug invasion in decades. The Chinese-born pests were attracted to homes and offices on warm fall days, anticipating colder days ahead. Like tiny brown shields, they crawled across the ceiling and upper walls, a welcome distraction from the anguish filling the room below.

Richard Pehle was our new family therapist, and he would turn out to be just what we needed. I had no idea what had brought him to the field of addiction counseling, but he was patient and soft-spoken. He quickly gained Jacob's respect and confidence. A very large man, he once alluded to having a food addiction. He was close with the staff at Pathways, who referred young people like Jacob. I liked him immediately. Something about his bigness invited comfort, so much flesh to absorb all the sorrow we brought to him.

Jacob began seeing him first. Now that he was twenty-one, Jacob had every right to prohibit Richard's telling me anything about their visits, and for the most part, Richard did not share what they discussed. Jacob did permit me to have occasional updates. It galled me, just as it had when he saw his first counselor, that I was paying for his care but had no right to know what that care exactly meant. Nevertheless, I respected the process and hoped, once more, that it might make a difference in Jacob's lives and ours.

For a brief spell, it did. Jacob began school, went to work, and saw Richard twice a month, and I was able to focus on work. Facing the fall months, my staff and I geared up for a final push to reach our fundraising goal by year's end. We were still more than two million dollars shy of the campaign's $44 million target, and the ribbon cutting for the new patient tower was just seven months away. The fall of 2010 held enormous pressures for me. Running underneath it all was the constant worry about my son and the fear that someone might find out what was happening in my family.

That fear arose often. One evening, as part of the CEO transition at the hospital, Tori pulled together her senior team for dinner at a nearby steak house. The ten high-level professionals who sat around the table rarely had time to relax, let alone spend a few minutes getting to know one another personally. This was the opportunity to discover that our VP of physician practices had a rare woodworking talent and that our compliance officer was buying a house in downtown Annapolis. The talk soon turned to our children. The human resources VP was celebrating her son's final year in engineering at the University of Maryland.

Sipping a glass of wine, I tried hard to deflect attention. When it was my turn, I talked about Heidi and Jon and Josh, focusing on my grandson. In that group, grandchildren were sainted. I was one of few who'd achieved that life's milestone, and it was enough to avoid any mention of Jacob.

But deep inside, I was hurting. So much jabbering. So many happy references to children off doing exciting things. A daughter at Cornell in her third year, likely med school beyond. A son who was thinking about the Peace Corps. Another son who'd won a sailing competition over the weekend and might go to Spain this winter for his next challenge. And meanwhile, my son—who was easily as capable and talented as these kids—was shuffling between community college and a coffee shop, with stops along the way at Richard's office. Why wasn't *he* off doing exciting things? Why wasn't *his* life full and rich and rewarding like others his age? What had other mothers done that I hadn't? Where had I missed a step?

I questioned everything. Should I have sent him to private school instead of letting him be among the first IB students in the public high schools' new program? Did I ever actually say to him, you know, Jacob, your Dad and I don't approve of drugs, and we do not want you to use them? Did we ever say, Jacob, we do not want you to smoke. Your grandmother died from smoking, and that aside, it is very dangerous to your health. Do not smoke.

Did we ever even give Jacob a "do not?" Did we just expect he would get all this from watching us, from how we lived and how his sister had turned out? That he would get it just from being a Hillman, understanding that because he had it better than many kids, his role in life would be to help care for others? Were we at fault because we'd just presumed all this and never sat him down and spelled it out for him?

So here I was, sitting quietly in Richard's office. It was my turn. Jacob had approved my meeting with him, a begrudging, "Ma, you can do whatever you want." I was both eager to meet privately with Richard and more than a little anxious. I'd never met with a therapist and had no idea what to expect.

Richard was as gentle and patient with me as he must have been with Jacob. His office was in a church annex set in a pastoral enclave just south of Annapolis. You entered through a basement door and climbed a set of narrow stairs. It was serene and secluded, and for that alone I was grateful. No one would see me coming or going.

I laughed when I saw the first stink bug. Richard apologized and tried to swat it away. It was such an incongruous sight in this otherwise carefully planned office, tidy with books on one tall shelf, two chairs that faced one another, a big, tweedy couch with deep indentations in its thick cushions. High windows on two walls framed the tips of leafy, age-old oaks against a sky clouding over with an impending late-summer storm. I felt the vague stirrings of a headache, something I had often these days between the pressures of the campaign and the unrelenting anxieties over my son.

Coupled with the comic relief of the stink bugs, Richard offered me the first comforting words I'd heard since becoming aware of

Jacob's problem.

"You know," he began patiently, "you didn't cause this. You and Dick are not users, and there's no substance abuse in your family. We really don't know why some kids can use and not get addicted and others try it and it becomes a full-blown addiction. In Jacob's case, he could be just wired for this. There's nothing you said or did or didn't do that caused it."

I wanted to believe what he said, but couldn't. Not then, not yet. For that first meeting, I couldn't speak without crying. Richard did most of the talking. My eyes filled with water and my body sagged with grief, my sorrow bottomless. I wondered how many other mothers sat in those deeply imprinted cushions, crying for their lost sons and daughters, while stink bugs skittered across the walls and treetops outside swayed beneath clouds. Here, finally, I was no longer alone. I could be myself and unload the terribly anxiety I felt.

Having Richard in our lives was a salve. Jacob continued to see him, and for a brief time, we all seemed better.

The Jewish holidays came early that year. We were not a deeply religious family and failed miserably as regular synagogue attendees. But we always observed the high holidays of Rosh Hashanah and Yom Kippur. When they rolled around each year, I marked off the dates, firmly letting work colleagues know I wouldn't be available. If they couldn't reach me by text or email, they knew I took it pretty seriously.

Yom Kippur was the traditional holiday when we invited family and many friends to our home to break the fast. After the twenty-four-hour fast to cleanse one's self of sins and begin the new year fresh, we enjoyed serving a lavish, traditional buffet of blintzes, eggs, bagels and lox, smoked whitefish and whitefish salad, cinnamon coffee cake, chocolate-covered macaroons, and lots of sweets to celebrate the end of the fast.

Jacob always enjoyed gatherings in our home. Since our family was small, he appreciated being with our friends, who treated him like a son. Especially at holidays, I felt even sadder that Jacob had never known Dick's parents or mine. That summer evening in Rehoboth, when he had mourned the absence of grandparents, haunted me. In my mounting guilt over Jacob's illness and brutal self-questioning about my role in causing it, I even piled on blame for not having him earlier in life. I sometimes wondered, if he had known his grandparents, would that have helped prevent his turning to drugs? Such sad, sick, crazy thoughts. Still searching for what I did wrong, I failed to accept the most basic fact: Jacob's birth was meant to be when it was. In my saner moments, I was certain of that, but these days I was certain of so little.

Jacob enjoyed the holiday weekend, attending services with us, sitting next to me, quiet and aware as the Torah was carried aloft by congregation members honored with performing that task. In his dark, pin-stripe suit and pale pink shirt, his hair and face smooth and shiny, he looked pensive but content. I beamed just to have him beside me. Such is the fickle face of addiction. One minute, you panic over droopy eyelids and slurred speech. The next, you're standing in a crowd of people you've known for years, your son, tall and all grown up, by your side, acknowledging the admiring glances from others across the room.

During the Yom Kippur service, there is a prayer the rabbi says for children. He asks parents to stand with their sons and daughters, regardless of age. It was mid-morning. The sun glinted golden through the ceiling-high windows that framed the pulpit adorned with urns of white lilies, casting a warm, rich glow on the ruby red carpet and blue-tweed, padded chairs. We stood, Dick and I, on either side of Jacob. I fixed my eyes on the rabbi, aware that some fifty or sixty mothers and fathers also were standing with their children, from infants and toddlers to strapping young men and beautiful young women. Ours is a small congregation of about 120 families, and we know many of these families well.

We kept our attention on the rabbi. He was smiling. He loved this part of the service, too. He asked the parents to place their hands on their child and repeat after him the threefold, ancient blessing:

May God bless you and protect you;

May God cause His face to shine upon you and be gracious unto you;

May God lift His face to you and grant you peace.

My eyes were closed, and in the flickering dark behind my lids I silently intoned a fervent prayer to God, who surely must have been present in that gorgeous sanctuary on that most holy of days. *Please be listening to me, aching to save the soul of this beautiful child standing tall and straight today next to me and his father. This boy you brought me twenty-one years ago to love with all my life for my life. This child who is so lost. Dear Lord, please bless him and protect him. Please, please help him to find his way.*

I opened my eyes, and Jacob was looking at me. We were still standing. The golden moment was fading, but I knew he knew. He knew how much I loved him and hurt for him. He knew.

That night my journal records this prayer:

> *A few promises I now make: to back off a little,*
> *not to hover or accuse, because it does no good. To say*
> *less, but love more. To know it must be his way. There*
> *really is so little I can do. So much promise when he*
> *is clean. May he get well. May he know the beautiful*
> *man he is. May his life be a blessing. May the new*
> *Jewish Year begin thus.*

Chapter 22

Is He Still Breathing?

Throughout Jacob's illness, there were times he and I had intense conversations. They usually began with something provocative and then, without fail, they sucked me into the whirl of his craziness. Suddenly I'd remember that I was talking with an addict.

A few weeks after the Jewish holidays, we were sitting alone at the kitchen table. I'd just placed a pile of linguine in front of him, made the way he liked it—plain, with lots of butter.

"Jacob, I forgot to ask. What were the results of your urine test at Pathways?" Even as the question dropped on his plate, I regretted it and tensed for his answer.

"I never did it, Ma. And if I had, it would've been positive."

"Positive? For what?"

"Percocet and OxyContin."

The kitchen was absent sound, not even the scrape of a fork.

"Jacob, what are we going to do about this?"

"I dunno, Ma. I want to finish school. Maybe I'll go to California next spring for school. I could be near Heidi."

"Yes, but have you forgotten she's moving here?" We had just learned the Navy had assigned Jon to a three-year tour in Washington. Heidi, Jon, and Josh would be moving to Silver Spring in November. I could barely contain my joy at knowing they'd be close.

"Oh yeah, right. Well, it's not safe in California anyway, with the earthquakes and floods."

Abruptly, he switched topics.

"I may lose my job."

"Why? What's happening?"

"I dunno. They're tightening the rules, and this other guy, Rob, and I can't conform. If I lose this job, I'll have been let go from every job I've ever had. That will be emotionally devastating. I really don't want to lose this job."

So the conversation moved to how to keep the job—keep your head down, listen to your manager, shave more often. My son was drowning in addiction and depression, and I was giving him advice on facial hair? These conversations always erupted in the kitchen. Not long afterwards, he stood against the counter while I cleaned up from supper. Without provocation, he simply announced that he'd had a horrible dream the previous night.

"Yeah, I had this really bad nightmare. I don't know where I was or anything, but I saw myself shooting someone." He was holding a glass of water, leaning back against the counter. He took a big gulp and kept staring at the floor. "And that someone was me. I was shooting myself!"

What then poured out was a tale of uncontrollable drug use— $3,700 worth in the last sixty days. He named two "friends" who'd been more than happy to supply the pills, often showing up at work.

"Ma, I don't even like it anymore, but I can't stop doing it!"

At one point, he cried. We both did. He said he wasn't suicidal, and I didn't think he was either, but there were times he thought drugs could end his life. He admitted he was closer to going away for treatment, but it was only six weeks until the end of the semester and he was focused on getting his degree.

During this increasingly bizarre time, Jacob still attended AA meetings and saw the therapist. In the nuttiness of how addiction takes hold of whole families, Dick and I even offered to give Jacob his Suboxone. Dutifully, we executed the ritual of dropping the little pill on our son's tongue each evening. It felt good to do this small act. As responsible, loving parents, surely administering our son's daily medication would help to cure him, right? How could we know that Jacob often spit out the pill as soon as he left the room?

On a cool, clear, crisp day in early October, we got a reprieve. Heidi flew to Maryland to find a rental home and stayed with us overnight. Jacob always perked up for Heidi. Born nearly a generation apart, the two still held a close relationship. He went to her for advice on matters he didn't with me—often about girls, although with his drug use there was little of that now. But the brief time we were all together was as sweet as the scented autumn air. I awoke that morning, Dick beside me, both my children asleep in the house, savoring the momentary joy of knowing everyone was safe, all of us under one roof, secure in the love of family,

The feeling of contentment faded swiftly as a dream. My eyes teared. No, this isn't right. Everyone isn't safe. Jacob is in trouble. My beautiful son is in so much trouble.

Days later, after Heidi had made a deposit on a rental home in Silver Spring and returned to California, our therapist, Richard, phoned me. It was a typically hectic day at the hospital. Tori was planning a retreat with her senior team and had asked for my help. Whenever Tori wanted my advice, I was flattered and thrilled to oblige. The call from Jacob's counselor caught me as I walked to her office through the glass-enclosed walkway that connected our buildings. Two hospital volunteers in their bright blue jackets breezed by and said hello. The director of nursing education paused to introduce two student nurses. A radiologist hurrying back to his suite gave me a wide smile.

It was that way whenever Jacob's illness pierced the bubble of my rushing, intense life at the hospital. Inevitably, I'd be walking off to some fairly high-level meeting, passing through brightly lit hallways with colleagues and visitors streaming by. Here I was happy. Here I was in control and could make things happen. These people passing me I respected and admired, and I hoped they felt the same about me. What would they ever think if they knew? My smile belied the panic rising in my chest. They had no idea I was desperate to find some quiet, dark place to take Richard's call. His phoning in the middle of the day could never be good news.

"Lisa, hi, it's Richard," he began.

No kidding, I thought impatiently. I know it's you. Just tell me why you're calling.

"Jacob's not really doing well, and I'm a little worried about him."

Hell. I knew this was coming.

"He needs a higher level of care than I can provide. I'm sorry to say this, but the outpatient plan isn't working. He's still using, and I'm afraid he's going to get into more trouble if it goes on much longer."

Okay. We agreed there. So what's next?

"I'm strongly recommending an inpatient stay for Jacob, perhaps at Pathways since you know the program. But there are other places, too. Would you want me to do some looking around for you? I think it needs to be pretty soon."

Richard suggested a thirty-day program, at least. And by soon, he meant immediately. The trick was, how to get Jacob to agree?

I buried the call deep inside my gut. I had to. There were still hours in the workday until I could get home and huddle with Dick. I would soon learn that "immediately" in the field of addiction treatment had many meanings. Actually, there was no "immediately" unless, God forbid, the addict was seizing or not breathing. Then you immediately dialed 911 and raced to the emergency room to save his life. Fortunately, we weren't facing that kind of crisis. In the world I lived in, "immediately" meant scheduling a visit with Richard as soon as the three of us could meet in his office to talk, yet again, about inpatient treatment.

That happened the following week. By then, I'd had another conversation with Jacob, where he acknowledged that Richard wanted him to "go inside."

"If you insist that I go," my son said to me, "I will."

The sound of his quiet, straightforward statement bumped up my hope. There was no need to say anything else.

As I prepped myself for the next visit with Richard, I wondered if Jacob was also prepping himself to go inside—somewhere—for treatment. My thoughts were focused only on getting him somewhere where he would be safe from harming himself or someone else. But once again, despite the serious tone of Richard's warning ringing in my head, I continued to delude myself over how serious Jacob's situation was. What was worse was what I let him do just a day later. My car was in the shop and Dick was tied up, so Jacob came to pick me up in the Trailblazer. It was only a short drive home. I hopped into the passenger seat, and we exchanged greetings. It wasn't until we nearly ran into a line of stopped cars at a traffic light three blocks from home that I realized he was high.

"Jacob, what in the hell are you doing?" I cried.

He hit the brake and joked that he hadn't seen the cars because we were talking, but don't worry, everything is okay. "Chill, Ma, I got this."

When I stared at his profile as we drove on, I thought, How nuts am I to let him drive? He's high on something! Fortunately, we got home safely, but that incident, although brief, rattled me into recognizing the idiocy of letting him have the car at all. Would Dick and I now need to prohibit his use of our cars?

Gradually, more and more, we tried to control Jacob's life. From giving him the Suboxone each evening to driving him wherever he needed to go, Dick and I tended to our son's everyday activities, as we had when he was an infant. Surprisingly, he accepted all our efforts. With the instinctual love good parents show their children, we tried everything we could to cushion his world. We did it without discussion or forethought. We just did it.

Often, it meant one of us stayed home. One of Dick's favorite activities was to plan monthly hikes in the DC-Maryland-Virginia area. Both of us enjoyed hiking. We were active members of the Appalachian Mountain Club and had taken Heidi and Jacob on hiking treks in the White Mountains of New Hampshire as children. Dick's monthly excursions typically attracted an eclectic group of ten to twenty people in the area, and I always enjoyed them. For me, the day-long climbs up and down mountain trails provided cathartic relief from the pressures at home and work.

Discussion of Jacob's going to inpatient treatment remained on hold. Jacob had balked at the idea again, so again, we were at an impasse. He insisted he wanted to finish the semester; he was so close to getting his associate's degree. Richard urged us to stay close, to have Jacob continue his biweekly therapy sessions, and to contact him if any emergency arose—as he knew inevitably it would.

One Saturday, a hiking day, it was impossible for me to leave to join Dick and others. Jacob had come home from work the night before very groggy, more sluggish than usual, his body heavy and his speech slurred. He went straight to his room. It scared me. Before going to bed, I tiptoed down the hallway to his room, listening for any sound, and gently pushed open the door. He was lying on his stomach, his head facing the doorway, hanging off the pillow. Slowly, careful not to wake him, I crept over to the bed and knelt down. My face was near his, as close as possible without our foreheads touching. I bent in close, closer, sensing the warmth of his skin, the stale smell of him, that gave me the slightest relief. But I needed more. Was there breath from his parted lips? Was there a flutter behind his eyelids? I need proof, please, God, that my son is alive.

I was just about to shake him when he slurred, "I'm okay, Ma," eyes opening for a few brief seconds. "I'm okay. Leave me alone."

But of course, I couldn't. I checked on him before going to bed and several times during the night. A maternal urge, like what I'd felt when I nursed him as an infant, repeatedly broke my slumber, but this time it was for something far more urgent — to make sure my son was still breathing. I came as close that night to calling 911 or rushing Jacob to the emergency room as in any of the sleepless nights leading up to it. But somehow the hours passed.

The next morning, with Jacob still passed out in his room, Dick and I looked at each other without saying a word. He would go on the hike, and it was obvious that I needed to remain at home. Dick would cover for me, telling our hiking friends some excuse like, "Lisa had work to do." When Jacob got up hours later, it didn't register with him at first that this was a hiking day and I should be away with his father.

"Where's Dad?"

"Hiking. You know this was our hiking day."

"Oh, yeah, that's right." He rubbed his eyes, acclimating himself to Saturday. "Well, how come you didn't go with him? Just didn't feel like it, or what?"

"No, I'm fine. You know I always like to go with Dad, but honestly, Jacob," I paused, scanning his face to be sure he was alert enough for this conversation, "I was worried about you. Last night you seemed so, so . . . out of it. I mean, really out of it. Maybe the worst I've ever seen you. I wasn't even sure you were breathing."

"Yeah, well, you shouldn't worry about me, Ma. Really? You didn't go on the hike today because of me? Aw, that's crazy." His tone rose. "Ma, don't do that. Don't change your life because of me. That's just nuts!" And he strode off.

The horror of the previous long night hovered over me for days. Was it possible Jacob could have stopped breathing? And if this happened once, what was to prevent it from happening again?

Chapter 23

What To Tell the Dentist

While my personal life was crashing, my professional life was soaring. Not only was I working to complete the capital campaign and support the CEO transition at the hospital, but I also continued leadership within my professional association. In 2009 I chaired the Association for Healthcare Philanthropy (AHP), an international organization for healthcare fundraisers. Like any professional association, AHP offered the opportunity to network with colleagues and keep my skills sharp. As past chair, I enjoyed attending conferences with friends from around the country. It was after an AHP meeting in Cleveland the previous year that Jacob had broken down on our flight home, setting the plan in motion for him to leave the University of Maryland and live at home.

This time, I was attending an international conference and board meeting in San Antonio, Texas. As I started to leave my hotel room for an early-morning meeting, my cell phone rang. The caller ID read "Jacob Hillman." Odd time for him to call, I thought. It was only 8:30 at home.

"Lis?" It was Dick. "Jacob has something he needs to tell you."

This couldn't be good.

What came next was Jacob's voice, garbled, faltering, far away. "Ma, I got fired."

I knew this was bad. His job meant so much to him. I couldn't calculate fast enough how much of a blow this must be for him, nor guess the truth of why he was let go. He mumbled something about missing money, messing up the register, but the connection was poor and there was no point belaboring the conversation. Before hanging up—as an added punch to my gut and at Dick's urging—he admitted that he had used the past weekend, despite yet one more promise to stop.

I hung up, desperately late for a meeting where my absence would matter. This was the morning for oral exams for candidates seeking AHP's highest level of credentialing, and I was one of the few examiners. Quickly and smartly, I had to bury this new, awful knowledge about my son, slap on my professional smile, and forge through the next six hours of testing. When the president of the association ran into me in the hallway, he could see something was wrong. I looked into his kind, blue eyes and choked back the lump that filled my throat. "Thanks, but it's just something at the hospital," I murmured, and hurried past him to my session.

Kindness hurt. If someone tried to penetrate the wall I had carefully built around me, I became panicky. I couldn't let anyone know about Jacob. Women like me with high-level professional jobs and respect from colleagues didn't have sons who were drug addicts. Crazily, even then I still thought or hoped that Jacob's drug use might be some passing fad, some high school thing he hadn't quite kicked, that was just taking him a tad longer to give up than most kids. So why blather to everyone that my son is using drugs, since that could harm the bright future I still held out for him?

Denial and delusion had become my watchwords. For Dick, too. Sometimes I phoned him from work just to hear the voice of someone who understood. I poured out to him how hard it was to wear a pleasant face and act "normal" with others when you are screaming inside. Across the phone line, his quiet "I know" was as good as a hug.

The only place we couldn't hide was with Richard. When the three of us met with him next, he was alarmed about Jacob's job loss. It was one more giant step in the wrong direction.

Richard laid it out for us very clearly. I was almost grateful for the stink bugs skittering across the ceiling, distracting us from the dead seriousness inside that small, closed room. Richard warned Jacob of what lay ahead. He'd never brought up the possibility of trouble with the law until now. Jacob's firing and the real cause behind it prompted this new discussion. I wanted Jacob to understand that his drug use was starting to have far more serious consequences and prodded Richard to detail what "problem with the law" meant. Dick, after all, was a lawyer, and Jacob had been around lawyers enough to know that legal issues spelled lots of problems he didn't have yet and might still avoid. Jacob sat very still on the big, soft couch, barely looking at us, but occasionally watching Richard's large, lion-like face as he drew a description of the court system, jail, prison, the loss of rights, and the impact on the rest of his life. Richard mentioned the words "convicted felon" and drove hard on what that meant. For some reason, Jacob focused on the possible loss of his right to vote. It seemed almost humorous, but it also made sense. At twenty-one, he had yet to exercise that right. Given that he lived in a household where elections and politics were regular topics, it certainly was important to him.

Despite Richard's graphic description of what could lie ahead, Jacob wasn't hearing that he had to go inside for treatment, not yet. He reiterated his determination to finish school. That was his default to avoid facing his addiction. There also was a new issue. He needed wisdom-tooth surgery. Richard pulled up a calendar and let his finger glide over the seven weeks remaining until graduation. He might as well have pulled up a road map to the North Pole. The distance across that calendar was a very long time, given Jacob's current drug use.

Jacob finally agreed that he would go "inside" after December 15, when school ended. He also wanted to get the surgery out of the way. Listening to him bargain with Richard, I found his behavior both ludicrous and hopeful. He was at once a maturing adult plotting his best path, and a child grasping at impossible dreams.

After our session, Richard privately reminded Dick and me, "Your son is not a child. He needs inpatient treatment, but obviously we can't force him to go. If you ask him to leave, he will find a place. He can take care of himself."

Could he? He was my son. I knew him best. And the Jacob I knew was extremely dependent on us. He needed to grow up, that I understood. But I was slowly realizing that we couldn't do it for him.

We left that meeting with a new plan: (1) Richard and I would research inpatient places; (2) Jacob would meet with Richard next week; (3) we would meet again as a group in about a week; and (4) our family needed to talk more.

My journal that evening had this simple note:

> One thing is for certain. Doing THIS, living
> THIS as a parent—as a person—is the hardest thing
> I have ever had to do in my entire life. Nothing pre-
> pares you for this. This is just hard. It hurts so badly.

The very next day I was all over it. Give me a project, and I'm happy. After calling Pathways and speaking directly with the executive director, I had my list of inpatient places to research. The list included both in-state and out-of-state facilities. All were on the pricey side. At the time, I assumed the better places were also the more expensive, and if my son was going for treatment, it would be the best. We were entering the world of inpatient addiction treatment, trusting the counselors and therapists who advised us, ready to open the checkbook and pay anything if it meant Jacob would get well.

The irony wasn't lost on me that Dick and I had made a similar point regarding Jacob's choices for college. Money wouldn't be the deciding factor. If our only son chose an Ivy League school or a major university where tuition was forty thousand dollars or more, somehow we'd find the money. What mattered was his happiness, his future. We wanted him to experience his college years to the fullest, reveling in learning with fellow students, and enjoying the full, leafy campus life. Now, instead of colleges, I was scanning websites for treatment centers— and with much the same criteria. I searched for a place where he would be happy, surrounded by others his age, amid clean, comfortable surroundings.

This time I ruled out anything too far away, like California or Arizona. It had to be within driving distance so we could check it out before he was admitted and make sure it was the right place for him. And we needed it near enough to visit.

The absurdity of addiction. If I couldn't control Jacob's drug use, damn it, then I'd control his treatment. Were we really going to drive to each of these places to screen them before Jacob was admitted? I pictured Dick and me meeting the director, taking a walking tour of the facility and grounds, the guide walking backwards while he proudly pointed out favorite spots on campus, just like the campus tours we'd taken when Jacob was applying to college. It wasn't until many years afterwards that I understood how silly this was. Not only was there never time to pre-screen these facilities, but as Jacob later told me, "You can get clean anywhere."

My research led me to places in Pennsylvania, Virginia, and Maryland. Finally, I settled on a highly respected treatment center about an hour's drive from Annapolis. It boasted a superb reputation. People I respected gave it a thumbs up. Situated on some one hundred acres of quiet, tree-lined countryside along the shores of a Chesapeake Bay tributary, Father Martin's Ashley was an idyllic place, just the spot for my son to give up drugs, get clean, and come home the person he was meant to be. Just like that.

The nice-sounding counselor on the phone was kind and patient, albeit persistent. After we talked the first time, he agreed to call me back to "check in" and determine when Jacob might be admitted. He understood how delicate our lives were, that Jacob's admission depended so much on his willingness. During one of these calls with the counselor, I huddled in my office, hoping no one could hear the desperation in my voice, when my eye caught a tiny movement on the outer glass of the windowpane. Darn it if wasn't a stink bug. Do stink bugs trail drug counselors and haunt the hearts of mothers who have drug-addicted sons?

Meanwhile, Jacob was trying hard to stay out of trouble. He was going to classes, but without a job he was spending more time home alone in his room.

At the end of October it was time for wisdom-tooth surgery. As we walked into the dental office, I knew my role was to satisfy the rule that "the patient must have someone accompany him after surgery." But was there another for me? I wasn't just dropping off a "normal" patient for surgery. How would Jacob's addiction affect anesthesia and pain medication afterwards? Was it up to me to tell the oral surgeon, "No, he had no major childhood illnesses, but you probably should know he has this one thing now that could be a problem, this drug addiction, so please don't give him anything for pain that he can get addicted to because he gets addicted really easily . . ."

My worries were needless. Jacob surprised me by doing this himself without even a whisper from me. I marveled at how he shared his drug history with the oral surgeon, again someone I knew well from the hospital, whom I trusted as a professional to keep this confidential. I had the distinct feeling that Jacob wasn't the first "child" with a drug issue he'd treated.

Once home, after the anesthesia wore off, Jacob took nothing stronger than high-dose Tylenol, or so I thought. Much later he told me he actually switched the pills and swallowed most of the Vicodin from the dental office before Dick or I were aware. Regardless, he was as relieved as I to have the surgery behind him. Check off one more rite of passage into adulthood. His spirits were boosted even more when he pulled up his grades online that afternoon and saw that he got an "A" on his final psychology exam.

The relative euphoria wouldn't last long— for either of us.

Chapter 24

The Call from the Bank

Sunday morning, November 7, my eyes opened at the sound of Dick's voice. Calmly, he was telling me that Jacob was leaving. The sound faded. It had been a dream.

That evening, the dream edged closer to life. Jacob left for his Sunday night meeting, a large gathering in the Pathways gym of more than one hundred alumni of the program. Incredibly, we were trusting him to drive to and from the meeting, clocking the minutes until he returned home. I was in the kitchen, cleaning up from supper, mentally preparing myself for the workweek ahead. Dick was at his computer in the library.

"Lis, you might want to come in here," he called. His tone said *come now.*

The computer screen displayed Dick's checking account and a long list of recent transactions. I leaned in to see where he was pointing. It was easy to spot. The numbers practically shimmered off the screen. From a credit card Dick shared with Jacob there were several withdrawals of two hundred to three hundred dollars—all over the past five days.

It didn't make sense. Jacob had been doing well since the surgery. There were no obvious signs of drug use. He seemed more upbeat, not groggy or hung over. He knew Thanksgiving was just two weeks away, and in early December he would finish school. Heidi, Jon, and Josh were moving back to Maryland, and in days they would settle into their new Silver Spring home. Life was too good to mess up now. The end was in sight.

But it was all an illusion.

When Jacob got home, Dick leveled him. Not with yelling or profanity, but with that stern, tight-lipped, steady command that, when they were growing up, both children knew meant, this is serious.

"Jacob, no more," Dick said, "I'm done. Tomorrow I'm closing the account."

More illusion and denial. Jacob argued the withdrawals didn't mean a relapse. He claimed he'd had to pay back "Charlie" and "Wes" for past debts. He was obviously rattled. We told him it didn't matter why he'd taken the money. He was caught stealing from his father, an act so vile and out of character for him and our family that none of us knew what to say.

Except for Dick's simple statement, we said nothing.

Breaking the terrible silence hours later, Jacob told me he didn't tell us about the withdrawals because "things were going so well." My heart broke again. Was he that out of touch with reality? He stole from us and hid it because things were going well?

Sure, I argued with myself, it was entirely plausible that he took the money to pay off debts. Maybe he really was trying to come clean in his life, to close out the bad and welcome the good. But to do so behind our backs stirred an ugly feeling of betrayal and deceit. It was a feeling I didn't like. For the first time I could sense a wall going up between us, something harsh and impenetrable. Down the road, that wall would give me strength to make the hardest decision of my life.

The next day it happened again. In my office, surrounded by typical Monday morning matters, I got a call that was anything but typical.

"Hello, Mrs. Hillman? Hi, this is Lindsey from the bank. I have a young man here who says you made out a check to him. Did you write a check for $360 to Jacob Hillman? Because this doesn't look like your signature on the check."

A stink bug skittered on my outer window. This didn't make sense.

"Is the young man there?" I asked. "That's my son. I don't quite follow . . ."

"Oh, I see," said Lindsey. "Now I understand. He's standing right here. Would you want to speak to him?"

The bank was less than a mile away. I pictured Jacob there, doing—what?

"Yes, please put him on."

"Ma?" Jacob's voice, low and dark. "I need help."

"Jacob, have you been using?"

"Yes."

"You have?"

"Yes."

"Jacob, leave the bank and go directly home. I'll meet you there."

I mumbled a thanks to Lindsey, shot "I'll be back shortly" to my assistant, and raced home. From the car I phoned Richard. When I told him of the two thefts within the past twenty-four hours, he didn't seem surprised. He agreed to meet the three of us that afternoon.

Before we left for Richard's office, Dick and I had one more try with Jacob. Cloistered in our warm, copper-carpeted library, the thin November sun slatting through the wooden blinds, I took a long, close look at my son. He was so skinny and pale that his skin was almost translucent. His arms looked like the hiking poles hanging in our closet, his wrists so thin a strong handshake might snap them. He stared at the floor, never looking at either of us. His whole body reeked of misery. On the phone he'd told me, "Ma, I need help." Would he sustain that thought? Could we keep him on a path towards the life he was born to have? Or would we lose him again, hidden and folded away in the cave of his room?

"Jacob," I began, knowing the next words would be the hardest I'd ever have to say to my son, perhaps in his entire life, "this is it. You can't live here and use. Not anymore. If you choose to go for treatment, Dad and I will pay for that. But you can't stay here and use. It's up to you. It's your choice."

His eyes blinked sheer terror. "Yeah, Ma, I know, but where would I go?"

The question was a plea for help—not from a twenty-one-year-old man, but from a very small boy, alone and frightened.

"I don't know. But you can't stay here." Where those words came from, I'll never know. It was as though I were playing a role in a bad, one-act play—the stern and proper English matron who banishes her son from the family homestead. Even my voice didn't sound like mine. But the lines came out strong and clear: "I won't have drugs in my house. You'll have to figure that out. It's up to you."

There really was nowhere for Jacob to go. We both knew that. He had few real friends in town, and those he had juggled their own tenuous living situations. No one could just take him in. His options were limited.

For a few, mind-screaming seconds an ugly scenario played out in my head: my son, even thinner and paler, wearing filthy, khaki-colored pants frayed at the cuffs and knees, sitting in a gutter downtown, lost and unrecognizable, shunned, a leper, a creature to avoid. I'd seen men like that on our streets. They emerged out of nowhere to trek aimlessly up and down Main Street, sometimes with frantic energy, other times barely shuffling, sifting through trash cans, or huddled on curbside benches, but not for long lest the police or shop owner confront them and warn them to move on. Gnats to be shooed away, specs of dirt on streets thick with tourists.

Lately, I looked at these men with new eyes. One especially was hard to avoid. Tall and thin, a stick figure clad in dirty pants stringy at the cuffs, so skinny his pants hung off his backside, baring white skin, he rambled all over downtown streets and passed me often. I was told he was schizophrenic. The police knew him well. They tried to help him and dropped him off at a shelter, but he always left and headed back downtown. So he just wandered the streets, surviving on scraps he found on sidewalks or in trash cans, or on leftovers that restaurants fed him. Passersby—me included—would see him, but not really. Coming upon him sometimes late at night when I walked the dog and he emerged from shadows, I would eye him as he muttered past.

The thought struck me: this man has a mother, or he did at some time. He is someone's son. I shuddered, envisioning him now: could this someday be *my* son?

But the wall had gone up. Stealing from us had laid the last brick. I stuffed the image of my child homeless, starving, and afraid deep into the duffel bag of my soul. Homeless or not, this young man who sat in my library would have to find some other way to support his habit. Not in my home. Not anymore.

The hour had arrived. The meeting in Richard's office held no tears or fright, not even anger. Even the stink bugs stayed away. That afternoon, only resignation filled the little room.

Quietly, collaboratively, we made the plan. Jacob would withdraw from classes and take an incomplete rather than a failing grade. He would enter Father Martin's Ashley this week, or as soon as we could make arrangements. He would give inpatient treatment a try.

That evening—at the end of the long, painful day—my journal has this entry:

Here's what I know.

That I've known for a long time we would get to this point.

That today's events surprise me not at all.

That each time brings a "revelation" that's really

not that but just more of the same.

And that the dream I had two nights ago was no dream.

Chapter 25

Recovery Begins

Once the decision was made, getting Jacob into Father Martin's was easy. The politely persistent counselor on the phone said, "Oh, good," when I called to lock in admission.

"Good?" His reaction stunned me. "How can this possibly be good?"

"Because," he said, "your son is beginning his recovery. And that's good."

The night before he left, Jacob spent hours cleaning his room. The symbolism wasn't lost on any of us. None of us knew when or if he'd ever be back. Giant green trash bags gradually filled up with gum wrappers, loose-leaf pages, faded test papers, paper coffee cups, stained and tattered tee shirts, plastic soda bottles—the litter of a life so unhappily led. Staying out of his way, but observing how intently Jacob focused on the task, Dick mused that he seemed like a "condemned man."

Our house, which had been riddled with sadness and despair, was now filled with apprehension for what lay ahead. This was all new. We had no idea what tomorrow would bring.

Despite the anxieties, a new emotion was emerging. For the first time, I felt hope. Real hope. The kind that painted a picture of my son standing tall, shoulders back, flashing that shy, smart-ass grin, his hazel eyes twinkling, handsome and sure, taking life as it comes, sweet and sassy and all grown up. I held on to that picture, even when Jacob was at his worst. Inside the downcast, pale, sullen child was a loving and charming man. Jacob's willingness to try inpatient treatment gave me the faintest hope that he might emerge as the warm, smiling son

I once knew.

At the very least, I welcomed the treatment center as a chance for him to learn more about his addiction and, I hoped, to grow up a little more. Jacob still seemed so lost, unable to care for himself, even to do simple things like manage laundry or keep track of money. Perhaps time away from us and the only home he'd ever known would force him to learn such basic life functions, compel him to take care of himself, because—as I was fast learning—he was the only one who could.

Driving through the gates of Father Martin's, Dick and I couldn't help but feel hopeful. Fields of trees and shrubbery stretched for acres on either side of the car. The scene was straight out of the movies— a pastoral paradise where the rich and famous slide in for a few weeks of burnishing away any taint of drugs or alcohol. Clean me up, and send me back to the world where I can shine again.

Like many treatment centers, this one was based on a twelve-step program. It promoted a minimum thirty-day inpatient stay with strict rules and regular group therapy. The campus-like feel, with several stone buildings set amid towering trees alongside a gentle river, added to the peacefulness. I couldn't shake the "upscale" image, no doubt fueled by the hefty, non-refundable down payment. But when we left Jacob in the hands of the intake counselor, and gave him a final hug that would have to sustain me for the ten days until I could see him again, I would have paid anything.

For that next week, Dick and I at least knew that Jacob was safe. He was inside a tightly knit community, beginning his rehabilitation. Certainly no harm could find him there.

Work continued to be my relief. The week before Thanksgiving, Tori called her team together for a retreat at an Eastern Shore site an hour's drive from the hospital. She dubbed the off-site gathering "forced fun" to belie the seriousness of our time together. Our goal was to forecast the next three to five years. No easy task. With the passage of the Affordable Care Act earlier that year, every forward-thinking health system in the country was doing just what we were: scrambling to assess its impact and planning for ultimate flexibility.

Inevitably, the session opened with self-introductions and talk of our families. I hated these times. Was there anyone else in the room with a shame greater than mine? Did anyone else have a child in rehab? As each person spoke and my turn neared, I sought a safe haven. The only grandparent on the team, I shared that Heidi, Jon, and Josh were arriving in a few days from San Diego to live in the DC area for the next three years. It was the perfect story, extracting acclamations of joy from my colleagues that my grandson soon would be close.

Meanwhile, Jacob was in his sixth day in treatment. The night before, I'd gotten a call from his counselor, Melinda, who sounded impossibly young. She told me Jacob was having difficulty sleeping, but that wasn't unusual and they were giving him something for that. Otherwise, "He is on time for everything." She made that sound significant. I had no idea what she meant. It conjured up visits to the pediatrician the first few years of your child's check-ups. Yup, he's on time.

"One more thing, Mrs. Hillman." I could easily have been this woman's grandmother. "I think he's homesick." Oh, really? Like he's away at summer camp? "He's very concerned about you and his family. He doesn't want to lose you. You are very important to him."

Okay. Finally we were on ground I could understand.

"So, that's a good thing, yes?" I asked.

"Yes, it is."

What I didn't learn until later, hadn't known even after years of association with our own drug treatment center at the hospital, was that the people who work in drug rehabilitation and treatment are often in recovery themselves. In certified programs there are rules about years of sobriety prior to hiring, but who better to treat addiction than someone who has lived through it? So it was common to find young people, not much older than Jacob, treating my son.

Melinda became my new hope. I tried to picture her talking with Jacob. Assuming she had counseled many young people, I prayed she might show some genuine interest in him.

Early on, she suggested that the next step for Jacob after his twenty-eight-day-stay might be a sixty-to-ninety-day program at a men's halfway house. Frankly, I was surprised that Jacob had just arrived but already Melinda was talking about his leaving. There was a lot I needed to learn. I hadn't thought beyond getting him into treatment. It was a great relief to me that someone else was thinking about what was best for Jacob and what would come next. She was very interested in assessing how much we were willing to help him financially.

"After all," she said, "this is just the beginning of his recovery."

Really? Just the beginning? Did she have any idea what we'd already lived through?

But she was right. This was an entirely new phase of addiction. We now had a new word in our addiction vocabulary—recovery—and it would mark an even longer journey.

Chapter 26

Recovery Tested

Except for our two greyhounds rushing to meet me at the door each night, the house was quiet. Dick had flown to San Diego to help Heidi bundle up her household for the move to Silver Spring. For the first time in a long while, I was alone.

Annapolis was reveling in one of its typical fall football weekends. The town was ablaze with gold and blue banners waving from streetlamps and "Go Navy" bunting flapping from porches and second-story windows. Even the weather wore Navy colors, bright yellow sunshine and a cloudless blue sky. From my kitchen windows I watched young couples parade arm-in-arm on their way to the game, families toting blankets and pompoms, children dancing ahead, lightness in the air.

Inside, my house was still. The dogs slept in their soft doughnut beds in the library, oblivious to the ruckus outside. My briefcase beckoned with reading I had no time for during the week. The cuckoo clock in the front hallway clucked each hour. I sat on the floor with the hounds, watching them breathe. Melinda had asked me to tell her more about Jacob. Was there anything about him she should know, anything that might help her to help him? What do you tell a stranger about someone whose life means more to you than your own? Whose life you began? I told her he was born on his sister's fifteenth birthday. That we love him and think this break is good for him, that he needs to be separated from us to learn to be independent and to finish—to start—growing up.

When Jacob left for treatment, the last thing he did was drop to the floor and hug the greyhounds. He nuzzled their soft necks and stroked their sleek, small brows. They blinked up at him, barely moving, as greyhounds do. He was saying goodbye to them, to this house, to his childhood.

The doubts assailed me. What had I done wrong? The counselors all said, you are not to blame. Right. How the hell did they know? The "what-ifs" taunted me. What if I had not been a full-time working parent? What if I had sent him to a private school where he would have gotten the close attention from teachers that he needed? What if I'd spent more time directly with him? What if I'd had him earlier so he could have known his grandparents? What if I'd understood sooner how shy he was, how hesitant about so many things? And what if, when that first call came from Greenfield four years ago, I'd just stopped *my* life and focused on *his*?

The sudden roar of jets flying low overhead—the traditional salute to open a Navy home game—rumbled the house, startling me out of my reverie. I put aside the painful self-doubts and picked up the stack of professional journals, losing myself, again, in work.

A few days later I heard Jacob's voice for the first time since he'd left. It was the obligatory "call your family after the first week" call. By then, Heidi and her family were safely ensconced in their new home in Silver Spring about forty-five minutes away, Dick was back, and we were all planning a trip to Philadelphia to be with my brother and his family for Thanksgiving. There were plans to visit Jacob at Father Martin's the Sunday before the holiday, the first day visitors were allowed. I told Jacob that his father, sister, and I would be coming.

Although I didn't see it then, his reaction was odd.

"Oh, you're coming this Sunday? Okay, but you don't really have to," my son said to me after a week's absence.

"Jacob, what do you mean? Of course we want to see you. Heidi does too."

"Really? Heidi wants to come? Okay, that's great. If she'd like to come, I'd love to see her. You know she doesn't have the hammer you all do."

He asked if we could "smuggle" in a Dr. Pepper or some peanut M&Ms. No, that was against the rules, and he knew it. How about some money? Another odd request. When he'd been admitted we left twenty-five dollars, which was supposed to last until we saw him. How had he ripped through that so quickly? I brushed it off to the high cost of soda and candy from the machines and promised to bring additional cash.

He gave me a picture of his routine. Awake at 6. Breakfast at 6:45. Lecture 8:30. Group 10 to 12 and again 1 to 2. Free time from 2 to 5. Dinner at 5:15. Another lecture at 6:30. And a men's group at 8, often with speakers "from the outside."

"The 1 p.m. is the only one for young people," he shared. "If you're old, it's alcohol. If you're young, it's Oxy or IV heroin."

He'd been sleeping better and was still on some medication to stop his legs from shaking, part of the detox process. I also learned that Melinda was short and fat. The way he said it, I wondered if he'd already crossed her off as his therapist. But amid the recounting of his routine, he revealed something that for Jacob was anything but routine.

"Mom, they call this God's place," he said, "and if we want to, we can talk with a priest here about spirituality."

In all our conversations together, even during the Jewish holidays, I couldn't recall the word "God" ever coming from Jacob's lips. The same for "spirituality." At the time, I wasn't knowledgeable enough about the twelve steps to understand what this implied and the promise it held, but it was just as well. My hopeful meter might have skittered way too far ahead.

That Sunday, Heidi, Dick, and I drove out to Father Martin's, excited to see Jacob but apprehensive after ten days of separation. The crowd surprised me. We fell in with some fifty to sixty people herding into the auditorium for an hour's orientation, required before we could join our loved ones. In line, a tall, handsome man nodded to me. He was a surgeon from the hospital, someone with whom I'd worked recently on the campaign. Self-consciously, we greeted one another and explained our presence: I for my son, he for his brother.

It happens like that with addiction. You meet someone who has a family member, and from that instant on, you have this eternal bond. Many times after that incident, I would see this doctor at the hospital, often in the stairwell of the building where we both had offices. If we were close enough to speak, we'd always ask about the other's loved one. If it was across a room, we'd simply smile to one another, comrades forever in this anonymous world of addiction.

I couldn't wait to get my hands on Jacob. When I first spotted him across the crowded auditorium lobby after the orientation, what caught me first was his shy smile, his striking, good looks, and how thin he was. He hugged me almost as hard as I hugged him. My eyes welled up. He smelled new, medicinal, but still like Jacob, earthy and boyish with a dab of Axe to mask it all.

The four of us wandered across the lawns that stretched out to the Chesapeake Bay and savored our brief time together. It was a beautiful day, high clouds alternating with vivid sun, warm for November with a cool, pleasant breeze. Jacob confessed that he knew nearly a year before that his addiction was out of control. It was just a few months afterwards that he and Chelsea broke up. He'd isolated himself while dating her and when she disappeared, he isolated himself even further. In high school, to be popular, it was easy to pick up a couple of six packs and be the guy who delivered the beer. And at College Park, he was just lost.

When Heidi and Dick wandered off for a few minutes, I had Jacob to myself.

"So, this is a good place for you now?"

"Yeah, for now it is." He paused. "But I'm just asking, and please don't read anything into this . . . what if I can't make it the full twenty-eight days?"

"Well, I don't know." I tried hard to do as he said. "What do you think?"

"I don't know. I'm just asking."

"Well, I'm not sure, Jacob. I can't say we would be able to support you."

"Where would I go? What would I do?"

"I don't know, Honey. That would be up to you."

A blue heron, its great wide wings flapping on the breeze, landed on a piling in the water. We watched it glide silently to its perch.

"Jacob, why don't you ask someone here that question?"

"Yeah. That's good advice."

When we hugged goodbye, I saw tears in his eyes. I couldn't honor his request not to read anything into his questions. That, plus the twenty-five dollars I handed over to him, made me read everything into it.

On the way home I phoned a counselor at the center. Something is wrong, I told him. Please check on my son. Yes, we will, the counselor assured me. But don't worry. A little sadness, being homesick, this is all normal. Check him, I repeated. Something is wrong.

The next morning the call came into my office at nine. This time there weren't any pleasantries from Melinda.

"Hi, Mrs. Hillman? I'm sorry to tell you that Jacob's been using." My heart sank. "He used here Friday. As he knows, that's grounds for immediate dismissal. I'm really so very sorry, but he will have to leave."

She put Jacob on the line.

"Ma?" my son asked in a tremulous voice. "Can Dad come and get me?"

Apparently, they had worked out that Jacob could transfer to Pathways. He was willing to go, and Pathways was willing to take him. This actually was a big step since Jacob had shunned Pathways initially, for the same reason it had worried me. He knew I was known there, and he either felt ashamed or embarrassed to be in his "mother's" place for rehab.

At that moment, I was too stunned to even think about what

came next. My mind quickly replayed the previous afternoon, the odd behavior for someone supposedly in rehab, the tears in his eyes as we parted. Hating myself for being right, affirming that a mother knows her child best, the next emotion was anger. Hell, how had he gotten drugs into a place like this? Wasn't this supposed to be the pastoral paradise of recovery? Couldn't they do a better job of policing their patients and protecting them from the very reason they're there?

Of course, I knew better. Addicts who want to use can get drugs anywhere, anytime. It happens in rehab centers all the time, even the most cloistered. But the fact didn't subdue my rage. This time, it was happening to *my* kid.

As it turned out, despite the rule that cell phones were prohibited, Jacob had hidden one in the lining of his backpack. He and another patient arranged to buy heroin from someone who simply left it tucked inside the fence that bordered the property. It was that easy.

Pathways couldn't accept Jacob until the next day. Dick had to drive up to Father Martin's and bring him home to spend the night with us. I cancelled my late afternoon meetings and got home early so the three of us could discuss this latest turn.

Jacob was openly contrite. He hung back, unsure if he should hug me or not. The only sure thing was that he wasn't supposed to be home, and he knew it. Seeing him standing in the library, waiting for my first words, I felt my resolve strengthen. No, my head said. He's not supposed to be here. This is wrong. He cleared out his bedroom and left for rehab, and now he's screwed that up. This is on him.

During one of our counseling sessions with Richard, he had asked if I ever showed Jacob that I was angry. If every household has its tone, ours was generally quiet. Even when we were angry with Heidi or Jacob, Dick and I lowered our voices rather than raise them. Jacob's addiction intensified that. It turned down the sound in every room, set a deep hush over how we moved through the house, how we trudged silently up and down stairs, set the table, lounged wordlessly with the greyhounds on the library floor, or spotted dust motes in silent riot when the sun caught them through the blinds. His illness had a terrible deafening effect on everything that went on in our house, and it only got worse as he did.

This time, I let him have it.

"Jacob," I started, feeling my voice rise, "you need to know that I'm really angry. I don't usually get pissed off, but I'm really pissed off now. Damn it, Jacob, being an addict doesn't mean you're powerless. You *can* make decisions. You *have* that power. Dad and I will support you at Pathways and as long as you're in recovery. But we won't have you in this house unless you're clean and sober. I'm serious. We won't. You have to know that, if you don't already."

For me, pretty strong words, especially then. But the years of anxiety and frustration with how he was wasting his life, and the hell it was creating for Dick and me, finally erupted, especially when we were offering him the gift of a new life through rehab.

"I know, Mom, I know," he said. He leaned against the fireplace, looked directly at me, and said the strangest thing. "And I'm going to be a leader at Pathways."

It was such an odd response. The line ricocheted in my head. Was it a vain, shallow promise, or had he really learned something at Father Martin's?

Reflecting on that strange night, having Jacob back in the house one last time before he went off to another rehab center, I realized that as a family we had made some progress. After ten days at the treatment center, despite using that weekend, Jacob's eyes looked clear. There was no nodding off. And now there were new ground rules. No longer would we hand our son any cash, even for incidentals. Instead, payment would go directly to those providing his care. It was a huge lesson learned and a big step in Jacob's ultimate recovery, and our own.

Another big step, for me, was talking about it. I still felt so desperately alone. Dick and I consoled each other, but I didn't want to overburden him with my feelings of despair and guilt. My sister-in-law

Helaine, a family counselor, was always just at the end of a phone line. But even with her, shame silenced me. I felt trapped. Sadness, worry, and anger consumed me.

At the hospital I moved through my days caught up in the swirl of the fast-paced campaign. The need to stay sharp and focused—the meetings with donors where I stared intently at their faces and listened hard to the intonation of their voices, trying to read and hear their reactions to our requests for large pledges—swept away thoughts of Jacob, at least for a time. But when my mind slipped, when I walked back to my office alone or caught sight of the clouds through the glass walkway waving over the hospital's rooftop helipad, it hurt so badly tears welled up. I had to tamp down those feelings because just around the corner was another donor-couple who knew me only as a gracious, genuine professional. There was no outlet for the anguish and grief that was never far from the surface, no matter how hard I tried to bury it deep inside.

I knew I needed to talk with someone. I was grasping at anything to help me understand why my son was an addict, where had this come from, whether I was to blame. In my sea of misery, I would swim towards any life raft. Once more, Richard became my rescuer. In one of our last private sessions, just before Jacob left Father Martin's and entered Pathways, Richard said, "Lisa, you have to tell someone at work." He didn't elaborate. It was a straightforward command, from one professional to another. With his years of experience counseling and consoling women just like me, he understood my situation. I had a highly responsible job, countless people depended on me to do it well, and someone needed to know that my ability to perform that job could be affected.

And there was something else Richard understood that I couldn't. He wasn't just trying to save Jacob. He was trying to save me.

Chapter 27

Telling the Boss

Given the peculiarities of the time, technically I had two bosses. Chip was in his last six months as CEO, and Tori would follow. So I reported to both of them. It was a tricky, if not highly sensitive, challenge. It meant staying in very close communication with them both, ensuring that each was equally informed. Chip had picked up how awkward this was for those who reported to him. He established a routine for his direct reports to meet at least once a month with him and once a month with him and Tori.

Two days before Thanksgiving — the day after Jacob was admitted to Pathways— Chip, Tori, and I were having our monthly meeting in Tori's office. These meetings usually lasted an hour. Put in a room three high-functioning healthcare professionals who like, respect, and know one another, and it's easy to let minutes melt into chatter. I always came to these meetings fully prepared, with both a keen sense of how time-starved these executives were and a need to get sign-offs on certain projects. And because it was the end of the year, a critical time when many donors make final commitments, I needed to match Chip and Tori with specific donors, confirm calendars, and determine how we would play it. With a neatly set list of bulleted topics—Board, Staffing, Campaign, Key Donors, Upcoming Events, and CEO Transition—I tried to keep them on track.

These monthly meetings were not without a certain tension. While Chip had hand-picked Tori to be his successor, it was hard for him to relinquish the reins. He was like the graying chieftain of a large, tribal village who eyed the bright, young warrior and chose him above all others to lead his people. While he would forever be revered as the wise chieftain, he would never sit inside the tent again.

The business of our meeting ended. Abruptly, before Chip or Tori stood and I lost my nerve, I blurted out, "Guys, if you can give me just another minute, please. I have something I need to tell you."

They froze. Bad news normally came at the end of meetings, and from the tone of my voice their faces said, uh oh, something bad is coming. Their backs stiffened. They remained seated, motionless.

"It's intensely personal, and it's about my son . . ." At the word "son," my voice cracked. I've never cried in front of a boss. Keeping emotions in check had been a badge of professional honor, a promise I'd made years ago to the sisterhood who made it to the executive suite. I wouldn't be caught betraying years of struggle to rise in the professional ranks by breaking down in tears. Grace under fire was my mantra, and I was determined not to falter now.

Long before my career at AAMC, I enjoyed a few years as a broadcast journalist for a prominent Baltimore radio station. Low person on the on-air totem pole, I worked weekends. One Saturday, minutes before delivering the noon news, I phoned home and learned that my grandmother, my Bubbe, had died. While it was expected, it was still a shock. The huge, unforgiving round clock on the newsroom wall blinked the time: 11:59:30. I shuffled the papers holding my freshly written newscast, scurried into the sound booth, adjusted my mike, and delivered the four-minute newscast flawlessly. The second I signed off, I burst into tears.

It was that same professionalism I struggled to hold on to now. I stood up from the table. Chip and Tori just stared at one another, silent, apprehensive, giving me time to collect myself. Pacing, I let my shame tumble out.

"It's my son. He's got a very serious problem, and I'm so sorry. I don't know where this came from. He's at Pathways right now. He was admitted yesterday, and the therapist said it was time for me to tell someone, so I just wanted you both to know. But you know I will do everything possible not to let this interfere with the campaign or my work here, and I don't think it will, but I just wanted you to know."

Chip spoke first. Still the chieftain, he offered consoling and instructive words. "Lisa, first, I am very, very sorry. You aren't the first person to have a problem like this. I'm sorry for Jacob, too, because I'm sure he's going through a lot. Knowing you, I'm sure it won't interfere with your work. But I do think you need to tell someone in your office. Maybe not specifically what's wrong, but just something in case for any reason you have to leave suddenly and they have to take over. You want some coverage there. But what's more important is that it will give you some peace of mind. You deserve that. Again, just in case you need it."

Standing there, desperate to end the meeting lest I break down, I fought off the intense kindness of his words. All I could do was nod, numbly. Of course, he was right. I would need to expand the circle around me and tell someone in my office. Tori also offered her help in any way.

"Is there anything either Tori or I can do?" Chip asked, his gaze serious and soft. "If not right now, please let us know. That's what we're here for."

I would be sad when this man was no longer inside the tent.

Now that Chip and Tori knew, I felt a huge relief. The circle of "the knowing" was gradually expanding. As I walked back to my office, my head was filled with how fortunate I was. In that top floor suite I had two bosses who had shown nothing but empathy, despite how strange and uncomfortable it must have been for them to witness their chief development officer, and a colleague they depended on, dissolve in front of them. Chip's suggestion to confide in someone in my office also helped. Carefully avoiding letting the meeting morph into a therapy session—which was easy and often happened in our caring environment—he had adroitly brought the three of us back to the larger goal: we had a health system to run, and thousands of people counted on us to do it well, regardless of our personal miseries. But I also knew he cared about me personally, just as he did so many others who worked with him, and he hoped that by suggesting I share this burden with others, it might lessen its weight on me.

That afternoon, before I lost nerve, I called my two top directors into my office. Larry had been with the Foundation nearly six years and had my total trust. There was little I didn't share with him. Jan was relatively new. Smart, aggressive, adept at marketing, and a fast-learner, she was just what we needed to close the campaign and get us moving after that. Today I very much needed them both just to listen.

Nestled in my corner office with the wrap-around windows that faced the hospital campus, Jan and Larry stared at me apprehensively.

"What's up?" Jan asked.

"Listen, guys, I won't keep you long. I just need you to know something. I'm going through a situation now that's very personal. It's a health issue in my family, and I don't know what's going to happen. I just need for you both to know this. There could come a time when—for some reason—I need to excuse myself suddenly. I don't think that's going to happen, but just in case it does, I wanted you to know."

They glanced at one another, neither speaking right away. Larry was first.

"No problem, Lisa. We're here. Whatever you need. You know that."

Jan: "Yes, of course! Anytime. Don't worry; we have it covered."

And without questioning me or dragging out our three-minute meeting, they exited my office.

Just like that. It made me wonder if they already knew about the problem in my family, but I didn't want to elaborate. Once more, the circle of "the knowing" grew, even though I had not spelled it out for them. Once more, I was thankful that I worked in healthcare, where the culture of caring for patients extended to caring for colleagues. Larry and Jan had my back. That was another huge relief. Chip had been so right in suggesting I confide in them. The man had been a mentor to me throughout my career at the hospital and even more so during the fifteen years that he had been president of the entire health system and I reported directly to him. I admired how he suggested ideas, rather than issued directives, to his staff. "You might want to consider . . ." or "Have you thought about trying . . ." were typical responses when you presented him a problem. Today he had "suggested" I tell Jan and Larry, and it gave me huge comfort during an otherwise hugely uncomfortable time.

Years later I would realize that addiction isn't a disease anyone can face alone. And yet millions do. Not only does addiction isolate the addict, it isolates those who love him. If you're new to the illness, as I was, and you know only what you've seen in bad movies or TV mini-series, then you feel even more frightened and alone. Add to that a responsible job in a relatively small town, where gossip is as certain to fuel the day as the second cup of coffee. Shame takes over, enshrouding you in secrecy, sealing you off from the comfort sharing often brings.

Even though my bosses and two direct reports now knew, I was petrified that others would discover my secret. My son was a drug addict, and he now was a patient in—of all places—my very own health system.

Fueling the fear were snatches of conversations I'd had over the years with board members and donors who failed to show any interest in Pathways' mission. One corporate CEO even referred to alcoholics and addicts as "bums." It was often the biggest drinkers on the board who were the least compassionate. Nevertheless, each year at budget time, when board members confronted the large deficit Pathways carried, they voted unanimously to approve another year's funding.

They almost had to. Survey after survey in Maryland and in our own county cited alcohol and substance abuse as a number one health problem. There were few treatment centers in Maryland and only a handful in our area. Too many nights there was nowhere to send the alcoholics or drug abusers once they were detoxed. If board members were going to be true to their credo that "we respond to the health needs of the community," then there was no way they could shut down Pathways, and they knew it.

Living under the threat of curtailed funding year after year took its toll on the Pathways staff. Many were themselves recovering addicts. You couldn't help but wonder if their self-confidence was strong enough to sustain their own sobriety while society beat them down. But instead of defeating them, the battle energized them. Morale at Pathways sometimes faltered, but it quickly rallied. Staff knew that each patient discharged to a halfway house, a long-term program, or even back home was a small victory. They celebrated every hard-won achievement.

Of all the places within the health system, Pathways was the strictest regarding confidentiality. State and federal laws demanded it. But the staff went well beyond that, knowing that any breach of confidentiality would jeopardize their ability to attract those who needed their services.

As Jacob entered his second day there, I was counting on that strict adherence to protect my privacy. If someone were to find out he was there, I could only imagine the shock and scuttlebutt that would follow. My mind played out conversations that would erupt around town, like fragile pipes bursting underground, spewing dirty water at parties, lunchtime cafés, board rooms, gymnasiums. Did you hear about the Hillmans? No, what? Their son is an addict. No? Really? The Hillmans? You're kidding me, right? No, it's true. I think he's away at rehab somewhere. But they're such an upright couple. Isn't he a former mayor? And she runs that hospital foundation? How could they have a son who uses drugs? No, I don't believe it. Tell me you're joking. You are, right?

Worse, I imagined what a board member might say. Do you know about Lisa? About her son? Think we should get together? Have a special executive committee to discuss this? Are we okay with her leading the Foundation now? What about our image? Will people trust us to give us money if they know her son's an addict? I'm uncomfortable with this; are you? Maybe we should talk.

The shame and panic over secrecy even extended to my closest colleagues on the senior executive team. As a separate nonprofit under the larger health system umbrella, Pathways had its own board of directors. It was a management board populated by the executive officers—the CEO, COO, CFO, CMO, and me. Chip had appointed me to the board as part of his transition. I was the only player who knew Pathways' history, and I had an abiding interest in seeing it survive long before Jacob's addiction surfaced.

While I have no idea how it started, I'd always had an interest in mental health and addiction. My first full-time job was with the Maryland Department of Vocational Rehabilitation as a counselor at Crownsville State Hospital. The goal was to help recovering alcoholics and schizophrenics gain work skills and find jobs when they left the hospital. Through off-site intensives and staff meetings with experienced social workers and trained psychiatrists, I acquired a great deal of knowledge about mental illness and the cruel cycle of addiction, made more difficult when there is no family or social support. Mostly in their forties and fifties, the patients were compliant, beaten-down men who had lost everything. It astonishes me today that they behaved so gentlemanly when a young woman in her twenties drove them to downtown Baltimore, escorted them into a halfway house, dropped off papers outlining their new job location and supervisor, and with a handshake wished them well.

Maybe they knew their time in the city was short-lived. More often than not, I'd see them reappear on the ward within weeks or months. In much later years, many of these men would populate city streets and spur the new social outcry to help the homeless. Under the banner of merging mentally ill patients with healthier populations and providing more outpatient treatment centers—which failed to happen in the numbers required—the government simply shut down its mental hospitals in the early 1990s. One day, Crownsville closed its doors. The next, the emergency room at Anne Arundel Medical Center was treating alcoholics and mentally ill men and women who had nowhere else to go.

It was partly because of this new, harsh environment that the need for Pathways emerged. While it was founded to ensure that young people, ages sixteen to twenty-one, could find care, it evolved to treat older patients as well. On average, some thirty to thirty-five patients from ages eighteen to sixty-five spent two weeks as inpatients and followed a strict daily routine of group and individual therapy based on AA's twelve-step program.

I was an odd appointee to the Pathways board. I had no clinical skills, nor the financial acumen to render much scrutiny. But Tori welcomed me for my historical perspective and passion for the mission. Plus, I wasn't shy about challenging others and insisting that each board meeting open with a "mission moment"—a story that allowed the staff to share a recent success and inspire board members to remember why we were there. These often were the best parts of the meeting, tying the board to the people it was charged to help, reminding everyone that behind the minutes and the financials were real men and women.

Board meetings were held at the Pathways facility, a two-story building about three miles from the main hospital campus, in a first floor room with windows overlooking an outdoor patio where patients held smoke breaks or relaxed between activities. Window blinds shuttered the view, but we could still catch glimpses of the men and women who were the focus of our work.

When we convened for our November board meeting, my son was one of thirty-some inpatients upstairs. Certainly Helen, the executive director, the medical director, and Tori knew. But I hoped the others didn't. My sense of shame about having addiction in my family and my frantic need to keep it secret made it easy to be paranoid. Who else knew? The secretary quietly tapping out the minutes? How about the social worker? Did anyone realize that the mother of a patient was sitting at this table, making decisions that could affect the organization's future?

How very strange to be in the board room while my son was elsewhere in the building. It was, at the very least, quite unsettling. Certainly there was no conflict of interest, was there? It should make me a better board member, right? I wondered if those who knew my situation might question my emotional ability to handle the board seat. I wanted to scream out loud, "Don't you all realize that my son is one of the statistics you are talking about today? He's only twenty-one, his bright future is ahead of him, and he shouldn't be here."

Silently, I applauded my poise at making it though the meeting. It amused me to remember a former president. During his more tumultuous years, Bill Clinton was famous for his ability to compartmentalize his life. I felt like Bill, able to focus on the board agenda, yet half-hoping I might catch a fleeting look of my son through one of the narrow window-blind slats. Fortunately, I never did. It was just as well, lest my face betray the professional demeanor I was trying so hard to maintain.

That evening I got a phone call from Richard, our therapist. He told me Jacob had phoned him and they'd had a twenty-minute conversation. He was astonished. It was one of the few times that a former patient had voluntarily called him, and he took this as a good sign. When Dick and I sat down to dinner, the phone rang. This time it was Jacob for us.

"The others have gone outside to smoke, but I've stayed here so I could call you," he began. My mind flashed to the patio the board could see through the blinds. I knew well where those "others" were going "outside to smoke."

His voice was strong, clear.

"Yeah, I'm doing okay, Mom. My counselor's pretty good." He told me she was there with him. Among the many rules, patients couldn't make calls to anyone without a counselor present.

"Sometime, maybe next week, she's gonna want to talk with you about what happens next with me. I really don't know what's gonna happen, but I'm just letting you know."

The sound of his voice was immeasurably consoling. His call was only five minutes, the maximum allowed, but it was the first time I'd heard his voice since he had been admitted forty-eight hours before. Against the pounding, feverish worry, it was a cooling balm. The few minutes we talked reminded me that there might be a reprieve, if ever so brief, from fear and despair. Was he feeling that too? I pictured the counselor beside him, monitoring our conversation, and hoped she was experienced and self-assured. Jacob might pay more attention if she were.

As it turned out, Traci, his counselor, was tall, attractive and very smart. She would have an enormous impact on Jacob's life—and ours.

Chapter 28

Letting Go

Among holidays, Thanksgiving is my favorite. It holds such sweet memories. As a girl, I tried to help my mother any way I could. She took great pride in laying out a beautiful table, complete with crisp white linens, fresh flowers, and a stunning turkey that was always impossibly huge for our small family. My grandparents, Bubbe, Nanny, and Pop, always joined us, and their thick Russian accents lent an old-world feel to our traditional American feast. I could hardly wait until the sweet potato casserole topped with melted marshmallows made its way around the table to me. My father hogged the steaming bowl of sauerkraut, pungent and overbearing, which was fine with my brother and me. In later years, as adolescence and young adulthood overtook us, we added friends and finally fiancés to our circle. Aside from the Jewish holidays, Thanksgiving was our one day to pause and savor the pure joy of simply being together.

The year Jacob was at Pathways, Dick and I celebrated the holiday at my brother's home in Pennsylvania. Despite my sister-in-law's perfect meal and the treat of being with my niece and nephew and their families, the holiday felt empty. I didn't even have Heidi and her family there, since they were committed to Jon's parents in New Jersey. Seated at the table, candles glowing, chatter and laughter surrounding me, I felt terribly cheated, like the playgoer who buys a ticket to a favorite show, only to discover his seat is high up in the top balcony behind a pole. I couldn't see the show or feel like I was any part of it.

Addiction does that. Little by little, it cheats you of even the most basic elements of normalcy. The Norman Rockwell Thanksgiving was just one more expectation unmet, like all the others: the happy high school graduation, excitement of the first day of college, successful completion of freshman year, even finishing community college. Addiction means life interrupted. The addict's growth stops when the addiction starts. Research says a young person's development actually arrests at the age the addiction takes hold. If that's true, Jacob was still seventeen, and I was still the mom of an adolescent, expecting him to grow up. Even worse, I had had such high expectations for him. He was my only son, a tiny gift that came with a message: it's okay. Your mom is dying, but you will be all right. She will die before she sees your new baby. But you will have this son to comfort you, and in caring for him and watching him grow, you will find solace from your loss.

Over time, I would learn that addiction means it's best to have no expectations. None. Erase them. Forget waiting for the good grades or news of the job promotion. Don't even look for the goodnight kiss or listen for "I love you" at the end of a phone call. If you expect any normal, loving reaction or deed from someone who is sick, whose only thought every day is where to get his next high, then you become the victim as much as he. But how does a parent give up those longings? Then there were my totally unreasonable expectations for Jacob from his near-mystical birth, and I was destined for an even harder fall. Forget MIT and engineering new space technology, wipe away visions of award-winning treatises, an adoring wife at his side, two children, a clique of brilliant friends who talked of saving the world and just might do it. Replace these with the thin small hope that he will awake safely in his bed in the morning, get up and get dressed, eat breakfast, go to group, and talk with his counselor later in the day.

While expectations tumbled like a hiker's bad spill on a high mountain pass, hope somehow survived. Even at Jacob's worst moments, when I wasn't sure where he was or what he was doing with whom, I never lost hope. When it faltered, I pulled up the words of the mother I talked to at the gym that morning when I was feeling deeply sad and depressed: "Where there is life, there is hope."

Jacob managed to stay at Pathways for the full fourteen days. Although that was hardly long enough to make any dramatic change in his disease, Pathways would live up to its name. He was about to travel down a totally new road.

About halfway through his stay, Traci arranged a critical phone meeting for the four of us. It was the conversation that each counselor has with each patient and family about "what comes next." Within thirty minutes we agreed that Jacob would go from "bed to bed"—to another treatment center, this one in Delray Beach, Florida. Apparently, Jacob thought I would balk at his leaving Maryland, but the idea had never occurred to me. Actually, I'd given little thought to what would happen post-Pathways. I'd given up trying to look too far ahead. Instead, I simply tried hard to focus on each day, grateful that he remained in treatment, trusting the staff there to know better than I what was best for my son.

"Mom, are you okay with this? I mean, it's Florida. I'd be going to Florida." He sounded like a kid asking for permission to go on spring break rather than an inpatient drug addict entering his next phase of treatment. Traci took over.

"Mrs. Hillman, would you be okay with Jacob's going to Florida? He seems to think you might not like the idea. There's a treatment center there we know well. We've sent people there before. It would be a good next step for Jacob, and he likes the idea too, but he's not sure you will."

Traci's gentle, kind words conjured up those of another counselor about a year before, when Jacob was an outpatient. His had not been so kind.

"Hey, Jacob," this gruff, burly man told my son as he left Pathways one evening after group, "You know what you need, man? You need to get yourself to a halfway house. Get out of your mama's house and grow up a little, you understand? You gotta' man up!"

At the time, his words bristled. Who was he to talk to my son that way? And yet, a year later, I knew he was right. I had to let Jacob go.

"Jacob," I asked, "how do you feel about this? Do you want to go?"

A pause, then, "I'm scared. Excited. Unsure."

Simple. Honest. Pure. His response fanned my hope. Clearly, he had learned something in his short stay at Pathways and even during his brief time at Father Martin's. For the first time in four years, my son was talking about his sobriety, his next step, what he needed to do, without direction from his parents. He was learning that recovery is a process, not an "event." It would take time and be up to him. He would get support and tools along the way, but ultimately, his recovery was up to him. He was "manning up."

Before we sealed the deal, I had one more question for Traci.

"Okay, so he's in Florida. What do I do if he uses again? Do I go down and get him?"

"No," she replied firmly, both of us aware Jacob was sitting near her and hearing all this. "He'll have to figure out what to do. He'll have to face the consequences. But hopefully we are giving him the tools he needs to face this. And to learn that there's so much more to life than drugs."

The weekend before Jacob's discharge, there was one final family session at Pathways. This time the counselor was LaToya, a bright young woman who exuded energy. Just her smile cheered you. She seemed excited for this next phase of Jacob's recovery, far more than I.

"So I know you have concerns about Jacob's going to Florida," she began.

I sure did. While my immediate reaction had been surprise, doubts were creeping in. Admittedly, it probably would be best for Jacob—and us—to have him live apart from us, at least for now. A geographic separation would force him to grow up, face his condition, and learn how to do the basics in life, like laundry, food, managing money. It overwhelmed me to think all this would be thrown at him at once. If I felt that way, what was he thinking? What concerned me most, and I wondered if I was the only one among the four of us thinking this, was that he might not be able to sustain this next phase without a relapse. LaToya understood.

"Sure, that could happen, but maybe not," she said. "Maybe expecting the worst is just your way of coping. You expect it, so you're not shocked or disappointed when it happens."

So much of my facing Jacob's addiction was expecting the worst. During his earlier years, I had had such impossibly high expectations for him. When the drugs took over, I tried hard not to have any expectations at all. But more recently, if I braced myself for the worst, then if the worst never happened, I actually would be better off. What a goofy way to live.

For Jacob the focus was far different. He'd had a few days to think about the move, and he began to fuss about money. What would he do for food? Would there be enough? He sounded infantile again, maybe because it was nearing lunchtime and his hunger had rebounded now that his system was flushed of drugs. Regardless, I was glad that his complaining annoyed me. It was a throwback to normalcy, the typical adolescent irritating his mom about trivialities. We hadn't been in that place in years.

Details for the move got settled. Dick would take Jacob to the airport in a few days. Someone from the treatment center in Delray Beach would meet him, and he would begin an intensive outpatient program. He would live in a men's halfway house, where strict sobriety topped a long list of rules. Dick and I would pay for the halfway house and treatment center, sending the money directly to the people in charge. No longer would we give Jacob money. It was expected that he would find a job within weeks to pay for food, clothing, and transportation.

Looking back on this time, I don't know where I found the strength to let my only son board an airplane for a place unseen. I'd never been to Delray Beach and certainly never seen the halfway house, let alone the treatment center. Online, the treatment center looked respectable, but online they all did. Click on any facility in South Florida, and dozens more pop up. They offer a smorgasbord of services for any addiction imaginable. Drugs and alcohol take the lead, but you can find places that promise cures for addictions to food, sex, gambling, smoking, even hoarding. I had to trust the counselors at Pathways and accept that I'd entered a realm where they knew more than I.

And yet, I knew my son better than they. How could we send him away without being certain there would be someone on the other end to pick him up? The mother in me wouldn't stop. My boy had no money in his pocket. He carried only a small duffle bag stuffed with underwear, jeans, shorts, and a few tee shirts. I wasn't even sure he had a toothbrush. Would there be a bed for him his first night? Would the sheets be clean? What about the man who ran the house? What kind of person takes a job like that? Hard, hardened men who expect those in their charge to tow the line, make their beds, clean up after themselves in the kitchen, "man up?"

"Let it go," one of the counselors said to me. "Let it go, or it will take you down with it."

My spirits should have soared at letting Jacob go to a place where he needed to go. But the final few days before his flight filled me with anxiety and despair. Worried for him, I felt horribly sad for myself. With Jacob in Florida, I wouldn't see him for—we had no idea how long. He would be a thousand miles away, but the distance barely mattered if I couldn't reach out to feel his presence. His face and body would be gone from my sight. I wouldn't be able to lay my hand on his arm and feel its warmth, smell his skin, tussle his thick dark hair. Those hazel-brown eyes that sometimes flashed bemusement or bewilderment would no longer meet mine. It hurt to let him go. In all the years of shame, worry, and agony over my son, no moment was more agonizing than the decision to let him leave. It was the first day of preschool and freshman year in college all over again. There was no way of getting away from it. We were about to say a goodbye that would mark a parting like no other. It was time to let him grow up.

Letting Jacob go might have been the end of the story. But actually, it was the beginning—for both of us.

Chapter 29

Mama, You Need a Hug

While I suffered mounting fear and worry over Jacob's impending move to Florida, I made a final visit to our family therapist, Richard. He deserved to know about Jacob's plans, and it wouldn't hurt me to see him one more time either.

It was early December. Stink bug season was long gone. Richard's walls were plain and bare. Farewell to summertime crawlers and storms that rolled in beneath his sad windows. The view now framed trees shedding black and browning leaves in the winter wind. Astute, patient, his big face gazing at me, Richard sat back and listened as I recounted the plans for my son. I thanked him, of course. It's always been important to me to thank people who do a job well, and I was grateful to Richard for getting us this far. In his work I could only guess at the times he felt good about what he did. You could almost smell the sorrow in his office.

We stood and shook hands. I was about to leave when Richard stopped me cold.

"You know," he said, "your son's got a plan now. He'll be well taken care of. But what about you? What are you going to do?"

It was as though he'd sprouted three heads. I thought the man was crazy. Jacob was the sick one, not me. What was he suggesting?

"Alcoholism, substance abuse, it doesn't matter. It's a disease that affects the whole family, you know. So what are you going to do for yourself and for your husband?"

For a brief, crass second I wondered if this was his vain attempt to sign me up for continued therapy. I was a paying customer who paid on time. How many of those did he have? From the looks of his office, a new couch was long overdue.

Again, he was ready.

"I'm not saying necessarily that you should continue seeing me, although I'd be happy to help if you'd find that helpful. But you might try Al-Anon."

Driving home, I played back my final visit with Richard. For so long Jacob's addiction, and my shame and inability to handle it, had made me feel like a stranger in a strange land. This new mention of Al-Anon was just one more foreign phrase. Helen at Pathways also had mentioned it during one of our secret meetings in her office. But I'd never thought Al-Anon was for me. The name conjured up nothing that was appealing: wives of hopeless alcoholics who faced financial ruin, women with scraggly hair and stained housedresses, losers who chased after kids out of control and stoically slogged through the squalor and chaos in their lives until they, too, were as broken and beaten down as their errant husbands.

So it was no small miracle that led me to a nearby church that Sunday night to "try" Al-Anon. I also was desperate. Jacob was scheduled to leave in two days. What would confront him in Florida—squalid living conditions, unsafe neighborhoods, addicts as bed buddies—consumed my thoughts. Worried for him, distraught for myself, I sat in my car shielded by darkness, eyeing the people entering the church, trying to size them up, assessing if I wanted to be among them. A chilly rain pelted my windshield. If I didn't get out of the car and go inside soon, I'd be drenched by the upcoming storm.

Holding the hood of my raincoat over my head, as much to protect my identity as to ward off the rain, I hurried up the church steps. Terrified someone might recognize me, I spotted a young man at the door smoking a cigarette. He looked like any of the hundreds of young men I'd seen at Pathways. A single gold earring, shaved head, shirtsleeves rolled up past impressive biceps. He nodded to me, "Good evening, Ma'am," and held the door open. Apparently, there was an Alcoholics Anonymous meeting going on at the same time.

Cautiously, I walked past the large room where dozens of men were meeting, stopped in front of the next room, and peered through the closed door's small, upper windows. Only one woman was inside, and she was arranging chairs around a small square table. So far, no one knew me and no one knew I was there. Only Dick knew I was going to the meeting, and he was home watching Sunday night football. It would take just minutes to retreat down the church hallway, get in my car, and join him on the sofa.

Too late. The woman behind the closed doors looked up, saw me, flashed a huge grin, and yelled out, "Hi! Come on in!"

Her name was Daisy. I'd never seen her before, and I was pretty sure she didn't know me. So far, so good. But in a town where my husband and I knew nearly everyone, or everyone knew us, my antennae were up for any hint of recognition. It hadn't occurred to me that someone might worry I would see *them* at a meeting. That would come later.

The few chairs arranged, Daisy was now seated. Knitting a pale green and white blanket, she motioned for me to sit beside her. The blanket was for her newborn grandson. A large woman with big, fleshy arms that jiggled with every needle tap, she told me the baby's mother, her "alcoholic daughter," lived with her and her husband, and her house was always in an uproar. She laughed when she said this, and it caught me by surprise. You couldn't help but smile at her genial good nature, and by the time five others joined us, I was feeling slightly more comfortable.

In all there were seven of us, four women and three men. It was inevitable I would know someone. When Sam walked into the room, our eyes locked. Busted! I hadn't seen Sam for years, but our lives entwined decades ago when his wife was in journalism with me. He had been a bit of a raconteur about town, dabbling in development and real estate, making his money where opportunities presented. In later years, he entertained kids at parties and city events, a natural clown. Even though he had long disappeared from my daily life, once we had been close. We had history. And he was shocked to see me at an Al-Anon meeting. He nodded to me. I nodded to him. The meeting began.

Typically, Al-Anon meetings last one hour and follow a common framework set forth eons ago that mimics, almost exactly, how AA meetings are run. In fact, nearly all twelve-step programs follow the same format. For "AA," simply dub in whatever addiction is ruining your life: drugs, food, sex, gambling. Nar-Anon was another option, but I'd heard that sometimes their meetings tend to be harder to find. So for "alcohol," I simply substituted the word "drugs."

The leader, in this case Daisy, opened the meeting with a moment of silence and the Serenity Prayer:

> God, grant me the serenity
>
> to accept the things I cannot change,
>
> Courage to change the things I can,
>
> And wisdom to know the difference.

Members in the group, chosen randomly, read from standardized texts that explained the purpose of Al-Anon, the reason for the meeting, and what was expected from those attending. There also was a newcomer's welcome, the words of which, especially on my hearing them for the first time, were startlingly comforting:

"As a newcomer you may feel that you are here for the alcoholic . . . that your presence here may teach you how to stop his or her drinking. The truth is you are here because of the alcoholic and not for the alcoholic . . . The people around you are experiencing in varying degrees the hurt, the anger, the anxiety that you are experiencing. Al-Anon will work for you if you allow it to. It's as effective as you make it. It's the safe place, the right place to be."

Perhaps most comforting of all was the emphasis on anonymity. "Ours is an anonymous fellowship. Your anonymity is protected at all times. What is said here, whom you see here, when you leave here, let it stay here."

When it was time for self-introductions, Daisy stated her name, and each person followed, first names only. She explained that someone in the group signs up ahead to speak. After the speaker finishes, it's open sharing by whoever wants to talk next. Each Al-Anon meeting varies slightly in size, tenor, makeup—but the structure is the same, granting those who attend something sure and rock steady, a safe harbor for at least one hour in an otherwise chaotic life.

I'd been to a few AA meetings in my life—once with a friend who was a recovering alcoholic and years ago at the state mental hospital—but this was my first Al-Anon meeting, and to say I felt uncomfortable would be a huge understatement. Given my years as a broadcaster and as a spokesperson for the hospital, life in the political spotlight, and countless talks to civic and community groups, I could hardly be called a wallflower. And yet at this meeting, in this church classroom, seated on an uncomfortable folding chair at a well-worn, rectangular wooden table with a small group of people whom I'd never met—save for one—I wanted to shrink into the floor. I couldn't find my place. What was I doing here? It was so incongruous, so out of character for Lisa Hillman to be at an Al-Anon meeting. The only way to get comfortable was to fall back on what I knew: the professional journalist and fundraising executive, listening intently to all the stories, focusing in on each person as he or she spoke. And the stores were fascinating, albeit so very sad.

Two of the men were recovering alcoholics themselves but had come to Al-Anon worried about a son or nephew. Another young woman was the daughter of alcoholic parents, or an "adult child," who pursued academic achievements perhaps seeking the recognition she never got from her parents. There was a whole new lexicon of words and phrases, and on one level I found it totally absorbing. As long as I was the observer, the reporter looking in, I was fine. But by the end of the meeting, with the hour winding down, the group turned to me.

Daisy said, "As a newcomer, you don't have to say anything. You can just sit there, that's fine. But would you like to share anything?"

The group was so small that in an hour everyone had a chance to talk with just enough time left for the newcomer. That's what I had been afraid of. Out of respect for them, if nothing else, it felt like my turn had come.

Although I'm pretty good on my feet, until Al-Anon I'd never had to stand up for anything personal. It had never been about me. It was always about the hospital, or teaching a fundraising seminar, or urging others to support the myriad of causes Dick and I supported in town. While Dick and I are joiners, certainly for the organizations we care about, we were never "groupies." I still wasn't sure if coming into this Sunday night church meeting of Al-Anon meant we would become groupies. Did it mean we had to reveal deep, dark secrets about ourselves, let it all hang out? Our relationships, even among our closest friends, tended to be somewhat restrained and cautious, always preserving a natural dignity we felt we owed one another and ourselves. Besides, up until now, we had never had anything *to* hang out.

From "groupie" it's easy to get to "cult." Al-Anon members find it intensely humorous when outsiders suggest their organization is a cult. If it's a cult, the seasoned among them say, then the world would be a better place if everyone belonged.

All eyes were on me. It was now or never. None of these people knew me, and Sam, the one who did, had enough secrets in his closet that he surely wouldn't care about mine. And wasn't this why I had come here? To get some relief from the shame and burden of my secret?

But at that moment I felt an intense loyalty to Jacob. To share anything now about my torment might betray him. Even though he was headed for Florida, surely he would come home one day, and I didn't want to besmirch his reputation by labeling him as a drug addict. The doors to success in his hometown would slam shut in his face, even before he wrapped his fingers around the handles. Was it fair to seek a reprieve from my angst and worry at the risk of increasing his?

Such were the crazy, mixed-up feelings that swirled in my brain

during that sixty minutes of precious meeting time. Al-Anon under-
scores that it's a program for "relatives and friends of alcoholics" who
share their "experience, strength, and hope in order to solve their
common problems." It's for loved ones and friends who are affected
by the disease of alcoholism. It stresses that it's a program for you, not
for the alcoholic. You are here for your own well-being, not that of
the alcoholic. This is usually the first big "aha" that newcomers experience. Oh, so I'm not going to learn here what to say to my husband,
how to get him to stop drinking, to pay attention to his job or he's
going to lose it, to stay sober, please, at least around the kids. And
this is followed up closely with the next big lesson, the three Cs: "You
didn't cause it, you can't control it, and you can't cure it."

Even in this first meeting, the basics registered. My mind went to
Richard. So this is why he wanted me to consider Al-Anon. A program just for me. Not Jacob. This was for my recovery from the effects
of the disease of drug abuse.

I took a deep breath and plunged ahead.

"Okay, thanks, Daisy, I'll try. But I'm not sure I can do this without crying." Instantly my eyes welled up and bottom lip quivered.

"It's okay," she said, passing a big, rectangular box of tissues my
way. "We do a lot of crying here."

Summertimes, Dick and I frequently hike in the White Mountains
in New Hampshire. On my best days, I move along the trail at a happy
clip, secure with a hiking pole in either hand. That night in the church
I was alone, high up on a mountain trail strewn with sharp boulders,
without hiking poles to steady me. Shaky, insecure, I couldn't see far
enough ahead to know where my next footfall would land.

Over the next two or three minutes I blurted out, "It's my son.
His addiction is opiates. He's twenty-one. A kid and a man. A man
and a kid. He's in a treatment center, but on Tuesday he's going out
of state to continue his care away from home. I know he needs to do
this, but this is so hard. It's really hard. The thought of putting him
on a plane and not knowing when I will see him again is unbearable."

Dabbing a tissue to my eyes, I choked out, "But I know it's for the best."

When I looked up, I saw that the thin, pretty woman across the table from me was crying, too. She also had a son, a few years younger than Jacob, addicted to opiates, still living at home, refusing treatment, complicated by bipolar disease and other mental health problems. She was a single parent, her husband having skipped out years ago, unable to deal with it.

The meeting ended as many Al-Anon meetings do. Everyone stood in a circle, held hands, and said the Lord's Prayer. It closed with the simple phrase: "Keep coming back. It works if you work it!"

As people were leaving, Daisy swung her big body towards me and said, "C'mere, Mama. You need a hug!" And with that, her huge arms enfolded me in a big, squishy embrace.

Wiser people than I, those who have attended Al-Anon for years, say you come when you are ready, and it gives you what you need when you need it. As a newcomer, I was told to try at least six or seven meetings to decide what was best for me. Also, that Al-Anon is a spiritual, not a religious, program, and that the word "God" means "the God of your understanding."

I would meet Daisy again in other meetings, but her floppy, friendly hug that rainy Sunday evening at the conclusion of my first meeting meant I would return. Her warmth and big Mama cheerfulness was just what I needed to get me through the sorrowful days ahead and the stormy months that would follow.

Chapter 30

Departure Day

Have you ever worried about a day so much for so long that when it actually arrives you're curiously quite calm?

So it was the day Jacob left for Florida. It just happened to be December 7, and in my melodramatic moment, its significance wasn't lost on me. On that historic day the world changed in 1941 just as surely as mine did in 2010.

At the hospital, it turned out to be a far busier day than usual. Every three years the majority of hospitals in the United States undergo a rigorous credentialing survey by an independent, nonprofit organization formerly known as The Joint Commission on Accreditation of Healthcare Organizations, now simply The Joint Commission. The survey prompts a nervous time for anyone undergoing the three-day process. The stakes are high. A failing grade means the hospital is denied payment by the federal government's two healthcare programs, Medicare and Medicaid, the predominant revenue source for most institutions. At AAMC, nearly half of its funding comes from Medicare and Medicaid. The Joint Commission survey is the government's way of ensuring—or trying to ensure—that the nation's patients are receiving the best, highest-quality care according to strict, across-the-board standards. It's the Good Housekeeping Seal for healthcare, and every hospital works hard to earn it.

For AAMC this meant a state of continuous improvement. The survey is intended to uplift hospitals as much as to scrutinize them for failures. So when we knew a survey was due, near the end of our three-year period, every staff member was on heightened alert. Each day began with high anxiety. The Commission could show up unannounced at any time. A three-member panel, typically a nurse, physician, and former hospital administrator, would move in for a tense, three-day stay.

So naturally, on a day when I was anxious about Jacob's departure, the Commission arrived. Even though I had only a nominal role in the survey—the hard work fell to the clinical leaders and especially to nursing—it was ironic that now the people around me were as nervous as I was.

Lunch that day was with my board chair and a new businessman in town, someone who'd given large gifts to another charity. I didn't think this pleasant, loquacious guy would be a giver. He had lots of money, but no connection with the hospital—the capacity, but not the affinity. We might develop that over time, but time was ticking today. While the board chair chatted about the hospital's future, I kept glancing at my watch, restless to get out of there and get home. Dick had picked up Jacob at Pathways that morning. They were at the house doing laundry, sorting out his room, packing. I would have less than two hours with my son before he and Dick headed for the airport. I ached to be with them. Seconds became precious.

When I finally did arrive home, I got a wonderful surprise: my daughter greeted me. My journal records, "Her presence had to be sent from God." Actually, it was my husband's idea to invite Heidi over for the afternoon. He must have ordered her to "keep Mom busy." We had decided only Dick would take Jacob to the airport. The plan was for Heidi to take me back to her house for supper with her, Jon, and Josh, and Dick would join us there. The day held all the potential of erupting into torrents of anguish and fear—from both Jacob and me—as he faced a thousand-mile flight towards a future clouded with so many unknowns. Heidi was the foil we needed to maintain calm. She stayed by my side that entire afternoon and evening. Just her presence was so comforting. No loving daughter could have done more.

Although he never said so, Jacob also was happy to have her there. Somehow she lightened the tension. When Heidi was sixteen, she'd had a minor fling with alcohol, too many beers at a girlfriend's party. It made her sick, and from then on she never drank to excess. She wasn't an addict. Fifteen years older than Jacob, she matured rapidly after he was born, perhaps because I paid less attention to her. She even jokes with Jacob that she was glad he was born when he was because "you took the pressure off me!"

The two were as close as siblings fifteen years apart could be, but Jacob's addiction and the pain it caused Dick and me had driven a wedge between them. Heidi was frustrated with Jacob. She couldn't comprehend why someone who had everything would throw it all away for drugs. She didn't enjoy talking about him and never brought up his name unless I did, and I tried not to, knowing how he aggravated her. Too caught up in my own feelings of grief and loss, I didn't realize that she was feeling a huge loss, too.

That early December afternoon, while Dick busied himself downstairs, Heidi and I sat on the floor in Jacob's room, watching him decide which shirts or shorts or shoes to stuff into his duffle bags. The minutes passed in a surreal sweetness. Dreamlike, the three of us, so rarely together and "present" these past four years, savored the time. One of the most well-known AA and Al-Anon tenets is to live one day at a time. Sometimes, during moments of greatest stress, it can be one minute at a time. On this day, the serenity of each moment was so shocking and unexpected that it lit up the room like warm sunshine. I didn't want the afternoon to end. Heidi teased Jacob about what he was packing. Would he really need all his button-down polos? Jacob grinned back at her, quipped, "You can never have too many polos."

Then he opened up with us. Turning reflective, he said that Father Martin's had been a wonderful place, but too remote for him. He knew when he went there that he would use again and claimed he told me.

"But I'm not saying that now," he was quick to add. To my surprise, apparently Father Martin's had been good for him, and in a way I'd never expected.

"Yeah, I found God there," this thin, pale child of mine told me and his sister. "It was a very spiritual place. When I got to Pathways I thought I'd lost that. But then I got it back."

Heidi and I looked at each other. Surprised at Jacob's words, we liked what we were hearing. Jacob's mention of God and spirituality was new to her, too. Always sensitive, Jacob rarely voiced his feelings. He was far more like his father that way. But lately he'd begun to share snippets of conversations he'd had with counselors, insights gleaned from group meetings where he listened intently to other addicts, both what they said and didn't say. He particularly liked one pastoral counselor at Pathways who breezed in once a week to give the patients an hour of his wisdom. Nicknamed "the white wonder" for his shock of shoulder-length white hair pulled into a ponytail, Jay looked every bit a '60's icon. Years of graduate education in counseling and psychology, experience with addicts, and his own spiritual awakening lent him a religious, fatherly presence, like a preacher making rounds, a Moses down from the mountain, a man to heed. He only spoke once when Jacob was at Pathways, but he was the one person whose admonitions Jacob recited often. Jacob especially liked the phrase, "It doesn't matter where I go. I always meet myself there." And another, "Don't worry about yesterday. And tomorrow is too far away. Mind today, for it is tomorrow's history."

Thanks to people like Jay and Traci, and even his brief time at Father Martin's, tiny seedlings of sobriety had been planted within Jacob. I could see just the faintest glimmer of his awakening to a much larger world—one where he might find his place, if he could only latch on to something greater than drugs, greater than himself.

As he finished packing, a phone call came in from Tom, the man planning to meet him at the Palm Beach airport. The young guy who was supposed to fly down with Jacob had gone missing. Tom warned Jacob that if this kid showed up, "Stay away from him." Jacob didn't seem surprised, and I was reminded how tenuous the minutes and hours are in a recovering addict's life. Could we now call Jacob a "recovering" addict? At least he was trying to be, and with each rolled-up tee shirt and pair of socks, he was getting closer.

Suddenly, or so it seemed, it was time for the round of goodbyes. Just as he had when he left for treatment the first time, Jacob lay on the copper-colored carpet in the library, a lanky kid with coal-black hair, nuzzling the two sleeping greyhounds curled in their beds. The dogs never budged. He kissed their sweet heads, murmured into their downy ears. Standing up, he opened his arms wide and invited Heidi in. The two embraced. She mumbled something to him, and he whispered back, "I know." Dick, staying busy fiddling with the duffle bags and taking them out, announced it was time to go and told Jacob he'd meet him in the car. My husband was doing everything he could to move things along and lighten the load for the rest of his family.

Then Jacob opened his arms for me.

After a husband, what touch is more precious to a mother than a hug from her child? He held me long and tight. I breathed him in, shutting my eyes tight, wanting to remember this moment, hating that it had to end. He was so thin. Five foot eleven, less than 140 pounds, he locked his arms around me with a fierceness that belied his bony frame. Fresh from a fast shower, he smelled clean and woodsy. He could have been sixteen, asking for the car to take a girlfriend for movies, burgers and fries, and a giant milkshake. I reached up and kissed his cheek. He still hadn't let me go. When we finally stepped apart, he stood in front of me, checking my eyes to see if I was crying. We did this often after our hugs, checked each other's eyes to read emotions, to see how we really were doing. He shrugged his shoulders in the way he sometimes did to be sure we were both all right, as if to ask, "Everything okay? Anything else? Do I look okay? You all right?"—and he left.

My son walked out of the only home he'd ever known, armed with two duffle bags, a backpack, his laptop, and all the love twenty-one years of mothering could send with him.

Hours later, the phone rang.

"Tom wanted me to call you. I'm here."

Jacob's recovery had begun.

Now it was time to begin mine.

Chapter 31

Kindergarten

Every town has its seasons. In Annapolis, there are five. January to April is Maryland General Assembly session. April to June welcomes tourists. Summer means high temperatures and high humidity with sticky, ice-creamed streets teeming with even more tourists. October heralds Navy football and the United States Powerboat and Sailboat Shows. And then there is the holiday season.

December is as beautiful a month as any in Annapolis. Fresh, natural greens entwined with twinkling white lights adorn shops and historic homes. Carolers stroll cobblestone streets in period costumes, stores stay open until midnight three Thursdays in a row, and people generally are on their best behavior. For a few wintry weeks, we all shun naughty to be nice because Santa Claus is coming.

In this merriest of months I turned to Dick the evening after Jacob left, and asked, "Honey, would you consider going to an Al-Anon meeting with me?"

It was a heavily weighted question, and the word "consider" was intentional. I was only asking him to think about it. No commitment, yet. Just mull it over a bit and get back to me. The choice of the word came straight from my professional life. Instead of directly asking donors for a gift, it was better to ask them to "consider" making a gift. It allowed them to think about the request without undue pressure. They typically said yes, and frequently they later said "yes" to the gift as well.

So I tried it with my husband. I asked him to "consider" going with me because we did so much together, and because he might at least be curious about how Al-Anon worked, even intellectually. He'd listened patiently when I recounted parts of my first meeting. Even with Dick, I was careful to safeguard anonymity, so he knew no names of the people I'd met.

I really didn't expect him to say "yes." Imagining him sitting in a roomful of strangers, listening to painful, personal stories, let alone sharing ours, was so far removed from the Dick Hillman I knew that I couldn't fathom he would ever do it. He'd sooner stick needles into his eyes.

To my total amazement, he shrugged his shoulders and said, "Sure."

"Really, you'll go with me?"

"Yeah, why not?"

I was thrilled. This might be something we could do together, and who knew how it might help us. But I wanted to make my intention clear.

"Honey, thanks, that's really great. You can go the first time for me. After that, go only if it's for you."

Two nights later we drove to a church a few miles outside of Annapolis for Dick's first Al-Anon meeting, my second. I was on the path Al-Anon prescribed: try six to seven meetings to see which one was best for me. The meeting was held in a basement kindergarten absurdly cheerful with colorful, oversized alphabet letters dancing across the walls and child-made holiday ornaments on spindly wires dangling from the ceiling. Still anxious about being recognized, I'd just raised the stakes considerably higher with a well-known Annapolitan by my side. So, of course, the instant we entered the classroom at least three people stood up to greet us. One was a longtime friend of ours, someone whom Dick had known when he worked for the state. Pete tried hard to suppress his surprise at seeing us. He told us right away that he was there because of his son. We sat next to him, feeling instant comfort that here was someone we knew, someone we could trust, who was going through the same sad scenario. I also was grateful for the presence of several men, in sharp contrast with the female-dominated meeting I'd been to Sunday night. At least thirty-five people filled the room, shuffling the small chairs to make a wide circle. I was struck by how we must have looked to an outsider: adults sitting in little kids' chairs, talking about very grown-up problems. The setting was apt. Especially for newcomers, it felt very much like the first day in kindergarten.

Dick and I sat very still and very quiet. I don't think we even re-crossed our legs the entire hour. The meeting began with the Serenity Prayer, the welcome readings, a round of introductions by first names only, and the anonymity phrase. Stan led off the discussion with the theme "Let it begin with me." A college professor, he spoke calmly and intelligently, mostly staring at the floor but occasionally making eye contact with his "students." He recounted his struggles with a wife of more than forty years and her repeated failures at sobriety. Mostly he was searching for how to reconcile his relationship with himself, how to be a better father to his two adult sons, and how he could find some meaning and maybe even some joy in his life.

"If there's to be any kind of recovery from how this disease has affected me," he said, "it has to begin with me."

Stan opened up the meeting to anyone who wanted to speak, and many did. A young woman with school-aged children talked about having to ask her husband to leave, and how her six-year-old daughter couldn't understand why mommy kicked daddy out of the house. An older man said he and his wife, a thin woman with downcast eyes who sat next to him, were "sick with fear and worry over our stepson," twenty-eight years old, "but I mean, what can we do? The kid's gonna use, right, if he wants to, and that's all there is to it. Like it says here"—he pointed to slogans in bright colors on small billboard signs, scattered like little prayers on the floor—"we didn't cause it, we can't control it, and we certainly can't cure it." His soft, gentle voice kept us captivated. We sat mesmerized by the truth of his words. "I guess all we can do is take care of ourselves. That's what we're here to learn, right? I mean, all I can really do is take care of *my* self. So I guess that's it. Thanks for listening."

A pretty woman wrapped in a dark green shawl talked about her daughter, a scholarship-winner, who was throwing it all away in a haze of heroin. She began to cry. Someone reached for a large box of tissues, and with fierce intent it got passed from one person to the next until it reached her lap. "She's beautiful; she's brilliant. Her father thinks it's just an adolescent thing and she'll get over it, but I know it's more than that. We offered her rehab, but she won't go. What do you do if they won't go? I really have no idea what to do next."

We sat hunched together on those kindergarten chairs, bearing the weight of our heavy burdens, giving comfort just by our presence. I wondered what Dick was thinking, but I got lost in the grief around me. This night there was the added, looming presence of Christmas. Holidays are an especially hard time for the addict and for those around him. It's hard enough to live through a normal day, let alone when every American family is gaily singing yuletide carols and ripping into shiny red and green packages. Holidays simply exacerbate the sadness and deep feelings of loss that families of addicts endure yearlong. What lay ahead in coming weeks was having to explain to children why a parent was missing, or to face accusations of other family members who didn't understand why you weren't doing more to control the loved one's drinking: "Can't you just get him to stop?"

One woman, someone who impressed me as being particularly well-grounded, talked of how she handled holidays with her family.

"So, as a recovering addict myself, I can see all the telltale signs with my son. He's only nineteen but I know he's drinking a lot at school, and why the university doesn't do more about drinking on campus is a whole 'nother story. We're supposed to go to my brother's house Christmas Eve, and I know there will be alcohol there. My whole family drinks. It's quite pervasive in my family. There's so little recognition of their disease. So I told my son, let's all go to the party. We really would like to see everyone, and we'll stay awhile and if it gets too bad, we'll just leave."

Christmas, of course, was not a concern for Dick and me. The more meaningful family holiday for us, aside from the Jewish holidays in early fall, was Thanksgiving. I'd already lived through that sadness while Jacob was at Pathways. Now I sat silently, crying inside for these men and women who shared so much pain. The walls of the tiny kindergarten could barely contain their grief. No room would be big enough. Maybe I could absorb some of the pain just by sitting there.

Near the end of the meeting, we "newcomers" were asked if we wanted to say anything. Dick and I glanced at each other. No, not this time.

The meeting ended with everyone standing in a circle, hands held, to recite the Lord's Prayer. It did strike Dick and me odd that in this "non-religious" environment a Christian prayer closed each meeting, but if it gave solace to the majority, we didn't care. As always, everyone held hands and shouted, "Keep coming back. It works if you work it!"

Afterwards, people formed small clusters of conversation and comfort as they reached for their coats. Pete turned to us and point-edly asked about Jacob. We discovered his son also lived in Florida, very close to ours. He'd been clean almost a year and had a good job with a chain restaurant. Pete said, "Jacob's a good boy. He's smart. He'll do okay. Just be patient. It takes time. It takes a lot of time. Consider how long they've been using."

Driving home, Dick and I exchanged thoughts about the meeting. He was glad he'd come, and he would go again the next Thursday. Neither of us could understand why women whose husbands were alcoholics didn't just divorce them. But that was easy for us to say. You can't divorce a child.

Several others at the meeting were like us, parents with sons or daughters who were addicts. Like Jacob, their "drug of choice" wasn't alcohol, but pills or other drugs. I also learned that Jacob's path had an all-too-common theme. Marijuana came first, then a preference for opiates, then prescription drugs, like OxyContin. When that got too expensive, heroin was cheaper and more available. At that time

I didn't know for sure if Jacob had used heroin, or anything else. It didn't matter. That was supposed to be behind us. He was presumably clean now, living in a sober house in Florida. One mother came up to me as we left the church to tell me her son also had gone to Florida to live in a sober house. My antennae went up, anxious about where this was going. Still fragile with Jacob gone less than two weeks, I wasn't sure this was a story I wanted to hear. The son stayed clean three months, used again, and was found nearly unconscious on a beach. After an emergency room visit, he ended up in jail. Now he was home again, living with his mother, and had been sober since August.

Stories of pain and sorrow, of relapse, recovery, redemption.

There was one other man there that night who recognized us immediately. He seemed to have a certain seniority within the group. Apparently, he'd known Dick long before his mayoral days nearly thirty years before. If Huck was stunned to see us there, he was polite and appropriate enough to hide his surprise. Tall, maybe six foot two, bald, tan—even in December—he had the ruddy, viral good looks of a Yul Brynner. A recovering alcoholic, he was well into his seventies but had the physique of a much younger man. It was no wonder women were attracted to him. In addition to his hard face and body, he exuded an almost spiritual calm, an inner peace that radiated from his steady, blue gaze. Sexy but reserved, Huck was the consummate Zen master, the longest-standing member of the group, the one who, when he spoke, made every ear strain to absorb all his wisdom. After we'd known each other a few months, I began calling him Yoda, and he'd grin at that. He was the Wise One, the father figure, patiently and gently guiding his flock of troubled souls. He almost never missed a meeting, and we missed him when he did.

Years later, after I'd learned more about Al-Anon and focused more on my recovery—and not Jacob's—Huck came up to me at the end of a meeting with this astonishing observation. "Lisa, you're doing well."

"Thanks, Huck. From you that's a real compliment. I'm not so sure, but I am trying."

"No, you really are. I can see the progress every week. You're so much better than when you first came here. Can't you see it for yourself?"

Well, I couldn't.

"Yes, you are," Huck reassured me. "And I'll tell you one more thing."

Letting his blue gaze garner my full attention, he pointed his index finger at me for emphasis. "I bet you are now the best parent you've ever been in your life."

Chapter 32

Whose Recovery Is This?

Like a patient whose leg cast is removed, the first few weeks Jacob was in Florida I had to learn how to move again. Dick and I had to adjust to the new reality that our son was no longer living in our house, let alone our town. There were the obvious changes, like scaling back the grocery shopping or doing laundry less often. In that way it reminded us of Jacob's first days at college, adjusting to just the two of us again. Much harder were the other changes. I had to retrain my senses not to listen for Jacob's footstep on the stairs late at night or the soft thud of his bedroom door closing, or glance at the clock at 3 a.m. and wonder why he wasn't home. Hour by hour I had no idea what he was doing. I simply had to trust that someone else did.

The hospital was a blessed distraction, and in December it consumed me. December always is a huge fundraising month, and at AAMC it's when many donors make their gifts and renew pledges. This year was even more frenetic. At the annual holiday donor gathering we planned to honor Chip as outgoing CEO after forty years with the hospital. Clandestinely, the board had approved naming a new educational institute for him. At the conclusion of the event we would unveil an elegant, four-by-six-foot, copper-lettered plaque bearing his name.

I thrived on planning such events and welcomed the diversion to my missing Jacob. Photographs of that day show a radiant woman dressed in a knock-out black suit, open white collar, pearl earrings, black stockings, high heels, perfect hair, the reddest lipstick. I was "on" and enjoying the moment at my professional best, greeting and tending to the hundreds of guests, nearly all of whom I knew by first names, making certain Tori got to meet each one. Staff members handed everyone a copy of a book encapsulating Chip's accomplishments. At the end of the luncheon, when the last guest had gone, my staff and I collapsed around one of the linen-covered tables to review the evening in excruciating detail. As always, I reminded them that it's the details and follow-through that matter.

At intense times like these, I would try to push aside thoughts of my son, newly and totally on his own, in a place I couldn't imagine. While I navigated a December whirlwind of holiday events and personal phone calls to thank donors, Jacob was starting a new life. He phoned home frequently.

The first few calls were brief, giving us only the essentials. He needed money for food. Okay, that was easy. We would send him a purchasing card for the grocery store near the sober house, as directed by his house manager. He was applying for jobs and asked a question about how to put a resumé together. He was going to an AA meeting every day. Eight guys lived in the house, and the house manager was tough, but an "okay" guy. What we got were short bites of what could only be a strange new world for our son. He sounded—fine? Just as when he lived at home, I found myself listening hard, straining to hear beyond what his words were telling me. Were they clear? Was he slurring his sentences, mumbling at the end, swallowing his thoughts in any kind of drug-induced fog?

My fingers gripped the receiver so hard, they nearly cramped. Blissfully, I realized he sounded clear and level-headed. He had a bad cold, but otherwise said he felt all right.

The calls were calm, always brief, and a bit tenuous. I couldn't picture where he was, and it was hard to keep him on the phone very long. He seemed distracted, as though other forces were pulling him away. But when I texted him that his dad had gone to his first Al-Anon meeting, he called back within seconds.

"Really?" he began without introduction. "Dad went to an Al-Anon meeting?"

"Yup," I said. "And he liked it, too, and says he's going back with me next week. I think we found a place we like, Jacob. There are people there you would know, or whose kids you might know."

He seemed amazed that his father had gone to an Al-Anon meeting, but not so much that I had. He sounded pleased, and I was glad. For some reason I wanted his approval. It was important to me that he thought our going was okay. Going to Al-Anon had arisen out of my despair, not his. I was grasping for something to save me from drowning, yet it felt like I might be trespassing on Jacob's territory. In the fragile, tormented way I thought about our lives then, I feared I might be intruding, stepping where I shouldn't, and that this could drive my son farther away. Drugs were his thing, not mine. Would he be angry if I learned more about them?

In classic addiction sickness, the total opposite was true. Jacob seemed pleased that Dick and I both had found Al-Anon. It began a new and stronger bond among the three of us and filled many of our early phone conversations.

Jacob's first few weeks in Florida were as strange for me as they must have been for him. I felt shaky, nervous, a new fragility in my life that wasn't there when he was home. Each day that passed was another tiny victory—assuming he really was clean, and I had no way of knowing that for sure. If I just focused on my work and kept him in my prayers, would that be enough to sustain him during this tenuous time? Was there anything that I could do in Annapolis that would keep him clean and sober in Delray Beach?

In all our counseling, no therapist had ever used the word "codependent." But in those early days of separation, there was a "codependence" in how we both grappled with this new way of living. Jacob and I were finally and fully leading separated lives. I had to accept that my son was no longer a child. He was twenty-one, a man by all legal standards, and supposedly capable of taking care of himself. If the experts were right, then addiction had arrested his maturation at age seventeen. So whatever life skills he hadn't learned by seventeen he'd have to acquire now.

I also had to acknowledge that he was starting his recovery, and I was starting mine. We were two travelers, each toting a bag packed with fears and anxieties about the future. All we had to do was place one foot in front of the other, take one step at a time. How strange, I thought much later, to be on the same path as my son, and at the same time. Lisa and Jacob, learning a new way to live, together, separately.

I tested two more Al-Anon meetings. Both met in churches, one small and one a large Saturday morning gathering where I recognized several people from the weeknight group. The slogans helped. "Think." "One day at a time." "Easy does it." Early on, I heard a phrase that practically smacked my brain: "Detach with love." When I first heard it in a mother's tearful tale about her adult, alcoholic daughter, I blinked twice and stared to be sure I'd heard her right. Recounting how she'd failed to help her daughter for years, after all the ER visits and the pre-dawn calls from police, this sorrowful woman whispered to the group, "Al-Anon tells me to detach with love. I need to do that, or I'm gonna go down along with her."

Her words lifted heavy weights off my shoulders. I even felt myself sit up straighter in the tiny, kindergarten chair. You mean, I can still love Jacob, but let him go? The phrase ricocheted in my head, a ping-pong ball banging some common sense into the chaos that was up there. Loving Jacob meant letting him go. It was as simple and as impossible as that.

The following week, I phoned Jacob after we returned from yet another local Christmas party. Most of these gatherings were meaningless to me, especially that year. The gaiety—green and red-draped mantelpieces, gilded trees so tall they brushed chandeliers—all seemed gaudy and glaring to me, a frivolity and wassail-swigging season I felt no part of. I only wanted to hear my son's voice.

There was noise in the background.

"Hi, Ma. We're having a party at the lodge"—his treatment center. "It's the largest sober party I've ever been to!"

He sounded as upbeat as I'd heard him in years. There was a lot to celebrate. He'd just gotten a job at Starbucks, he had a sponsor, and he was at a party where everyone was in recovery. It sounded like a throng.

"I have to walk to my job. It's two and a half miles, but it's okay. It's good exercise," he said. The previous day he'd walked to the interview through a terrible rainstorm and gotten soaked, but when he got back, after getting the job, "the sun came out. I'm making good progress, I guess," he finished.

Another Al-Anon phrase popped into my head: "Progress, not perfection." My son was making progress.

My journal that night recorded this:

> *Trust the recovery community. Trust the process.*
> *Trust that for today, at least, my son seems almost*
> *happy—that he sounds upbeat and healthy, and that*
> *he is doing everything he is supposed to do right now,*
> *for now, and that's all that matters. Tomorrow nite*
> *I will go to an Al-Anon meeting. I will stay with*
> *people who are battling the same worries and fears*
> *as I. They comfort me. And I want soon to be able to*
> *comfort them. These silent helpers.*

The year would close on further good news. On December 23, Jacob texted me a photo. In AA, addicts celebrate recovery milestones. They pick up "chips" at meetings to recognize the time they've stayed clean, and all in attendance applaud, sometimes really whooping it up, to congratulate and encourage their fellow member. Demonstrating how hard it can be to enter recovery, the first milestone is the very first day an addict stays clean. The next comes at one month. The text Jacob sent me was a photograph of his open palm. In it he was holding his thirty-day chip.

Chapter 33

Cleaning House

With Jacob away, Dick and I felt free, for the first time in years, to enjoy our lives. Spontaneity even returned. On New Year's Eve day we did something we love: we went hiking. Across the Severn River from Annapolis is an old naval installation once used for protecting the Annapolis harbor. Today the North Severn Naval Station holds a hidden treasure—miles of hiking trails that edge the high banks of the Severn River with wide vistas of Annapolis, the Naval Academy, and the Chesapeake Bay.

After we'd been walking for several miles, chattering the entire time as we often do alone together, my cell phone jangled. Cutting the cold, clear day, the call was from Dan, Jacob's new counselor in Florida. I could barely breathe again until he said he was delivering good news. Dan knew I was anxious and just wanted to let us know that Jacob was "doing all the right things." Apparently, he was attending meetings and Dan had "gotten reports" that Jacob was "sharing" as well.

"That's a very good sign," Dan told me, in case I'd missed that tiny, encouraging note.

Jacob's progress continued. At the end of January he was still living at the men's sober house in Delray Beach, attending a meeting every day, going to intensive outpatient therapy three times a week, meeting with Dan once a week, and walking the two-plus miles each way to his job as a barista at Starbucks, all without complaint. We talked weekly. The sound of his voice, clear and crisp like the cold hiking air, thrilled me. Even so, the connection often was bad and I found our conversations sometimes strained, partly because of the poor connection, but mostly because I wasn't sure of what to say. I was so afraid of saying the wrong thing—as if an errant word might cut our tenuous line, send my son tumbling into space, and shut the phone into the blackest silence. I knew he was approaching sixty days of sobriety, but he hadn't mentioned it. Was it my place to say something?

"Jacob," I ventured near the end of our call, "aren't you coming up on sixty days?"

"Yup, Sunday!" he shot back, so quickly that obviously it was on his mind, too.

"Well, don't get angry with what I'm about to say, and I'm not sure what the right thing to say is, but that's awesome. And I am proud of you."

"Why wouldn't that be the right thing to say?"

Two people who had been so close, a mother who had known her son's every move, every mood, now physically separated, learning to *be* separated, we were finding our way. The awkwardness was more mine than his. In that simple conversation, Jacob had begun to take on the role of teacher, the child guiding the parent, so long as the parent was open, willing to listen and hear and learn. After only a few weeks of going to Al-Anon, I was thankful for every speck of wisdom that came from those meetings. "Live and let live." "Allow him the dignity to make his own mistakes." "Take it one day at a time." Al-Anon was bringing me closer to my son and not pushing him away as once I'd feared.

Meanwhile, the progress in our household also took one day at a time. One evening I came home from work to find a husband who could hardly contain his excitement. He called me upstairs to Jacob's room. Looking in from the doorway, I gasped. Jacob's sofa—the hulking, dark symbol of his isolation and long nights holed up in that room—was gone. Hideous images of his crushing pills into powder and burning powder into poison evaporated. With the simple removal of that couch, the dark, dank cave had been erased. The relief was physical: I could walk into the room and feel no panic. Together, we rearranged Jacob's bed, chest of drawers, bookshelf, and desk and built it all back into a bedroom. What a pure act of love this was from my husband. Unknown to me, Heidi had put the sofa on craigslist, but after three weeks of no-takers, Dick simply had it carted away. No more hiding place. I could breathe again in my own home.

Like Jacob, our family was taking action to free itself from the effects of addiction. As my journal noted:

We are freer . . . casting away the darkness and hiding
and fear and loss of control of the disease. We'll face it now,
whatever it is, and we'll deal with it in the open.

At the end of January Dick and I planned a three-day weekend to see Jacob. We stayed with close friends from Annapolis who now lived within a half hour's drive from Delray Beach. They'd known Jacob since he was a baby, cuddled him at his bris, and were pulling for him now. I could barely wait for the plane's wheels to touch ground. We drove straight into Delray and headed for Starbucks, texting en route so Jacob knew to expect us.

Imagine someone you see every day. It could be your spouse, your child, a cherished friend or co-worker. You love this person more than life, more than sunshine on a piercing blue day, or the giggles of small children, the swell of fans uproarious over a team win, a lobster dinner, the contract won, or whatever it is that makes you smile and rejoice that you are alive. Then, remove this person; take him a thousand miles away for days, a week, months. Now walk into a bustling, aromatic coffee shop in South Florida. Your eyes adjust to the dim light. And there, emerging from behind the high counter, there he is.

At first, I didn't recognize Jacob. This tall, clean-looking, striking young man walking towards me with the enormous grin looked—the word lit up my brain—healthy. Within seconds he threw his arms around me. Enfolded in his warm, strong hug, I felt overwhelming relief just to be with him. Time stopped. Tears filled my eyes. Two months had felt like two years. Here was proof that coming to Florida was the right decision for him. He already seemed older, steadier, more self-assured, like he knew where he was and what he had to do. With relative ease he introduced Dick and me to co-workers and to a man named "Bob" who also was in recovery. Bob was much older, closer to our age, gregarious and self-sufficient, a man who took young men like Jacob under his wing to encourage their sobriety. He was one of many such people we met that weekend.

We soon discovered that Delray was a hotbed for recovery. As we strolled with Jacob on Atlantic Avenue, the town's main street, past dress shops and restaurants, he'd nod to young men and women and later explain he knew them from AA meetings or his treatment center. Many frequented Starbucks, which itself seemed both a meeting place and recovery central for men and women of all ages and all stages of recovery. The town pulsed with a certain electric energy, like an underground current that ran from one end of the avenue to the other, capable of blowing at any point. Except for tourists and retired seniors from up north, Delray vibrated with young adults in recovery, many who would make it clean through that day, and some who wouldn't. Recovery also meant relapse, and there was plenty of that in Delray, too.

That weekend we met Jacob's disease close-up. He wasn't shy about telling us about new friends, their stories, and their "clean" time. He already admired men who had many years of sobriety, like Bob, or Dean, his sponsor, who'd been clean more than forty years. We met his house manager, a tough, thick-necked man who shook our hands formally and acknowledged that Jacob was doing what he was supposed to do. The house wasn't in the best neighborhood, and I tried to ignore how sparsely furnished it was inside. But it seemed neat and clean, and after all, this was where Jacob's life had led him. We sensed the cold, harsh reality of keeping a houseful of men minding the rules, day in and out. At his workplace Jacob's supervisor told us "what a great guy Jacob is" and "you should be very proud of him." Over supper at a trendy sports bar, Jacob showed us his sixty-day chip.

He talked about the near future: he wanted to buy a car, find an apartment, and move out of the sober house. Even though this all felt a bit too soon, I held my thoughts, just so happy at the change in him and how he was thinking of the future for the first time in years.

One of the highlights of our weekend together, odd though it seems, was going to AA meetings with him. In Delray, meetings are so commonplace there's even a designated building for them called Crossroads. A single-story, nondescript structure alongside railroad tracks, Crossroads offers meetings all day, every day. Depending on the type of meeting, the crowd tends to look a little rough—lots of earrings and tattoos, men in jeans and black leather, girls in short skirts sporting streaks of fuchsia-colored hair. Seated next to my son, given a window on this anonymous world, I watched how both men and women hugged and high-fived one another. They sat next to those they knew, shook hands with some of the much older guys, settled down in the folding chairs for the formal start of the meeting, and it struck me: they're all the same. They may look tougher or rougher than Jacob, but they all have this very same thing in common. They're all addicts, like my son.

It makes me shudder today to recall how I first viewed that scene. It forced me to say the words to myself: my son is an addict. It felt so surreal. Staring at this diverse group of addicts in this well-worn building in South Florida, I had to work hard to put aside my normal, all-too-quick assessment of people. My pattern of being judgmental and quick to criticize or to size someone up just wouldn't work here, not if I was going to attend these meetings with the son I loved so much. If I was going to be the mother Jacob needed, I had to shed any illusions about where he was and scrub some very bad habits. Although open and caring, I could be harsh and demanding at times, with high expectations of how others should look or act. It hit me: sorry, that won't do here. Welcome to your new world of drug addiction, recovery, and relapse. Here you get the whole scene played out for you as you sit with your son in this first of many AA meetings you will attend with him—*if* you are invited.

Others told me later how flattered I should be, that it's a sign of love that your son invites you to meetings with him. So I told myself, if you are going to attend, keep your mouth shut, your eyes and ears and heart open. Remember what you are learning at Al-Anon. Listen. Learn. If you really love your son, you owe him that. Understand this now: the people around you, no matter how they look, are living through the same hell Jacob is.

The room slowly filled with more than a hundred people of all ages, the majority in their twenties and thirties, but several in their fifties and sixties, more men than women, all dressed very casually— jeans and tee shirts, an occasional coat and tie. My God, I thought, all these people with addictions. In our "normal" busy workaday lives, how would any of us know that this goes on in communities everywhere?

Just before the meeting began, a line of expressionless adolescents streamed in and huddled on the floor at one side of the room, their backs against the wall. Jacob leaned over to me and explained, "treatment center kids." I kept thinking this wasn't quite real and feeling that somehow we were "better" than this. What were we doing here? Jacob comes from a solid family who loves him. The very fact that his parents were here with him now was proof of that. Did these other kids have families, too?

Loving Jacob, I savored the minutes sitting next to him. The comforting routine of the AA format took hold. We said the Serenity Prayer, welcomed newcomers, and the leader began. I kept checking my judgment-meter and forcing it down. For the most part, everyone was paying attention to the speaker, taking in his story of addiction and recovery: a lawyer extolling how good his life was today after twenty-five years of sobriety, and how he keeps coming back to AA to sustain it. Each person there had the same disease as my son, comrades in their battle against an illness that many still do not recognize or, like me, for so many years tried to deny.

I eyed the treatment center kids, the group that was paying the least attention. Several looked bored or just adrift. One girl braided the hair of the girl in front of her. A young man with thick dreadlocks rested his head on his knees. So lost. So young. They made me feel very sad. What a waste. My throat choked up with images of what their lives must have been like before getting here. Each of these kids has a mother too, I thought. Each was someone's son or daughter.

Several of those in the room had become close friends and mentors to Jacob. We sat down with them at an after-meeting brunch at a favorite local diner. Dean, Jacob's sponsor, was there, as well as others who soon came alive through personal stories swapped over scrambled eggs, pancakes, piles of toast, and lots of coffee. One diminutive Asian woman with clear, dark eyes and sleek, long black hair told me, "You have a great boy there. You should be very proud of him."

I heard that often that three-day weekend, words that were so reassuring. They meant that others saw in Jacob what I always knew, that here was someone who was good, sweet, and smart, capable of being so much more.

We attended three meetings with Jacob, including one he'd cautioned us would be quite different. The group leader began the session, held in a small classroom in a Presbyterian church, by dimming the lights and announcing a fifteen-minute meditation. At the end, the lights remained lowered during the sharing. After several people spoke, to my amazement Jacob looked up. The leader called on him.

"Hello, my name is Jacob, and I'm an alcoholic and an addict," he said softly. It was the first time I'd heard him pronounce his addiction aloud. Dick and I cringed, but in the same moment I was immensely proud of him and wondered where he'd found the courage to say this. At these meetings? At Crossroads? In other church classrooms like this one?

After Jacob told a little of his story, he said, "I'm very grateful for all of you here. And I'm grateful that my parents came down to visit me. It feels peaceful and happy with them here, not like some of the times at home. I'll keep coming back."

The group leader smiled at us and nodded. Jack turned and gave us a big smile. I blinked back tears. Dick and I had to come to Florida to an AA meeting, of all places we'd never imagined we would be in our lives, to hear our son speak for the first time in years with honesty and emotion. In front of strangers and before a community of recovering addicts, we found our son again.

That afternoon we did what any parents might do visiting a son in a faraway town: shopped at the posh Boca Raton mall and went to see a movie, loving the time together, thirsting for this normalcy, gladly interspersing it with AA meetings to keep us all sane and grounded. One of the highlights of the weekend was dinner at an oceanside Italian restaurant with our friends and Dean. Jacob wanted to invite him, and I was eager to learn more about this man who was my son's sponsor. Of slight build, in his sixties, and with the vaguest hint of an Italian accent, Dean had lost nearly everything before he found sobriety—his career, wife, kids. He now lived in Delray and devoted his life to helping young people like Jacob achieve sobriety. After dinner, we wandered back up Atlantic Avenue and stopped at a hotel porch where a guitarist had drawn a small crowd. Jacob left us to bring back coffee. I had Dean all to myself for a few minutes.

Whether it was the journalist or the mother in me that took over, I tried hard not to assault him with too many questions. The weekend had aroused my curiosity and interest not only in addiction in general, but also in how Jacob was doing, specifically. I wanted reassurance. I wanted someone to say Jacob would be fine, that he was "cured" or at least on his way, and that I could put my worries aside for now, forever. Surely his sponsor would be the best person to ask.

Sitting next to Dean on the hotel porch, I asked him, "What is the difference between the kids who make it and those who don't?"

"The kids who make it apply themselves," Dean told me, "and work the steps." He added, "Jacob is not like the rest. He's a cut above. His speech, the way he talks...he's smart, your son. He digs deep.

Sometimes he even challenges me."

Before I could get too smug, Dean lowered his voice and said, "But there is a difference between alcohol and drugs. With the old guys, it's alcohol. With the younger ones, it's drugs. I worry about the kids with drugs. And Jacob is so young. Sometimes they just need to be kicked in the butt before they get better."

On Sunday afternoon Dick and I headed home to Maryland. We both were glad to have had three sunlit days with a healthy son who was just beginning to understand himself and the changes he had to make. But I couldn't shake Dean's words. Despite the relief at seeing Jacob healthy for the first time in years, and all the friends we'd met and the laughter and the painfully sweet words at the AA meetings that lingered like kisses, I worried. Dean had cautioned that the "younger" ones sometimes need to fall before they get better. I couldn't know if Jacob had already had that "kick in the butt" or whether it was still to come.

Chapter 34

The Second Thirty-Day Chip

It didn't take long. On Sunday night, April 10, his twenty-second birthday, Jacob phoned home.

"Mom, there's something I need to tell you." Dick was on one line, I on another, both of us tensed. "I'm holding a thirty-day chip."

He didn't share details, and it didn't matter. The raw fact affronted us: he'd used. His new clean date was now March 1. He was vague about the date and didn't explain what had happened or why, and we didn't ask. We didn't want to know. It was all too disheartening. I felt ill, sick that we were sliding backwards. But the four months in Al-Anon helped. This was Jacob's issue, not mine. The wisdom of other parents I'd met in meetings kicked in, and I found myself responding calmly, grateful that the right words came to me.

"Jacob, I am so sorry. Take care of yourself. I love you."

His reaction was quick and strong. "Yes, that's what I needed to hear. Thank you."

My journal for that night records a prayer:

22 years old. May he live to be healthy at 23. Please
God. I do believe and have to believe he will—that he
will cure himself—and have a good and healthy life. I
believe that. And that keeps me strong.

As I always do when a heavy burden hits me, I made it a mini-project. Jacob had relapsed, again. It sounded like a "small" one, and it sounded like he'd picked himself up and was back on track, but what did this mean? I needed to talk about it with someone other than Dick. I needed some expert advice to understand this and get myself moving through the workweek. Fortunately, first thing Monday morning I ran into Shirley Knelly, president of Pathways, and our substance-abuse guru.

"Are you kidding? That's great!" Shirley reacted when I told her about Jacob's call. I must have looked totally dumbfounded. How could Jacob's using again possibly be great?

She followed up quickly, "Do you know how important that is? Lisa, he didn't have to tell you that. That means he's really *getting* recovery. He's thinking of how his actions affect others. He's getting it." She closed the conversation with, "That's *very* good news."

Like a dog that comes inside from the rain, I tried shaking the muddy wetness out of my head. Just when you think you've learned something through AA and Al-Anon, you realize how little you know. When I mulled it over throughout the day, Shirley's reaction made sense. Jacob was being honest with himself and sharing that with us.

As happened repeatedly during the years of Jacob's active addiction, work was my refuge. That April, while Jacob struggled every day to pull himself out of addiction and into recovery, I fought each day to meet looming deadlines in one of the most intense, stressful times of my career.

The $44 million campaign was scheduled to conclude the end of April with a grand ribbon-cutting for the new hospital pavilion. Going into that month's board meeting, just days before the big event, we were still several hundred thousand dollars short of the goal. In my thirty years with the hospital, twenty-three as head of the Foundation, and four capital campaigns, I'd never finished a campaign short of goal. The thought was unacceptable not only to me, but also to my staff. They looked to me to solve this one.

The board meeting held the key. When I gave a campaign update and stated we were a few hundred thousand dollars shy of goal, the board members understood: with the celebration three days away, it was up to them to ensure our success. One of the members, a former social worker with a strong interest in pediatrics, was divorced with no children. She loved the new pediatric emergency suite. Right after the meeting and a tour of the suite she pledged an additional six-figure gift that not only would help sick children, but ensured the campaign would exceed its goal.

The opening itself was a huge success. Prior to the public open house, the invitation-only, ribbon-cutting ceremony allowed major contributors to see the results of their generosity first. Staff beamed with pride at what technology, teamwork, planning, and philanthropy had achieved. By the end of the three days, which included a Saturday afternoon for children to visit the new pediatric emergency department, complete with Elmo, more than three thousand people had toured the new eight-story pavilion. The weekend ended with a huge, collective sigh of relief. Everything had gone off perfectly. The building was turned back to the clinical staff, scrubbed, scoured and disinfected, and ready to receive patients the following week.

With the grand opening behind us, it was time for my staff to take some time off. That included their boss. For nearly a year, while I envisioned the ribbon-cutting and tours of the new hospital building, Dick and I were planning a very different kind of tour. Ever since our German exchange student, Martin, had returned to his home in Frankfurt, we had stayed close with his parents. Sigi and Gertrude shared many of our interests, including a passion for hiking. Four years before, we'd hiked with them through the Bavarian Alps. This time, Dick proposed one of the world's greatest excursions: the Tour du Mont Blanc, a seven-day trek up and down the ten-thousand-foot trails around the base of Mont Blanc, traversing Italy, Switzerland, and France. For Dick and me, it was a trip of dreams.

Sigi and Gertrude planned the journey with meticulous attention to every detail. As we climbed those glorious mountains each morning, I knew we were fueling memories for a lifetime: vistas of snow-capped peaks, herds of rushing sheep in the meadows, warm, wine-laced casseroles in roadside hostels, and the laughter of friends out for a European jaunt, weary in the evening, yet excited and ready for adventure each morning. As if that weren't enough, Dick and I bookended the trip with visits to Florence and Venice and a stopover in Paris to celebrate our forty-third wedding anniversary.

To assuage any guilt about such a glamorous excursion, I regarded it as a reward for the successful campaign. And with Heidi and her family in Maryland and Jacob in Florida, it felt safe to go. Despite a five-thousand-mile separation, thoughts of Jacob were never far. Frequently, Gertrude and I fell in together, walking at the same steady pace up the steep climbs. As a teacher she understood how young men can hit rough patches and face their own mountains growing up. While I never discussed Jacob's addiction with her, I think she knew and tried in her intuitive, intelligent way to comfort me and give me hope as we trudged, one foot at a time, up those high mountain trails.

Midway through the trip, we rested in the tiny Italian village of Planpincieux, and I phoned Heidi. Jacob wasn't answering my calls, and I wondered what she knew. She was vague. They'd spoken, everything was fine. Heidi was monitoring a situation at home for us. Larry, our fourteen-year-old fawn greyhound, was failing, and the dog sitter was worried. Heidi promised she'd stay on top of this for us. I hung up proud that my daughter was such a mature, capable young woman, but the call did nothing to alleviate worry over her brother.

When I finally did connect with Jacob—Heidi must have told him we were concerned—the conversation only fanned my growing sense of alarm. The connection was poor, and Jacob sounded sleepy. What I got were monosyllables. I blamed it on the time difference, Jacob's work schedule, and the poor line. I had to trek up the next hill, so there was no time to wallow in worry.

That time came once we got home. I could barely wait to clear Customs and get into the taxi back to Annapolis before phoning him. He answered with the same dull, monosyllabic tone that I knew too well. The deadpan voice swelled my worry. Waves of nausea gripped me and I froze, the flush of our journey fading like sunshine before a storm.

Once home, the roller coaster ride resumed. One minute Jacob sounded fine, the next, totally distant. My anxieties rose and fell with the sound of his voice. During one conversation he sounded clear, telling me his Starbucks was constantly busy despite the expected summer downturn. In April he had moved out of the sober house and into an apartment with a young man he'd met in rehab. His roommate was okay, and he got a kick out of walking the roommate's dog around their apartment complex. The next time, Jacob sounded off about the roommate and gave me single-word answers to questions, a one-sided conversation.

The days grew sad. We had to put our beloved greyhound to sleep. Jacob and Heidi knew how the sleek, fawn-colored ex-racer with doe-like eyes filled emptiness in the house, especially with both of them gone. We still had Topper, a stunning, black and white greyhound whose needle-nose and muscular body went into overdrive greeting us, even if we were gone only minutes. Greyhounds stirred life into our household. They'd become as much a part of our lives as our children. Heidi and Jacob often quipped that we loved the dogs more.

Summer bore down on Annapolis, its steamy heat wilting tourists and sizzling sailboats in the harbor. It was time to get away with the family. Rehoboth had become our family spot, and I was looking forward to all of us being together. Then Jacob called.

"Ma, I need to tell you something," he began. "First, you need to know I've been clean forty-eight hours." He went on to explain he'd been drinking something at a local hangout off the main street in Delray, a drink called "kava" that was popular with addicts. It wasn't alcoholic, but something about it was addictive. A lot of kids got hooked again after using it. In Jacob's case it too easily had started the quick slide into pills and then . . .

"But I pulled myself away from it, and I'm clean now," he finished.

Despite months of Al-Anon, I blurted out, "Oh, Jacob, no."

"Ma, I'm an addict. This happens!" he shot back. He said he'd borrowed money from someone at work and needed to repay the loan. It was more money than he had, and he was unsure what to do. He was behind on his rent. Dick and I were listening together to lines we'd all heard before. It was disappointing and disheartening, one more low point in Jacob's recovery. We looked at each other; Dick waited for me to respond.

"Jacob, thank you for being honest and telling us all this. Seriously. Being honest is a big step, and we appreciate that, and we love you." I sighed. This was so hard. "Here's what we'll do. We will send a rent check directly to your roommate, and you can pay us back. But, Jacob, no, we will not help you with the loan. That one's on you."

"Okay, Ma, thanks. That's really helpful."

"Jacob, one more thing." I reached deep inside my gut, calling up every snippet of wisdom Al-Anon had given me. "I want you to hear me carefully. If you are using," I paused, then pronounced each word clearly and slowly, "I don't want you coming to the beach."

Now it was his turn to pause. He understood. In as calm and steady a voice as I've ever heard from him, he said, "You will have your son at the beach."

Chapter 35

The Return of Fear

Summers at the beach held such precious memories. As a child, I always was happy there, and I wanted to give my own family these memories.

With two close friends, Dick and I rented a house in Rehoboth just a few doors from the ocean. Heidi, Jon, and Josh joined us for the week, along with Topper, our greyhound, and Mister, our friends' black lab. The house welcomed us with large bedrooms and a screened-in porch that soon became beach central for towels, flip flops, books, beach toys, and leftover pizza.

Into this happy chaos my son arrived midweek. We picked him up at the Philadelphia airport with the daughter of friends from Maine, where Jacob had visited for a few days. We'd known Anna from birth. Now a college freshman, she and Jacob had shared personal struggles and were naturally drawn together. Anna was strikingly beautiful, a turn-your-head young girl just beginning to blossom into a mature, self-confident woman. She had plans to spend an exchange year in China and wowed us all with her adeptness at the language.

It had been six months since I'd seen Jacob, the longest ever. Dick pulled the car up to the airport curb, and I texted, trying to find him. Suddenly, I spotted a tall, tan young man wearing navy shorts and an open-collared shirt alongside a lanky, show-stopping young woman with thick black hair, a short skirt, and a ruffled blouse. I hardly recognized them. They could have been actors posing for a photo shoot; the pair took my breath away. Within seconds, I threw my arms around Jacob and hugged Anna and told them how beautiful they both were. Jacob's grin was even wider than my own. They laughed at my exuberance and hugged me again, this stunning young couple, so healthy and full of promise, aglow with happiness. The memory of how they looked standing there that day, lighting up the dark tunnel of the airport pick-up area, lifts my heart still. It was the happiest I'd seen Jacob, maybe ever.

Their glow gilds the memories of that week as surely as sand seeps into suitcases and finds its way home. Jacob and Anna spent most of their time with all of us. Theirs was an odd and special relationship, born of childhood and adolescent adversity, a shared, personal, misfired chemistry that sent their brains spiraling off-kilter. At this rare moment in their lives, they could comfort one another. I was grateful to this gorgeous young woman just for her presence in my son's life. It wasn't complicated. I loved people who loved Jacob, and he was surrounded by them at Rehoboth. There wasn't a person in that household who wasn't rooting for him. He took late afternoon walks to the local Starbucks with our friend, Dave, whom Jacob liked and trusted. With no children of his own, Dave always treated Jacob like an adult and drew him into his banter with humor and sarcasm. Jacob spent quiet hours with Heidi, the two of them taking off down the boardwalk for fries or sodas, two siblings on the lam. He dug deep holes in the sand with Josh and sat quietly next to Anna on the beach or the screened-in front porch, our perch on the world.

The postcard-perfect week was interrupted only once: Heidi, Dick, Anna, and I joined Jacob for an AA meeting. As it turns out, there's an underbelly to Rehoboth just as there is in many seaside towns, and it shows itself in church basements as the sun rises and sets. Jacob didn't ask, but we offered to attend with him. It was a small meeting, some twenty people, mostly older men and women, but there were several young people like Jacob. We sat a few rows behind him, and when it came time to introduce ourselves, first names only, we each mentioned we were there for Jacob. The leader welcomed us and acknowledged Jacob especially because of his family's support. Jacob glanced back at us and flashed that stunning grin. We all beamed back, so glad we'd come. In future years, attending AA meetings with Jacob would become a beach-week staple. They were as reaffirming for us as they were lifesaving for Jacob.

At week's end we hugged Anna goodbye, and she flew home to Maine. A few hours later I was saying goodbye to Jacob. By now he and I were accustomed to the pattern of his visits and the rise and fall of emotions they elicited: pure elation on arrival, depression, if not despair, at departure. He'd had a great week, proven to all of us he could be drug-free, healthy, happy, and a genuine member of the family. He'd given us just a taste of what "normal" felt like, and I wanted more.

I didn't have to wait long. At the end of September I flew down to Delray for my birthday, wanting to spend it with Jacob. Since spring and fall were Dick's busiest seasons as a colonial tour guide for an Annapolis company, he stayed behind to work and keep Topper company. I would have Jacob all to myself.

Once more, my son looked tan and healthy, but without the brilliant shine of a gorgeous girl by his side. Jacob's life revolved around his battle against addiction and for now, as much as he craved it, he knew to shun serious relationships. Most of the girls he met also were in recovery, and every counselor and sponsor cautioned him to be careful. Given my son's propensity for falling in love, it was just safer to avoid serious dating.

He focused, instead, on work. Jacob had always liked making money. In the years of his heavy addiction, money meant freedom to buy drugs. But in Delray, money paid for basic support because Dick and I were no longer funding him. We'd made that point clear when he first boarded the plane for Florida. He was on his own financially. If he wanted to return to school, or had medical bills, that we'd do. But no more handing over cash directly to him. So it was no surprise that one of the first things we did that weekend was to visit a little cheesesteak joint across the street from Starbucks, where he applied for a second job. He knew the guys there, and they seemed eager for his help. Picking up extra work was easy for Jacob. The tourist trade in Delray fed the hospitality industry and, fortunately, it was an industry willing to help recovering addicts.

Jacob seemed to know every restaurant in town and which were open to giving addicts a chance. As we walked down Atlantic Avenue, he'd nod and tell me who that guy was or what was up with that gaggle of youngsters clustered around the corner. Starbucks remained a recovery anchor. All manner of humankind wandered through there, mostly men, many just seeking companionship, like the young guy with thick curly hair and a lopsided grin who sat outside holding a hand-written sign that read "Free hugs." Many were young adults Jacob met at meetings. There also were older men with years of sobriety who hovered around the younger guys like guardian angels, doing their best to encourage them, knowing how fragile sobriety can be in the young. As one of these men told me, "They just have to live it out until they're ready to stop."

Thanks to one such mentor, Bob, who had connections with a new, upscale hotel close to the beach, Jacob reserved a comfortable suite for me at a great price. I was touched by my son's thoughtfulness and planning. Wanting to maximize our time together, he moved in with me for the two nights.

The first morning I woke up feeling a quiet sense of peace, content to look at the bed next to mine and see my son sleeping soundly, safe and alive. Just his presence was so reassuring and affirming. I'd always liked waking up at home knowing my children were under the same roof, even when they were adults and slept over rarely. Some deep, instinctual, animal-like urge would nudge me awake, frantic to know where my cubs had wandered, only to discover, it's okay, Mama, they're all here, snuggled down deep in the den, whiskers and paws licked clean, eyes closed in baby bliss. Your family is safe. There is nothing to fear.

Fear was a constant companion when Jacob was using. It shadowed my every move, waiting to terrify me with another heart-stopping phone call like the time Jacob was so sick: "You need to get your son. Something is wrong." Where there is addiction, there is fear. It sickens both the user and those who love him. Fear is such an element of addiction that Al-Anon addresses it repeatedly. There's even a phrase that's recited frequently at meetings as a rejoinder to those who are suffering: "Courage is fear that has said its prayers."

I wanted to be done with fear. After our sweet week in Rehoboth that summer, I wanted more of the "normal." We'd had the Jacob we loved that week, and I looked again for that guy, the one who held his shoulders back, laughed at our jokes, and cracked his own. But fear hung on, a sticky furry thing I couldn't shake off, like a spider-web after a steamy summer shower, clinging, dissolving, only to rebuild again.

During that birthday weekend, my level of fear rose or fell with each acquaintance I met. Early one morning we had breakfast with Dan, the counselor whom Jacob met when he first came to Florida. Dan seemed to know Jacob well and in ways I never would. He'd met Jacob in the treatment center and had stayed close to advise him, thanks to a small retainer I paid him, but also, it seemed, from a genuine interest in seeing this young man make it. Like everyone in Jacob's life, Dan, too, was in recovery. Clean more than twenty years, he was a large man with the self-assurance that comes from years of winning the war against addiction. Jacob liked him and trusted his advice. So when Dan told me Jacob was doing well, my heart soared. "But," he added, "I don't want him to stagnate. He really needs to think about returning to school. Unless he pushes forward, he will roll backwards."

Everyone I met that weekend was in recovery or working in treatment. Meeting the people in Jacob's life over meals became routine, and why not? Mom was in town, footing the bill. But I didn't mind. I was with Jacob, and he was healthy and seemed as happy to be with me as I was with him. This same loving son corralled several friends, including his sponsor, his roommate, and Bob, for a birthday dinner at a main street Italian restaurant. I was delighted to be among a group of people who seemed so normal, laughed a lot, and loved Jacob. So it didn't strike me as odd when Jacob disappeared, saying he needed to go to the restroom, but took a little longer than necessary to get back. After dinner and my "surprise" birthday cake, Jacob, his roommate, Bob, and I walked down Atlantic Avenue. Jacob asked if he could go with the roommate for a quick stop at a nightspot across the street, and would I just hang with Bob for a few minutes? I tried to ignore the vague stirrings of fear and drown them in small talk with Bob. Bob kept glancing over his shoulder to the nightspot. I couldn't get him to engage on where the guys had gone or why. Jacob came back minutes later. I passed off his absence to something private he'd had to handle, not anything for my prying.

What happened the next day completely erased the previous evening's worry. Just as Jacob and I were heading for the beach, Dick phoned with jaw-dropping news: Topper was dead. Dick had found him collapsed in the front hallway, already gone. My husband was in shock, and so were we. Jacob held me, and we mourned for Topper and for ourselves. It had been only three months since we'd lost Larry, and we loved these dogs like children.

Jacob spent the rest of the day trying to console me. His tenderness and attentiveness were so genuine that they brushed aside the doubts over his brief disappearances during the weekend. He even took me to a special tea house for lunch, charmed the waitress, and asked her to bring me a selection of tea that was calming and comforting.

That afternoon, as my plane rose above the Florida coastline, I had time to ponder the long weekend. We had spent hours talking about everything, silly and serious, always coming back to the questions Jacob faced: his anxiety about making decisions, worries about making the wrong one, and what if he didn't like this second job? Or if he and his roommate didn't get along, and he'd have to find another place to live? Our conversations were never trivial. With Jacob, it was easy to go deep, and quickly. For nearly an hour in the hot sunshine outside Starbucks, we had talked about fear. Jacob had many fears, and right at the top was a fear of trying new things. By the time we finished talking, his optimism seemed to have returned. He said he would consider applying to college again and planned to ask Dan for help. He hugged me and thanked me for the weekend. He was thinking again about his future.

My final words to him that day were, "Jacob, take care of yourself. You are the only one who can." And he said, solemn as a prayer, "You're right, Mom. I know."

Gazing at the ocean far below, I prayed he did know. Charcoal clouds rolled in, stirring my sorrow at returning home to a house without Topper. I needed to console my husband and share this loss.

Shortly before we landed, while the skies blackened, something soft and unseen padded its way down the aisle. It was that old familiar shadow of fear, just beginning to creep up again, quickening my heart. I stared out the window, searching the clouds for answers. Where had Jacob gone when he left me? Was he still using? Was I only denying it, again, so eager to be done with all this? And worst of all, would I one day get that call that every parent of an addict fears the most?

Despite my anxiety, weeks later we learned that Jacob had made another major leap in his recovery. With Dan's help, he had applied to college. It was a huge step for him, but the four-year university took one glance at his poor academic record and rejected him. We were proud of him for trying and as disappointed as he was that he hadn't gotten accepted. I had no idea how this might affect him. He sounded depressed and mumbled something about possible courses at the community college. Rejection and loss were not new in Jacob's life, just part of the debris from years of drug use. If recovery mattered, I was learning, these were consequences he needed to face. Sobriety required him to confront the results of his actions, correct them where he could, and strive not to repeat them.

In December, he flew home for a weekend. Dick picked him up at the airport, and we met up at our weekly Al-Anon meeting. Entering the church basement straight from work, I spotted my son right away.

He stood out easily—a tall, tan, hip kid from South Florida, deep in conversation with Huck, our Yoda. As I walked over for a hug, Jacob saw me without turning his head. Flashing that brilliant smile I loved so much, he said to Huck, "And this one is my mom." During the meeting he sat between Dick and me, head down, taking it all in. I had difficulty focusing on the meeting, I was so happy to have my son, my "qualifier," there with me. It was Jacob's first Al-Anon meeting, and he was impressed with how the members shared and tried to keep the focus on themselves, not the addict.

"It's good you guys are going," he told us afterwards. "Huck's pretty cool. It's clear he's the leader, the main guy. It's all good."

We were glad Jacob had attended one of our regular meetings. Now he knew where we were each week, and what we were learning was adding a new dimension to our relationship. Al-Anon gave us an understanding of addiction we couldn't have gotten anywhere else, and our son seemed appreciative.

Jacob's brief visit home was filled with things our family loved to do at Christmastime: taking in an Annapolis Symphony Orchestra pops concert; walking downtown for coffee, bundled against the cold; engaging in long conversations over eggs and turkey bacon at the breakfast table; savoring dinner at his favorite steakhouse. The relative normalcy of Jacob's pre-holiday visit belied the danger that awaited him in Florida. If the signs of relapse were there, we totally missed them. How could we have known that everything we'd learned about addiction that first year Jacob was away was about to be tested?

Chapter 36

A Dangerous Liaison

A telephone seems like such an innocuous object. Essentially a small box, it's also a mini-miracle of modern technology. The telephone features prominently in addiction, and not just so that addicts can connect with suppliers. Al-Anon talks about the eight-hundred-pound phone. When you're deep in the despair addiction brings, it's hard to pick up the phone and call someone for help. But that's precisely what you are instructed to do. Addicts know this. They're told over and over again: call someone. Call your sponsor. That's why those in recovery so freely give out their phone numbers at meetings. A phone can save a life. In Al-Anon it's the same. When you need help, call another member. It can save your life, too.

But it's not the telephone as lifesaver that taunts me. It's the phone as a vehicle for bad news, a harbinger of sadness and worry that traces back to Jacob's birth: my brother calling just weeks before I learned of my pregnancy, telling me our mother's cancer had returned; Jacob's teacher calling to say, Lisa, your son is hanging out with the wrong crowd; a mother calling from North Carolina to alert me that Jacob had been arrested; Dick phoning me at work to say "Go get your son, something is wrong with him."

I should have known the call was coming. There was just the faintest whisper of fear haunting me again. Jacob had not said or done anything to cause it, but my ear, fine-tuned to the subtlest changes in my son's voice, registered the slightest minor key. Coupled with a certain restlessness when he was home, and the few times now when he didn't answer his phone right away, worry—like cicadas on a hot summer night—buzzed an unrelenting cacophony inside my head.

Was Jacob still using? If so, what? And how bad was it?

Just after Jacob returned to Florida, I had the rare opportunity to lunch with the son of a new friend I'd met through the hospital. Libby Cataldi, an internationally-known author and speaker, had come to the hospital that fall to celebrate Pathways' twentieth anniversary. She spoke to an audience of several hundred people along with her son, Jeff, about whom she wrote the book *Stay Close*. The two told their personal story about addiction and fielded unending questions from an audience all too eager to hear more. Libby and I grew close after that, and I consider myself fortunate to know her. She offered Jeff's help for Jacob if I ever needed it. That December, I did. I arranged to meet Jeff when he visited his mom during the holidays.

We met in a crowded Italian restaurant for lunch. For the record, Jeff is a doll. A slight man in his early thirties, he's trim and good-looking with an inner toughness—even though, like his mom, he looks like a wind gust off the bay could knock him over. Sitting across from him, staring into his clear eyes and clean face, I felt some hope. Maybe someday this could be my son. Likely that's why Libby so freely encouraged Jeff to meet with me. He offered insights that resonate today.

"Jacob is still young," Jeff began. "At twenty-two I was totally messed up, too. It's good that he stays in touch. It sounds like he doesn't lie to you. I would lie to get what I wanted. He seems in touch with who he is. These are all good signs."

I asked Jeff, "Could Jacob just glide along like this, live his life as a low-level addict, using, but not that much, working in a Starbucks? Could this be his life?"

"No, unlikely," he responded without hesitation. "With an addict something always happens. He'll get worse or lose his job, or something will happen. There are three places addicts wind up eventually: the hospital, jail, or they die."

Then my final question, "Will he have to get worse before he gets better?"

"Not necessarily, but maybe."

Forewarned by Jeff's admonition, it should have been no surprise when the call finally came. I'd been obsessed with Jacob since he returned to Florida, tracking him in my mind hourly every day, envisioning him at work or home, wondering where he was and with whom.

It was New Year's weekend. Dick and I were home, preparing for a quiet time together since we typically disliked the forced gaiety of the holiday—and certainly this year, with Jacob's condition so tenuous, we were in no mood for parties. The call was from Dan, Jacob's counselor and friend. Dan had alarmed me a few days earlier with a text saying he was "concerned for Jacob. He could be headed into full relapse." The text alone was enough to terrify us.

"Lisa," Dan began, "I have Jacob with me. We're in the car. He needs to go to detox. He's in pretty bad shape."

I was numb. Questions whirled in my brain, but I fought to stay calm. How does a parent respond to a call that your child is in "pretty bad shape?" If this were a car accident and a police officer calling, that I could comprehend. But my persistent denial over the depth of Jacob's drug habit, and the very real possibility that his addiction could kill him as surely as a car crash, thwarted my grasp of the life-saving scene playing out in Dan's car. What should I say to Dan or even ask him? And if *he* was calling and not Jacob, how bad was it? I had no idea then how perilously ill Jacob was. I heard Dan talking with my son and imagined them in Dan's car. Their voices were muffled, but I caught Jacob arguing that he couldn't go to detox because he was worried about losing his job. Dan persisted, and finally Jacob agreed to go, but only for "a few days." Dan turned the conversation back to me and said he needed my approval to admit Jacob. He had a place in mind, and someone would be calling me soon, but it was important to get Jacob there right now. There was an urgency that practically screamed through the line. He put Jacob on.

"Jacob, are you okay?" I asked, with no idea of how desperately sick he was, or if he could understand me.

"Yeah. No. Not really."

"So you'll go with Dan to this place?"

"Yeah, I guess. I think I need to."

Dan came back on the line and promised, again, that someone would phone me soon. We hung up, and Dick and I waited. There was nothing else we could do.

Less than an hour later, a call came from a man named Angelo, a representative of Recovery First in Ft. Lauderdale, the treatment center where Jacob was headed. Despite my fear and worry over Jacob's condition, I felt an instant distrust. My son was headed into his third treatment center, this time in a new city, and who could say this one would work? Who were these people who promised to take care of him and failed every time? Wasn't South Florida just a haven for addiction centers, people making a fast buck on the miseries of kids like mine? While my cynicism and mistrust may have been well-founded, this wasn't the time to deal with it. Assaulting the addiction treatment industry wasn't going to help my son, and Jacob really needed help, and fast. Little did I realize it, but my thinking was as sick and distorted as my son's. Much later I would learn that an addict can get clean anywhere, and that it's up to him. But detox had to come first, and doing that alone is never recommended. The same was true for me. Al-Anon would teach me to take care of myself, and that I didn't have to do that alone, either.

It was Angelo's job to penetrate my skepticism and anger. Despite—or perhaps because of—the real possibility that this time Jacob could have killed himself or someone else, I found myself growing increasingly angry that he had relapsed. Maybe the anger was my way of masking the real fear I couldn't face—that my son could have died, or still could. So I lashed out. Surely this was someone's fault, some failure of treatment. Someone who was paid to get him well had failed utterly. A rising fury simmered beneath our conversation. Angelo must have sensed it. Likely he'd heard it in many mothers' voices before mine. Patiently, he tried to convince me that Jacob needed to stay in treatment, that Recovery First was a good place for him and was where he needed to be. I almost felt sorry for Angelo. He sounded like a nice guy, but he was definitely a salesman, pushing another expensive rehab on a potential customer. He tried candor. He told me that he'd gotten clean "from this facility" five years ago. He hoped Jacob would stay the full 105 days "because that gives him the best chance at recovery." Jacob had never stayed that long in treatment, and the idea was appealing. At least he would be safe.

When Dan called me again, he told me that Jacob and a girl had been staying in some rented room in a shabby part of Delray. They were using together. This time it was heroin—needles and a sordid picture neither Dan nor Jacob ever thoroughly painted for me. I tried hard not to see it in my mind, but the images sickened me and made me gag. My son, living like that? And for how long? I was forced to face the fragility of Jacob's situation, where "using" might lead to a lethal overdose, all too common in addicts seeking only the next high. Jacob was living in an extremely dangerous world. If he stayed in treatment for an extended time, maybe he could get clean and clear enough in his head to remember who he was, that he came from a good family who loved him and wanted him well. It might be a fresh start. Still, there had been other fresh starts. How would I know that this one would work?

Once again, I was confronted with the issue of payment. Like the other treatment centers, this one wasn't cheap. If Jacob stayed the full ninety-days, at least, it would be thirty thousand dollars. But I knew we would pay it. Parents will pay anything to get their kid clean, and the treatment centers know that. What was different this time was Angelo's advice. He understood how a parent can get fed up with shelling out money without a guarantee. He was very clear about what I should tell my son.

"If we can convince Jacob to stay, and I think that would be best for him," Angelo instructed, "then you tell him this is the last time you will pay for rehab. The next time, if there is one, he will be on his own."

Years later, I was grateful that I hadn't seen Jacob that weekend. There's no doubt it would have terrified me to see him so sick. Our geographic separation spared Dick and me from many of the horrors other parents have faced with their sons and daughters, coming upon them in bedrooms or basements with bands tied around an arm or leg, a needle stuck in a vein. My reaction to such a hideous scene never got tested, and, again, I am exceedingly grateful for this. Except for the fear and constant worry, we have not had to carry the visual image of our son shooting up, smoking, or ingesting drugs. From the urgency in both Angelo's and Dan's voices, I knew that this time with Jacob was serious. This time, living in that shared room with the girl, he might well have killed her—or himself.

The year was winding down. With Jacob beyond my reach and the sickest I'd ever known, disappointment and worry threatened to take me down, too. That New Year's Eve, Dick and I wandered down Main Street. The night was cold and clear. White Christmas lights twinkled in front of storefronts. Throngs of visitors, locals, and kids home from college headed to City Dock for midnight fireworks to welcome in 2012. Against the rising tide of holiday cheer, I felt empty, emotionless. My son was in South Florida in a treatment center, while all around me was revelry and happy chaos. I felt cheated, angry, and sad. I was glad we had made no plans for New Year's. We huddled against each other as we forged through the crowds. Thanks to Al-Anon, although my heart ached, I stayed calm. We both did. The words of the program and the advice from people I'd met over the previous few years echoed in my head. Take it one day at a time. Let go and let God. Keep it simple. And most important of all, give up expectations, but never give up hope.

I didn't expect Jacob to stay in treatment. I tried hard not to expect anything from him. But after that first weekend, he agreed to stay longer. He called his manager at Starbucks, who was happy to hear where he was. She had seen all the signs and knew he was headed for disaster. She even told him that whenever he came back she'd have a job for him. With his job secure, Jacob relaxed. The first week melted into a second, and before he even knew how many days had passed, he agreed to give the full program a chance.

During Jacob's first week in treatment, his therapist asked me to write a letter telling him how his addiction had affected me. She asked me to read it to him over the phone during one of their sessions. I barely made it to the last lines before breaking down.

January 7, 2012

Dear Jacob,

Rena has asked me to send you this letter telling you how your addiction has affected me. As you know, I've kept an ongoing journal since that first telephone call from Mr. Greenfield nearly six years ago. But that's not what this letter is. Instead, it is supposed to focus on how your addiction affects me now. My fear is that this will hurt you more, add to the guilt you already may feel. But you asked me to "do this assignment."

So, here's how your addiction has affected me:

When the phone rings, I am afraid. Every time.

When you do not respond to a text, I worry until you do.

When I meet someone at a party or at the supermarket or at the hospital—anywhere—I find myself trying very hard to steer the conversation away from "How are your children?" or shorten it so as not to allow them to ask me, "How is your son?"

When they ask, I hope that I can make it through some unintelligible answer, something like he's ok, living in Florida, needed a change of pace, trying to figure out his life. And inevitably I get back, yeah, young people are like that . . . equally inane.

But if it is someone who is close—like our friends or family—I often cry.

When I meet someone with whom you went to high school, and I see them working or having fun with friends, or just living "normal" lives, I feel terribly sad. Not just for me. But for you—for all the fun and joy you are missing in your life. For what is missing in our lives together. And I feel sad for Heidi, who doesn't have the brother she wants.

When I hear all kinds of music, I think about you and how we love talking about music and listening together.

But mostly, your addiction makes me sad, worried, fearful, angry, and depressed. Lately, knowing how bad your addiction is, I even have felt physically ill—sick to my stomach—to think of what you have been doing to your body and how much physical and emotional harm you are bringing on yourself.

This past year—thanks to Al-Anon—your addiction has made me stronger, tougher. I have learned that addiction is a disease that affects the entire family. I have learned to say "no." I have learned you need to find your own way. So I guess that I should be grateful to you that your addiction has introduced me to a wonderful group of people, many of whom are going through what I am, and in some cases, perhaps worse (although lately I am not sure).

Al-Anon has been an incredible help. I read messages of hope from two books every day. I say the Serenity Prayer. I call someone when I am most worried or fearful. I go to a meeting, sometimes twice a week.

In the end, your addiction has taught me not to have any expectations, even though that is so very hard for me when it comes to you. Because I love the man you could be. And so, I have hope. Always, hope.

A few weeks later, Tori and I attended a healthcare conference in

Naples, Florida, with our respective board chairmen. I jumped at the opportunity to be with Tori and our top board members, but also because it meant I could see Jacob.

After picking up the rental car and buying bagel sandwiches for lunch, I arrived at the Recovery First lodge a little after 2 p.m. The place was hardly impressive—just a large, two-story, motel-looking place—but it was clean and carefully monitored. A staff member even gave me the once-over, making certain the bags I brought contained only lunch. Just three weeks into treatment, Jacob couldn't go off grounds, so we sat outside at a picnic table, munched on the bagels, and talked. He looked thin, but clear-eyed and reasonably healthy. Like his father, he now sported a neatly trimmed beard. It made him look older, and he seemed to like it. More interesting was the bandage over the inside of his left arm. Jacob told me it was only a small abscess, but it scared me. He shared more of the story. He'd been with a girl for months, and they'd been shooting up together. She finally told him that unless he stopped using the way he was, she would leave him. He preferred to use alone and had tried to inject a needle on his own. It made me sick to hear my son telling me all this, but I forced myself to be calm, knowing I should be thankful that he was opening up with me.

He unloaded a lot that day, and even though it made my stomach churn, I just sat and listened. He was worried over paying for treatment, so I assured him again that his father and I would cover it. Already he'd developed admiration for Angelo, who was encouraging him to stay. Mostly, we talked about what would come next. Return to Delray? Go into a halfway house there? His thoughts raced ahead. We had to remind each other, one day at a time. That afternoon, it was more like one minute at a time. The time flew. At 5:00 I had to hug him and wave goodbye from my car.

My journal that night notes:

Most of all today leaves me feeling hopeful. Not

> *that this is it for Jacob . . . but he is trying. And*
> *making choices that are good for him. For now. And*
> *that he is safe tonight.*

Not long afterwards, Angelo called to tell me Jacob wanted to stay for the full 105 days.

"Lisa, he's so smart. I just feel he will make it. He's a totally different kid than many of them we see down here." Angelo's words lit my heart. I wanted to believe him and felt the same, but did he tell every parent this?

"Thanks, Angelo. You know I won't enable him any longer. I'm just hoping for the best."

Angelo agreed. That's how they treated every patient, and he repeated that he had high hopes for Jacob. He lowered his voice, as though he were talking to himself, and gave me advice I follow to this day: "Support him. Tell him you're proud of him. I wish my mom could have been there for me."

Chapter 37

Moving On

Throughout Jacob's illness, there were many times when the challenges he faced mirrored challenges in my own life. That spring of 2012, he labored every hour of every day to stay clean. He did all the right things—attended meetings daily, obeyed the edicts of those he admired, like Angelo, and thought about the next phase of his recovery. Meanwhile, I faced changes at the hospital after the capital campaign—the need to redirect my team and to figure out the next phase of my own life.

Already the thought of retirement had seeped into conversations with Dick. He would turn seventy soon, and my sixty-fifth birthday was approaching. It didn't matter that I felt like forty and loved my job, or that Dick was still a runner, active on boards, and working part-time as a tour guide. We had to face the count of our years. There was so much we wanted to do together. It wouldn't happen if I were working full-time, because full-time for the hospital meant total commitment. It was the culture of the place. Those who worked in top leadership for Anne Arundel Medical Center gave our lives to it, by choice. We spent ten, twelve hours or more there each day, routinely attending nighttime meetings or events, and often giving up at least part of our weekends. Sometimes we laughed that we ate breakfast, lunch, and dinner at the hospital. We were always on call, emailing until 10:00 or 11:00 at night, then texting even later. It's how we lived, and we thrived on it.

That spring the Foundation board transitioned from a fast-paced, capital campaign to a new five-year plan to fund key programs. The goal was to support Tori's new vision, to continue raising millions of dollars each year, and to build on the Foundation's strong base that had been built over more than twenty-five years. What it needed most was a dose of fresh energy. With the plan in place, and Tori now completing her first year as CEO, maybe now was the right time for me to step aside.

Meanwhile, Jacob surprised me by staying in rehab and continuing to do all the right things. After an AA meeting, he found the courage to approach a young man a few years older who "had what I wanted" and who offered to be his sponsor and to take him through the twelve steps. Jacob entered the final phase of his treatment—outpatient treatment three nights a week—and suddenly faced free time. He was encouraged to find a job but learned that the door to Starbucks was closed.

"That's okay," said my son, "I need to go in a different direction now, anyway." He talked about working part-time and going to school part-time. It was the first time school had come up since his counselor, Dan, suggested it months ago.

His reaction surprised me. Instead of abject depression, he was handling the situation and examining his options. It was the first time in years I'd heard him turn adversity into opportunity, and it struck me that this time his rehab was different. Something was taking hold.

There was another sign that rehab was different this time. In any addict's life, the "clean date" is a milestone much celebrated. Ask any addict who's been clean a year or more, and he will tell you the precise date he "got clean." For Jacob, I assumed it was when he entered Recovery First, but he corrected me. During his first weeks in treatment, he'd been taking the sleeping pills other patients didn't want. On January 23 he confessed this to his counselor, gave up the extra pills, and went totally clean.

He told me that story during one of our many calls. His self-awareness and honesty, his humility—this was all new. I tried hard not to have any expectations, but each time we talked he sounded stronger, more self-aware, more open and eager to share his progress. With each phone call I took it all in, delighting in watching this new personality emerge, ever so slowly, one call at a time.

In April Dick and I flew to Ft. Lauderdale for Jacob's twenty-third birthday. He was living in a halfway house and working as a busboy at a beachfront hotel. He seemed as happy as I'd seen him in years. What was most striking was his physique. Shoulders back, he stood tall. He'd gained some weight, his eyes and skin were clear, and the abscess was healed. My son looked healthy, and for me, that was enough. The kid I'd once dreamed would go to MIT or design jets now thrilled me just by the fact that he was alive, healthy, and standing before me. It was everything.

No matter where we went that weekend, I couldn't take my eyes off him. He showed us his halfway house, a reconverted motel run by a Native American who had a thick black ponytail and nodded to us distantly. It wasn't a place where I envisioned my son would ever live, but it was his place, and for now, it was fine. Jacob introduced us to fellow workers at the hotel where he bussed tables and handled room service. Each co-worker praised us for raising such a "fine young man." We met Phil, his sponsor, an attractive young man in his late twenties, tall and thin, an ascetic figure with a certain mysticism from years of AA and his own Christian leanings. I was glad he was Jacob's sponsor, regardless of where it took Jacob in his religion. Phil had helped Jacob to find his own "higher power"—a term that was new for both of us—and I forever will be grateful for that. We visited the rehab center, where workers emerged to hug Jacob and tell us what a "fine young man" he was. And I finally met Angelo, the "salesman" I'd initially distrusted when he convinced me to admit Jacob over New Year's. I was able to thank him, this kind man whose drawn face told of a harsher time. With each hug and each compliment, Jacob stood a little taller, glancing at me to be sure I was taking it all in, giving me that shy, sweet grin that had disappeared for so long.

One morning we ate breakfast at a small, local café on Las Olas Boulevard, Ft. Lauderdale's busiest shopping street. We sat at an outdoor table, enjoying the warm weekday morning, feeling the promise of another full day together. When Dick left for the restroom, I had Jacob to myself. It was my moment to share something deep and personal.

"Jacob, I want you to know something. It seems strange to say it, but I think I'm happy. I know my happiness should not be dependent on you or how you are doing, but it is. It's just so difficult for a parent."

Jacob nodded, looked up from his thick black coffee, and stared directly into my eyes, hard. His eyes were clear, the pupils dark as his drink, steady and piercing.

"It makes me happy to know you are. Because I've done so much, it makes me happy to know that I can give you this now."

When we left that weekend, I felt a peace I hadn't experienced in years. When Heidi saw the pictures from our visit, she said, "Ma, you look happy!" The separation was different this time, too. After we hugged and boarded the plane, that same intense sadness welled up, but this time it felt as if the space around me shifted, as though the molecules where Jacob once stood had repositioned themselves and opened up the air around me. Al-Anon teaches "detach with love," and for the first time I was acutely aware that Jacob was a man—no longer a child, but a separate being from me. We each had to live our own life. I needed to think of him almost as a new person in my life, not just the son I'd raised and adored since his birth. He always would be my son. But now he was a man, out in the world, living independently and making his path—even if it wasn't the path I'd set for him. He had his program, and it was helping him to rebuild his life in ways I never could. Now it was time for me to do the same.

Chapter 38

Transition

"Tori, it's time."

That's how I opened the conversation with my CEO, planned in my head for months. Alone together in her office, we were nearing the end of our biweekly meeting. The first day of the fiscal year, July 1, 2012, was a good time to tell her of my plans to retire at the end of December. Tori was visibly surprised, and she fought back. In the full year since Chip's departure we'd become close, trusting and respecting one another. Expert at negotiating, she pressed hard, first on why I would retire at all, and secondly, on why in December.

"How about June 30?" she countered.

"No, December."

"June."

"Okay, let's compromise. How about March?"

"June."

So, of course, we agreed on June.

A year of transition lay ahead to work closely with Tori and ensure a smooth hand-off to my successor. It would be a huge transition for me personally, as well. I'd be leaving a place I loved, a staff and board I'd built, people who made me smile every day, and the incalculable worth of feeling a part of something larger than myself. But setting the alarm for 5:20 every morning and clicking off the bedside lamp at midnight most nights was something I wouldn't miss. Time was ticking away. I wanted more of it, and at least the illusion of some control over how I spent it.

Meanwhile, Jacob continued to recover. Minding Al-Anon's caution to let go of expectations but preserve hope, I was thrilled at every milestone he chose to share. With the geographic separation, and my focus on coaching my successor and planning retirement, I no longer obsessed over Jacob's every move. In fact, whole hours would pass by without my wondering where he was, what he was doing, with whom he was doing it, where it would lead, and when the phone would ring. When I thought of those earlier days, the old sick worry, that gnawing panicky feeling, would stir again in my gut, and I never wanted to go back there. Even as Jacob proudly told me one evening that he held in his hand a ninety-day chip, adding, "I'm healthier than maybe I've ever been," I kept hold of hope but refused to believe this could be it for him. It never would be "over." Jacob was an addict. He'd been a substance abuser for some five, six years, and although this was his longest attempt at sobriety, a time to celebrate for sure, it also was not a time to look too far ahead. The adage "one day at a time" clearly applied, and I tried hard to live it.

Dick and I stayed loyal to our weekly meetings. By now, this had become our "home group," a lovely phrase that AA or Al-Anon members apply to that one meeting where you feel most connected and where you give most of your service. We'd made many friends there. Huck, ever the teacher, repeated to me at one point, "I bet you're the best mother now that you've ever been." Two other men in our group, a former banker and an owner of a large business, also were savoring their sons' sobriety—each for a few years longer than Jacob. The three of us continued attending meetings because it grounded us. It reminded us of where we'd been and that we never knew where tomorrow would lead, nor how desperately we might need these meetings again. We also came to share our stories—as Al-Anon says, "our experience, strength and hope"—because it gave others hope. If our children had found sobriety, maybe theirs could, too.

During this incredible time, transition took on many meanings. While I pulled back the throttle on my nonstop professional life, Jacob was revving up his. He liked his job at the hotel, where he was learning about food service, how to please customers, and the ebb and flow of business in a town heavily dependent upon seasonal guests. Florida's warmth seemed to soothe him. He rounded out his days attending meetings and making friends in recovery. He even voiced thoughts about returning to school. But the most surprising change was his transition from a student of addiction to a teacher. Learning so much about the disease, he became not only startlingly self-aware, but willing to share his knowledge with others who might benefit, including his mother.

In July Dick and I visited him for a weekend. There was no special reason; we just missed him. Like other visits, this one, too, was filled with packing in as much time with him as possible, visiting with him at his hotel, taking him and his friends out for meals, and attending meetings. One particular meeting prompted heavy conversation. It was the Ft. Lauderdale Speakers' Meeting on Friday night in the City Council chamber. Jacob urged us to get there early, saying it filled up fast, and he was right. The meeting began at 7:00, but by 6:30 half the seats were filled or saved. The speaker, a former professional football player and recovered alcoholic, held the audience of 150 men and women rapt for nearly an hour. Afterwards, over Chinese food at an outdoor table, savoring the warm South Florida night, we talked about the meeting.

Jacob opened up about recovery in ways I'd not yet heard. He told us it wasn't enough just to stop using, but he had a hole inside him that *just* not using didn't fill. He needed something else. Now, after reading the Big Book—the addict's bible—and working the twelve steps again with a younger sponsor, he was "recovering." When Jacob talked about the twelve steps, it thrilled me to hear him say the word "God" and acknowledge a "higher power" and a spiritual part to his life. He could have been speaking Azerbaijani or Swahili, so foreign were those words coming from his mouth.

Many times throughout that year, Jacob and I continued these intense conversations. During our annual family vacation in Rehoboth, he and I took long walks on the boardwalk late at night when everyone else in the household had gone to a book or bed. I was content just to stroll alongside him, this tall, tanned young man, growing in self-confidence, now teaching me so much. There was one theme, in particular, that he kept repeating.

"It's not enough, Mom," he would begin patiently, "for the addict just to stop using or drinking. He has to replace that absence with something else—and that 'else' is the spiritual awakening."

Other times he told me, "Being clean and sober or dry isn't enough. You have to replace that, and that's where the program comes in, and a belief in something greater than yourself."

One sunny morning I was walking the boardwalk alone, thinking over all Jacob was teaching me, when a young father chasing two small children came up beside me. He warned them not to run too far ahead. As he passed, I said, "Learning the rules of the road?" Yes, he said, but it's hard. Indeed it is, I thought silently. They grow up so fast, run ahead of you, and break your heart. But it's so much worse when they leave before they grow up. I'd lost Jacob for so long. Now I hoped I had him back.

The next milestone came in January. Reaching the first year of sobriety is a huge accomplishment for any addict. Experts say achieving the first twelve months of "clean time" compounds the likelihood of beating the disease. It's a pivotal turning point in an addict's life, and Dick and I flew to Florida to witness it.

Once again, we sat in a large meeting room—this time at an AA meeting in Ft. Lauderdale—which was filled with men and women of all ages, most in their twenties and thirties, greeting each other, chewing gun, sipping coffee, some sitting cross-legged on the floor. The room was packed with fear and misery, hope and joy. Jacob was called up to the podium to receive his one-year medallion. Along with his friends and Phil, his sponsor, we cheered wildly. Jacob was allowed to speak briefly.

"Thank you to my parents, who are here tonight, to God, and to the twelve steps."

When he came back to his seat, he looked deeply into my eyes and handed me the medallion. My fingers closed over the half-dollar-size gold coin in my palm, emblazoned with the AA logo. To this day, I carry it with me everywhere.

The next morning I walked a two-mile stretch along A1A that skirts the ocean. It struck me that I could trace my journey with Jacob by towns and cities along the sea: Ft. Lauderdale, Delray, Rehoboth, even North Carolina at the outset. *We go to the sea, like lemmings*, I thought, *to find our way again.*

How far Jacob had come. At meetings with him, I marveled at how younger men thronged around him. He cares about these kids, Dick and I observed. I felt intense pride to know he was trying to help them. When Jacob was growing up, I wanted him to be a giver and a leader, as he was meant to be. Now here, outside AA meetings and in clusters of needy, recovering addicts, he was finding a way to do that—not as I ever could have imagined, but in his own way. I even laughed when he insisted we give two kids a ride back to their halfway houses, conscripting us into service as well.

What I most felt for my son that weekend, and in times since, was an intense pride in what he had achieved. Experts say the first year is the hardest. Others say every day is hard. I knew the rest of his life could be hard, but I'd learned not to think that far. Dick and I were grateful for this day and to be sharing this "graduation." We reveled in the moment of celebration, gratitude, and love.

Chapter 39

Giving Back

In June, the hospital insisted on throwing me a big party. My staff kept the details secret, realizing I'd drive them crazy. They knew I wanted my family to attend. Most of all, I wanted Jacob there. We hadn't seen each other for a few months, and I had no idea if his work schedule would allow him to fly home.

On a Thursday evening after a board of trustees meeting, the ground floor of our newest pavilion's glass-enclosed atrium was turned into a party site. An open stairwell served as a platform for those who insisted on saying nice things about me. I was instructed to stand on the landing while Tori, Chip, and others made complimentary and memorable comments in front of some two hundred board members, doctors, nurses, donors, elected officials, community leaders, my staff, and others. The crowd and the comments were humbling and overwhelming.

Amid all the glitter, two images stay with me. The first is Josh, three years old, sitting on his mom's lap and staring up at me with eyes as big as silver dollars, mouth open, sucking in all the words the grown-ups said about his Bubbe. The second, way off, towards the back of the room, there in the corner next to Dick, standing like a beacon, is my tanned, dark-haired son, flashing that knowing grin. Hi, Ma, it's me, I'm here, and I'm proud of you. And my grinning back. Hi, Jacob, I'm so glad you're here. You make this night for me. Thank you for getting here, for being here, for just being.

By then, Jacob was eighteen months clean, still working at the hotel, and planning to attend community college in the fall. Helen and Ida, staff leaders at Pathways, were among the few in the crowd that evening who knew about Jacob. After the speeches and gifts, they made a beeline for him, ogling over how healthy he looked, radiating in his confident demeanor. On the spot they asked if he would stop in that weekend to talk to the patients. Jacob glanced at me briefly, as if for permission, and said, "Sure!" They invited me to join him.

Jacob and I talked to the patients at Pathways that weekend, and it gradually led to scores of other talks. After we spoke that day, I offered Helen my willingness to talk with the families if it might help in any way. She jumped at the idea.

So began Dick's and my commitment to speaking at Pathways' family workshops, sharing our "experience, strength, and hope," to give hope to some of these families. At these Saturday workshops, I look at the faces of the mothers in the room, and I know each of them. My heart seizes at their red-rimmed eyes, the gray pallor of their skin, the tissues they clutch with twisting fingers. I was there. I stare into their faces and think, I was sitting right where you are, barely able to breathe, I loved my child so much. I ached to cure him. But you can't. I share with them: You can't control this disease, you didn't cause it, and you can't cure it. You can only take care of yourself. It begins with you.

When Jacob could, he flew home to attend Pathways with us. These sessions always proved meaningful for the families as well as for us. Jacob later confided he felt guilty because he got more out of the talks than he gave. But I could tell by the reactions in the room that he was fanning hope for these families and giving parents strength to face their child's addiction. He also gained strength from each session, sharing his story and how he found sobriety. The families couldn't get enough of him. They peppered him with questions, trying to measure where they were with their own son or daughter. After talking with the families, we went upstairs to speak with the patients. Now it was Dick's and my turn to be grilled. Apparently, it was unusual for addicts to see an "intact" family, and they often commented that they envisioned one day sitting there with their loved ones, as we were. At the very least, we were giving them something to aim for, a glimpse of health and hope.

After one session with the patients, Jacob told me gently, "Ma, you can't really talk about the steps until you do them yourself." So with his not-so-subtle nudge, I found a sponsor. Just like the addicts do, I worked through the steps. It took nearly nine months of reading, writing, thinking, and meeting with my sponsor to discuss my progress. It was all the more intense given that it stretched into my retirement, giving me time to think deeply about my life. Among the many character traits the process forced me to evaluate was my inclination to control. My entire career had been built on controlling others in some way—getting donors to give to the hospital, having my CEO follow a program's script, instructing my staff how to conduct an event and expecting them to follow it.

Al-Anon teaches us to "let go and let God." So much is out of our control, and sometimes events happen for a reason. How could I ever have known that Jacob's presence at my retirement party would prompt a new path? That weekend began an entirely new chapter in my life wrapped around Jacob's recovery—and my own. Like someone who prays for a loved one to heal after a near-fatal accident, I knew I had to give back in some way for having this healthy son return to my life.

Just as Jacob had to find something to fill that hole left without drugs or alcohol, so I, too, had to find something to fill the hole left after a thirty-year career. While I knew I would stay linked to the hospital and continue consulting in philanthropy, retirement would mostly be about service. Dick and I agreed we would continue speaking at Pathways. Focused on its patients, Pathways had not yet developed a strong program for families. It was easy to conscript friends through Al-Anon, and soon we had the burgeoning bud of a volunteer support network for families. Our goal was to help family members help themselves so that, in that counter-intuitive way, they might one day be able to help the addict as well.

Around this same time, I was asked to join the board of a six-teen-bed men's halfway house, which was undertaking a major capital expansion. Aside from the opportunity for service, what enticed me were the board members themselves. All were recovered addicts, and most had been clean for decades. They are remarkable people, each with a story to tell of a hellish journey that brought them to recovery and boundless joy in their lives. With them I can be honest about Jacob, and they, in turn, give me added hope and inspiration.

Applying my experience, strength, and hope to help others suffer-ing from addiction may not drive me forever, but "forever" is beyond my grasp. Focusing on giving back to families and addicts feels right for today.

Maybe we'll never know for sure what got Jacob clean—or what keeps him clean. But I do know that I had to get out of his way. I had to let him go. Sending him to Florida, ultimately, was a huge turning point in his life and mine. There were relapses and days upon days of heartache. But today I am grateful that he is healthy and grateful for the counselors and therapists who helped advise us. Most of all, I am grateful for Al-Anon. Al-Anon's not for everyone. But as I tell others, especially parents, when your heart is breaking and you're sick with worry, it's there for you.

There is a saying, "Addicts are angels in the making." If that's true, Jacob has become an angel in my life, keeping me honest, helping me to stay focused on the day, knowing what I can control, and feeling gratitude for all I have. Growing within me years ago when my mother lay dying, he was a reminder that life goes on. As an adult today, he reminds me of what's important. The child has become the teacher.

I tell Jacob often that I am proud of him and proud of my own progress as well. No one knows what tomorrow will bring; today is all we have. I still work hard to let go of expectations, but never of hope.

After all, if one angel can make it, others can, too.

Epilogue

Today, substance abuse—and in particular heroin—is a national epidemic. Across America, cities and states are proclaiming a crisis in deaths from opioid overdose.

While substance use has plagued mankind for centuries, the current wave of new drugs, often mixed with lethal substances, is alarming. Our modern ability to track and measure nearly everything may be increasing the reporting, and therefore the awareness, of addiction, an awareness that's further fueled by a rapid-fire media. Regardless of what is causing the increase in usage or attention to the disease, it is tragic to witness the loss of so many lives, many of them young men and women in the prime of adulthood.

My story of Jacob's journey is just one of thousands like it. With support from others, he continues in recovery. Clean and sober since January 23, 2012, he holds two jobs and is pursuing his education. At least once a week he attends an AA meeting, and he sponsors men in the program, young and not so young. Similarly, at least once a week my husband and I attend an Al-Anon meeting and welcome newcomers and old-timers alike. We often find an Al-Anon meeting when we travel. It keeps us grounded and reminds us we are still very much taking one day at a time.

Jacob continues to be my teacher. He often tells me that alcohol and drugs are not the problem for an addict, but rather a solution. And that ultimately, only belief in something greater than oneself can aide lasting recovery. Jacob prays every day, and so do I.

We know addiction will be a lifelong threat to our family. Relapse can happen at any age. But with prayer and programs like AA and Al-Anon, we look forward to each day with courage and joy.

There was a time when Jacob said, "Mom, if this book is meant to be published, it will be." If my story helps just one mom or dad survive the addiction crisis in their life, and prompts them to seek help for themselves, even if they cannot help their loved one, I will be glad to have shared it. Jacob will, too.

About the Author

Lisa Hillman has been a development professional for more than thirty-five years. She is the former President of Anne Arundel Medical Center Foundation and a former broadcast journalist. She serves as a board member of Pathways and Samaritan House, both programs that serve addicts. Lisa lives in Annapolis, Maryland with her husband  and greyhound and is the proud mother of two children, Heidi and Jacob. Please connect with Lisa at lisahillmansecret@gmail.com

Apprentice House is the country's only campus-based, student-staffed book publishing company. Directed by professors and industry professionals, it is a nonprofit activity of the Communication Department at Loyola University Maryland.

Using state-of-the-art technology and an experiential learning model of education, Apprentice House publishes books in untraditional ways. This dual responsibility as publishers and educators creates an unprecedented collaborative environment among faculty and students, while teaching tomorrow's editors, designers, and marketers.

Outside of class, progress on book projects is carried forth by the AH Book Publishing Club, a co-curricular campus organization supported by Loyola University Maryland's Office of Student Activities.

Eclectic and provocative, Apprentice House titles intend to entertain as well as spark dialogue on a variety of topics. Financial contributions to sustain the press's work are welcomed. Contributions are tax deductible to the fullest extent allowed by the IRS.

To learn more about Apprentice House books or to obtain submission guidelines, please visit www.apprenticehouse.com.

Apprentice House
Communication Department
Loyola University Maryland
4501 N. Charles Street
Baltimore, MD 21210
Ph: 410-617-5265 • Fax: 410-617-2198
info@apprenticehouse.com • www.apprenticehouse.com

CPSIA information can be obtained
at www.ICGtesting.com
Printed in the USA
BVOW04*1816010517
482835BV00004B/17/P